THE FIRST ADMINISTRATION

OF

JAMES MADISON

1809—1813

HISTORY OF THE UNITED STATES.

BY

HENRY ADAMS.

Vols. I. and II.—The First Administration of Jefferson. 1801–1805.

Vols. III. and IV.—The Second Administration of Jefferson. 1805–1809.

Vols. V. and VI.—The First Administration of Madison. 1809–1813.

Vols. VII., VIII., and IX.—The Second Administration of Madison. 1813–1817. With an Index to the Entire Work.

HISTORY

OF THE

UNITED STATES OF AMERICA

DURING THE FIRST ADMINISTRATION OF

JAMES MADISON

By HENRY ADAMS

Vol. I.

ANTIQUARIAN PRESS LTD.
New York
1962

First Published
1891-1896
by
Charles Scribner's Sons

————

Reprinted 1962
by
Antiquarian Press, Ltd.
New York, N.Y.

Edition Limited to 750 Sets

115473

Library of Congress Catalog Card Number: 61-8054

Printed in the U.S.A.

————

NOBLE OFFSET PRINTERS, INC.
NEW YORK 3, N.Y.

CONTENTS OF VOL. I.

HISTORY OF THE UNITED STATES.

CHAPTER I.

THE " National Intelligencer," which called public attention only to such points of interest as the Government wished to accent, noticed that President Madison was " dressed in a full suit of cloth of American manufacture " when he appeared at noon, March 4, 1809, under escort of the " troops of cavalry of the city and Georgetown," amid a crowd of ten thousand people, to take the oath of office at the Capitol. The suit of American clothes told more of Madison's tendencies than was to be learned from the language of the Inaugural Address, which he delivered in a tone of voice so low as not to be heard by the large audience gathered in the new and imposing Representatives' Hall.[1] Indeed, the Address suggested a doubt whether the new President wished to be understood. The conventionality of his thought nowhere betrayed itself more plainly than in this speech on the greatest

[1] Diary of J. Q. Adams, March 4, 1809; i. 544.

occasion of Madison's life, when he was required to explain the means by which he should retrieve the failures of Jefferson.

"It is a precious reflection," said Madison to his anxious audience, "that the transition from this prosperous condition of our country to the scene which has for some time been distressing us, is not chargeable on any unwarrantable views, nor as I trust on any voluntary errors, in the public councils. Indulging no passions which trespass on the rights or the repose of other nations, it has been the true glory of the United States to cultivate peace by observing justice, and to entitle themselves to the respect of the nations at war by fulfilling their neutral obligations with the most scrupulous impartiality. If there be candor in the world, the truth of these assertions will not be questioned; posterity at least will do justice to them."

Since none of Madison's enemies, either abroad or at home, intended to show him candor, his only hope was in posterity; yet the judgment of posterity depended chiefly on the course which the new President might take to remedy the misfortunes of his predecessor. The nation expected from him some impulse toward the end he had in mind; foreign nations were also waiting to learn whether they should have to reckon with a new force in politics; but Madison seemed to show his contentment with the policy hitherto pursued, rather than his wish to change it.

"This unexceptionable course," he continued, "could not avail against the injustice and violence of the belligerent Powers. In their rage against each other, or impelled by more direct motives, principles of retaliation have been introduced equally contrary to universal reason and acknowledged law. How long their arbitrary edicts will be continued, in spite of the demonstrations that not even a pretext for them has been given by the United States, and of the fair and liberal attempt to induce a revocation of them, cannot be anticipated. Assuring myself that under every vicissitude the determined spirit and united councils of the nation will be safeguards to its honor and essential interests, I repair to the post assigned me, with no other discouragement than what springs from my own inadequacy to its high duties."

Neither the actual world nor posterity could find much in these expressions on which to approve or condemn the policy of Madison, for no policy could be deduced from them. The same iteration of commonplaces marked the list of general principles which filled the next paragraph of the Address. Balancing every suggestion of energy by a corresponding limitation of scope, Madison showed only a wish to remain within the limits defined by his predecessor. " To cherish peace and friendly intercourse with all nations having corresponding dispositions " seemed to imply possible recourse to war with other nations ; but " to prefer in all cases amicable discussion and reasonable accommodation of differences to a decision of them by an appeal to arms" seemed to exclude the use of force. " To promote by authorized means improvements friendly to agriculture, to manufactures, and to external as well as internal commerce " was a phrase so cautiously framed that no one could attack it. " To support the Constitution, which is the cement of the Union, as well in its limitations as in its authorities," seemed a duty so guarded as to need no further antithesis; yet Madison did not omit the usual obligation " to respect the rights and authorities reserved to the States and to the people, as equally incorporated with, and essential to, the success of the general system." No one could object to the phrases with which the Address defined Executive duties; but no one could point out a syllable implying that Madison would bend his energies with sterner purpose to maintain the nation's rights.

At the close of the speech Chief-Justice Marshall administered the oath; the new President then passed the militia in review, and in the evening Madison and Jefferson attended an inauguration ball, where " the crowd was excessive, the heat oppressive, and the entertainment bad." [1] With this complaint, so familiar on the occasion, the day ended, and President Madison's troubles began.

About March 1, Wilson Cary Nicholas had called on the President elect to warn him that he must look for serious opposition to the expected appointment of Gallatin as Secretary of State. Nicholas had the best reason to know that Giles, Samuel Smith, and Leib were bent on defeating Gallatin.

[1] Diary of J. Q. Adams, i. 544.

" I believed from what I heard he would be rejected,"
wrote Nicholas two years afterward;[1] " and that at all
events, if he was not, his confirmation would be by a
bare majority.   During my public service but one event
had ever occurred that gave me as much uneasiness :
I mean the degradation of the country at that very
moment by the abandonment of [the embargo]."

The two events were in fact somewhat alike in
character.   That Gallatin should become Secretary
of State seemed a point of little consequence, even
though it were the only remaining chance for honorable peace ; but that another secretary should be
forced on the President by a faction in the Senate,
for the selfish objects of men like Samuel Smith and
Giles, foreboded revolution in the form of government.
Nicholas saw chiefly the danger which threatened his
friends ; but the remoter peril to Executive independence promised worse evils than could be caused even
by the overthrow of the party in power at a moment
of foreign aggression.

The effort of Giles and Smith to control Madison
had no excuse.   Gallatin's foreign birth, the only
objection urged against him, warranted doubt, not
indeed of his fitness, but of difficulty in obliging
European powers to deal with a native of Geneva,
who was in their eyes either a subject of their own
or an enemy at war; but neither Napoleon nor King
George in the year 1809 showed so much regard to
American feelings that the United States needed to

[1] W. C. Nicholas to ——.   Nicholas MSS.

affect delicacy in respect to theirs; and Gallatin's foreign birth became a signal advantage if it should force England to accept the fact, even though she refused to admit the law, of American naturalization. Gallatin's fitness was undisputed, and the last men who could question it were Giles and Samuel Smith, who had been his friends for twenty years, had trusted their greatest party interests in his hands, had helped to put the Treasury under his control, and were at the moment keeping him at its head when they might remove him to the less responsible post of minister for foreign affairs. Any question of Gallatin's patriotism suggested ideas even more delicate than those raised by doubts of his fitness. A party which had once trusted Burr and which still trusted Wilkinson, not to mention Giles himself, had little right to discuss Gallatin's patriotism, or the honesty of foreign-born citizens. Even the mild-spoken Wilson Cary Nicholas almost lost his temper at this point. " I honestly believe," he wrote in 1811, " if all our *native* citizens had as well discharged their duty to their country, that we should by our energy have extorted from both England and France a respect for our rights, and that before this day we should have extricated ourselves from all our embarrassments instead of having increased them." The men who doubted Gallatin's patriotism were for the most part themselves habitually factious, or actually dallying with ideas of treason.

Had any competent native American been pressed

for the Department of State, the Senate might still
have had some pretext for excluding Gallatin; but
no such candidate could be suggested.   Giles was
alone in thinking himself the proper secretary; Samuel Smith probably stood in the same position;
Monroe still sulked in opposition and discredit; Armstrong, never quite trusted, was in Paris; William
Pinkney and J. Q. Adams were converts too recent
for such lofty promotion; G. W. Campbell and W. H.
Crawford had neither experience nor natural fitness
for the post.   The appointment of Gallatin not only
seemed to be, but actually was, necessary to Madison's
Administration.

No argument affected the resistance of Giles and
Samuel Smith, and during the early days of March
Madison could see no means of avoiding a party
schism.   From that evil, at such a stage, he shrank.
While the subject still stood unsettled, some unknown person suggested a new idea.   If Robert
Smith could be put in the Treasury, his brother
Samuel would vote to confirm Gallatin as Secretary
of State.   The character of such a transaction needed
no epithet; but Madison went to Robert Smith and
offered him the Treasury.[1]   He knew Smith to be
incompetent, but he thought that with Gallatin's
aid even an incompetent person might manage the
finances; and perhaps his astuteness went so far as
to foresee what was to happen, — that he should deal
with the Smiths on some better occasion in a more

[1] Robert Smith's Address to the People, June 7, 1811.

summary manner. Madison's resemblance to a cardinal was not wholly imaginary.[1]

While Robert Smith went to inquire into the details of Treasury business before accepting the offered post, the President consulted with Gallatin, who rejected the scheme at once. He could not, he said, undertake the charge of both departments ; the President would do better to appoint Robert Smith Secretary of State, and leave the Treasury as it was. Madison seized this outlet of escape. He returned to Robert Smith with the offer of the State Department, which Smith accepted. In making this arrangement Madison knew that he must himself supply Smith's deficiencies ; but stronger wills than that of Madison had yielded to party discontent, and he gained much if he gained only time.

The true victim of the bargain was Gallatin, who might wisely have chosen the moment for retiring from the Cabinet; but after declining an arrangement in his favor, he could not fairly desert the President, who had offered to sacrifice much for him, and he was too proud to avow a personal slight as the motive of his public action. Weakened already by the unexpected decline of his influence in the Senate, his usefulness was sure to be still further lessened by the charge of clinging to office ; but after weighing the arguments for retirement he decided to remain,[2] although he could not, even if he would, forget that

[1] First Administration of Jefferson, vol. i. p. 188.

[2] Gallatin to Jefferson, Nov. 8, 1809; Adams's Gallatin, p. 408.

the quarrel which had been forced upon him must be met as vigorously as it was made.

The War and Navy Departments remained to be filled. Dearborn, who had continued in the War Department chiefly to oblige President Jefferson, retired in the month of February to become Collector of the port of Boston. As his successor, Madison selected William Eustis, of Boston, who had served in Congress during Jefferson's first Administration. Eustis was about fifty-six years old; in the Revolutionary War he had filled the post of hospital surgeon, and since the peace he had practised his profession in Boston. Little could be said of the appointment, except that no other candidate was suggested who seemed better qualified for the place.[1]

To succeed Robert Smith at the Navy Department, Madison selected Paul Hamilton, of South Carolina. Nothing was known of Hamilton, except that he had been governor of his State some ten years before. No one seemed aware why he had attracted the President's attention, or what qualities fitted him for the charge of naval affairs; but he appeared in due time at Washington, — a South Carolinian gentleman, little known in society or even to his colleagues in the government, and little felt as an active force in the struggle of parties and opinions.

From the outset Madison's Cabinet was the least satisfactory that any President had known. More than once the Federalist cabinets had been convulsed

[1] Madison to Henry Lee, February, 1827; Works, iii. 562, 564.

by disagreements, but the Administration of Madison
had hardly strength to support two sides of a dispute.
Gallatin alone gave it character, but was himself in
a sort of disgrace. The Secretary of State, the Secretary of War, and the Secretary of the Navy, overshadowed in the Cabinet by Gallatin, stood in a
position of inevitable hostility to his influence, although they represented neither ideas nor constituents. While Gallatin exacted economy, the army
and navy required expenditures, and the two secretaries necessarily looked to Robert Smith as their
friend. Toward Robert Smith Gallatin could feel
only antipathy, which was certainly shared by Madison. "We had all been astonished at his appointment," said Joel Barlow two years afterward; [1] "we
all learned the history of that miserable intrigue by
which it was effected." Looking upon Robert Smith's
position as the result of a "miserable intrigue," Gallatin could make no secret of his contempt. The
social relations between them, which had once been
intimate, wholly ceased.

To embroil matters further, the defalcation of a
navy agent at Leghorn revealed business relations
between the Navy Department and Senator Samuel
Smith's mercantile firm which scandalized Gallatin
and drew from him a sharp criticism. He told
Samuel Smith that the transactions of the firm of
Smith and Buchanan were the most extraordinary
that had fallen within his knowledge since he had

[1] National Intelligencer, July, 1811.

been in the Treasury, and had left very unfavorable impressions on his mind.[1]   Smith was then struggling for a re-election to the Senate, and felt the hand of Gallatin as a chief obstacle in his way.   The feud became almost mortal under these reciprocal injuries ; but Samuel Smith gained all his objects, and for the time held Gallatin and Madison at his mercy.   Had he been able to separate them, his influence would have had no bounds, except his want of ability.

Yet Madison was always a dangerous enemy, gifted with a quality of persistence singularly sure in its results.   An example of this persistence occurred at the moment of yielding to the Smiths' intrigues, when, perhaps partly in the hope of profiting by his sacrifice, he approached the Senate once more on the subject of the mission to Russia.   February 27, the nomination of William Short to St. Petersburg had been unanimously rejected.   March 6, with the nominations of Robert Smith and William Eustis to the Cabinet, Madison sent the names of J. Q. Adams as minister at St. Petersburg, and of Thomas Sumter as minister to Brazil.   He asked the Senate to establish two new missions at once.   March 7 the Senate confirmed all the other nominations, but by a vote of seventeen to fifteen, adhered to the opinion that a mission to Russia was inexpedient.   Both Giles and Samuel Smith supported the Government;

[1] Gallatin to Samuel Smith, June 26, 1809 ; Adams's Gallatin, p. 402.

but the two senators from Pennsylvania, the two
from Kentucky, together with Anderson of Tennessee and William H. Crawford, persisted in aiding
the Federalists to defeat the President's wish. Yet
the majority was so small as to prove that Madison
would carry his point in the end. Senators who
rejected the services of Gallatin and John Quincy
Adams in order to employ those of Robert Smith,
Dr. Eustis, and Governor Hamilton could not but
suffer discredit. Faction which had no capacity of
its own, and which showed only dislike of ability
in others, could never rule a government in times
of danger or distress.

After thus embarrassing the President in organ-
izing his service the Senate rose, leaving Madison
in peace until May 22, when the Eleventh Congress
was to meet in special session. The outlook was
more discouraging than at the beginning of any
previous Administration. President Jefferson had
strained his authority to breaking, and the sudden
reaction threw society as well as government into
disorder. The factiousness at Washington reflected
only in a mild form the worse factiousness elsewhere. The Legislature of Massachusetts, having
issued its Address to the People, adjourned; and a
few days afterward the people, by an election which
called out more than ninety thousand votes, dismissed their Republican governor, and by a majority
of two or three thousand chose Christopher Gore
in his place. The new Legislature was more decid-

edly Federalist than the old one. New Hampshire effected the same revolution. Rhode Island followed. In New York the Federalists carried the Legislature, as they did also in Maryland.

Even in Pennsylvania, although nothing shook the fixed political character of the State, the epidemic of faction broke out. While the legislatures of Massachusetts and Connecticut declared Acts of Congress unconstitutional, and refused aid to execute them, the legislature of Pennsylvania authorized Governor Snyder to resist by armed force a mandate of the Supreme Court; and when the United States marshal attempted to serve process on the person of certain respondents at the suit of Gideon Olmstead, he found himself stopped by State militia acting under orders.

In a country where popular temper had easier means of concentrating its violence, government might have been paralyzed by these proofs of low esteem; but America had not by far reached such a stage, and dark as the prospect was both within and without, Madison could safely disregard dangers on which most rulers had habitually to count. His difficulties were only an inheritance from the old Administration, and began to disappear as quickly as they had risen. At a word from the President the State of Pennsylvania recovered its natural common-sense, and with some little sacrifice of dignity gave way. The popular successes won by the Federalists were hardly more serious than the momentary

folly of Pennsylvania. As yet, the Union stood in
no danger. The Federalists gained many votes ; but
these were the votes of moderate men who would
desert their new companions on the first sign of a
treasonable act, and their presence tended to make
the party cautious rather than rash. John Henry,
the secret agent of Sir James Craig, reported with
truth to the governor-general that the Federalist
leaders at Boston found disunion a very delicate
topic, and that " an unpopular war . . . can alone
produce a sudden separation of any section of this
country from the common head." [1] In public, the
most violent Federalists curbed their tongues whenever the Union was discussed, and instead of threatening to dissolve it, contented themselves by charging
the blame on the Southern States in case it should
fall to pieces. Success sobered them ; the repeal of
the embargo seemed so great a triumph that they
were almost tempted into good humor.

On the people of New England other motives
more directly selfish began to have effect. The
chief sources of their wealth were shipping and
manufactures. The embargo destroyed the value
of the shipping after it had been diminished by the
belligerent edicts ; the repeal of the embargo restored
the value. The Federalist newspapers tried to prove
that this was not the case, and that the Non-intercourse Act, which prohibited commerce with England, France, or their dependencies, was as ruinous

[1] Henry to Craig, March 13, 1809 ; State Papers, iii. 550.

as embargo itself; but the shipping soon showed
that Gottenburg, Riga, Lisbon, and the Spanish ports
in America were markets almost as convenient as
London or Havre for the sale of American produce.
The Yankee ship-owner received freights to Europe
by circuitous routes, on the accumulations of two
years in grain, cotton, tobacco, and timber, of the
whole United States, besides the freights of an extended coast-trade.   Massachusetts owned more than
a third of the American registered tonnage, and the
returns for 1809 and 1810 proved that her profits
were great.   The registered tonnage of Massachusetts employed in foreign trade was 213,000 tons in
1800, and rose to 310,000 tons in 1807 before the
embargo; in 1809 it rose again to 324,000; in 1810
it made another leap to 352,000 tons.   The coasting
trade employed in 1807 about 90,000 tons of Massachusetts shipping which was much increased by the
embargo, and again reduced by its repeal; but in
1809 and 1810 this enrolled shipping still stood far
above the prosperous level of 1807, and averaged
110,000 tons for the two years.[1]

Such rapid and general improvement in shipping
proved that New England had better employment
than political factiousness to occupy the thoughts
of her citizens; but large as the profits on freights
might be, they hardly equalled the profits on manufactures.   In truth, the manufactories of New England were created by the embargo, which obliged

[1] State Papers, Commerce and Navigation, pp. 897, 898.

the whole nation to consume their products or to go
without. The first American cotton mills, begun as
early as 1787, met with so little success that when
the embargo was imposed in 1807, only fifteen mills
with about eight thousand spindles were in operation,
producing some three hundred thousand pounds of
yarn a year. These eight thousand spindles, representing a capital of half a million dollars, were chiefly
in or near Rhode Island.

The embargo and non-importation Acts went into
effect in the last days of 1807. Within less than
two years the number of spindles was increased, or
arrangements were made for increasing it, from eight
thousand to eighty thousand.[1] Nearly four million
dollars of capital were invested in mills, and four
thousand persons were in their employ, or expected
soon to be employed in them. The cotton cost about
twenty cents a pound; the yarn sold on an average
at about $1.12½ a pound. Besides these mills, which
were worked mostly by water but partly by horse-
power, the domestic manufacture of cotton and linen
supplied a much larger part of the market. Two
thirds of the clothing and house-linen used in the
United States outside of the cities was made in
farm-houses, and nearly every farmer in New England sold some portion of the stock woven every
year by the women of his household. Much of this
coarse but strong flaxen material, sold at about

[1] Gallatin's Report, April 17, 1810 ; State Papers, Finance,
ii. 427.

fifteen or twenty cents a yard by the spinner, was sent to the Southern States.[1]

While the cotton and linen industries of the North became profitable, the manufactures of wool lagged little behind. William Whittemore, who owned the patent for a machine which manufactured wool and cotton cards, reported from Cambridge in Massachusetts, Nov. 24, 1809, that only the want of card-wire prevented him from using all his machines to the full extent of their power.[2] " Since the obstructions to our foreign trade, the manufactures of our country have increased astonishingly," he wrote. " The demand for wool and cotton cards the present season has been twice as great as it has been any year preceding." Scarcity of good wool checked the growth of this industry, and the demand soon roused a mania among farmers for improving the breed of sheep. Between one hundred and three hundred per cent of profit attended all these industries, and little or no capital was required.

All the Northern and Eastern States shared in the advantages of this production, for which Virginia with the Western and Southern States paid ; but in the whole Union New England fared best. Already the development of small industries had taken place, which, by making a varied aggregate,

[1] Gallatin's Report, April 17, 1810 ; State Papers, Finance, ii. 435.

[2] Gallatin's Report, April 17, 1810; State Papers, Finance, ii. 436.

became the foundation and the security of Yankee wealth. Massachusetts taxed her neighbors on many small articles of daily use. She employed in the single manufacture of hats four thousand persons, — more than were yet engaged in the cotton mills. More than a million and a half of hats were annually made, and three fourths of these were sold beyond the State; between three and four million dollars a year flowed into Massachusetts in exchange for hats alone.[1] At Lynn, in Massachusetts, were made one hundred thousand pairs of women's shoes every year. The town of Roxbury made eight hundred thousand pounds of soap. Massachusetts supplied the country with cut-iron nails to the value of twelve hundred thousand dollars a year. Connecticut supplied the whole country with tin-ware.

New industries sprang up rapidly on a soil and in a climate where the struggle of life was more severe than elsewhere in the Union, and where already capital existed in quantities that made production easy. One industry stimulated another. Women had much to do with the work, and their quickness and patience of details added largely to the income of New England at the cost of less active communities. Their hands wove most of the cotton and woollen cloths sent in large quantities to the West and South; but they were inventors as well as workmen. In 1801, when English straw-bonnets were in fashion,

[1] Gallatin's Report, April 17, 1810; State Papers, Finance, ii. 428.

a girl of Wrentham, not far from Boston, found that she could make for herself a straw-hat as good as the imported one. In a few months every girl in the county of Norfolk made her own straw-bonnet; and soon the South and West paid two hundred thousand dollars a year to the county of Norfolk for straw hats and bonnets.[1]

At no time could such industries have been established without the stimulus of a handsome profit; but when Virginia compelled Massachusetts and the Northern States to accept a monopoly of the American market, the Yankee manufacturer must have expected to get, and actually got, great profits for his cottons and woollens, his hats, shoes, soap, and nails. As though this were not more than enough, Virginia gave the Northern shipowners the whole freight on Southern produce, two thirds of which in one form or another went into the hands of New England shipbuilders, shippers, and merchants. Slowly the specie capital of the Union drifted towards the Banks of Boston and New Haven, until, as the story will show, the steady drain of specie eastward bankrupted the other States and the national government. Never, before or since, was the country so racked to create and support monopolies as in 1808, 1809, and 1810, under Southern rule, and under the system of the President who began his career by declaring that if he could prevent the government

[1] Gallatin's Report, April 17, 1810; State Papers, Finance, ii. 439.

from wasting the labors of the people under the pretence of protecting them, they must become happy.[1] The navy and army of the United States were employed, and were paid millions of dollars, during these years in order to shut out foreign competition, and compel New England at the cannon's mouth to accept these enormous bribes.

The Yankee, however ill-tempered he might be, was shrewd enough to see where his profit lay. The Federalist leaders and newspapers grumbled without intermission that their life-blood was drained to support a negro-slave aristocracy, " baser than its own slaves," as their phrase went ; but they took the profits thrust upon them ; and what they could not clutch was taken by New York and Pennsylvania, while Virginia slowly sank into ruin. Virginia paid the price to gratify her passion for political power ; and at the time, she paid it knowingly and willingly. John Randolph protested almost alone. American manufactures owed more to Jefferson and Virginians, who disliked them, than to Northern statesmen, who merely encouraged them after they were established.

These movements and tendencies were rather felt than understood amid the uproar of personal and local interests ; but the repeal of the embargo had the effect intended by the Virginians, — it paralyzed Pickering and the party of forcible resistance. New England quickly turned from revolutionary thoughts

[1] History of First Administration of Jefferson, i. 224.

while she engaged in money-making; and as though the tide of fortune had at last set in Madison's favor, a stroke of his diplomacy raised the tottering Administration to a sudden height of popularity such as Jefferson himself had never reached.

CHAPTER II.

WHEN Napoleon, Aug. 3, 1808, heard at Bordeaux
that the Spaniards had captured Dupont's army at Bay-
len and Rosily's ships at Cadiz, and had thrown eighty
thousand French troops back upon the Pyrenees, his
anger was great; but his perplexity was much greater.
In a character so interesting as that of Napoleon, the
moments of perplexity were best worth study; and
in his career no single moment occurred when he had
more reason to call upon his genius for a resource
than when he faced at Bordeaux the failure of his
greatest scheme. From St. Petersburg to Gibraltar
every shopkeeper knew that England had escaped,
and all believed that no combination either of force
or fraud could again be made with reasonable hope
of driving her commerce from its channels. On this
belief every merchant, as well as every government
in the world, was actually shaping calculations.
Napoleon also must shape his calculations on theirs,
since he had failed to force theirs into the path of
his own. The escape of England made useless the
machinery he had created for her ruin. Spain,
Russia, and Austria had little value for his immedi-

ate object, except as their control was necessary for the subjection of England; and the military occupation of Spain beyond the Ebro became worse than a blunder from the moment when Cadiz and Lisbon, Cuba and Mexico, Brazil and Peru threw themselves into England's arms.[1]

More than once this history has shown that Napoleon never hesitated to throw aside a plan which had miscarried. If he did not in the autumn of 1808 throw aside his Spanish schemes, the reason could only be that he saw no other resource, and that in his belief his power would suffer too much from the shock of admitting failure. He showed unusual signs of vacillation, and of a desire to escape the position into which his miscalculations had led him. Instead of going at once to Spain and restoring order to his armies, he left his brother helpless at Vittoria while he passed three months in negotiations looking toward peace with England. In September he went to Germany, where he met the Czar of Russia at Erfurt, and induced Alexander, or consented to his inducement, to join in an autograph letter to the King of England, marked by the usual Napoleonic character, and offering the principle of *uti possidetis* as the preliminary to a general peace. England regarded this advance as deceptive, and George Canning was never more successful than in the gesture of self-restrained contempt with which he tossed back the letter that Napoleon and Alexander had presumed to address to

[1] Correspondance de Napoléon, xxxii. 265, 272, 359-370.

a constitutional King of England; but even Canning
could hardly suppose that Napoleon would invite an
insult without a motive. From whatever side Napoleon approached the situation he could invent no
line of conduct which did not imply the triumph of
England. Study the problem as he might, he could
not escape from the political and military disadvan-
tages he incurred from the Spanish uprising. Without the consent of England he could neither free his
civil government from the system of commercial restriction, nor free his military strength from partial
paralysis in Spain; and England refused to help him,
or even to hear reason from Alexander.

Thenceforward a want of distinct purpose showed
itself in Napoleon's acts. Unable either to enforce or
to abandon his Continental system, he began to use it
for momentary objects, — sometimes to weaken England, sometimes to obtain money, or as the pretext
for conquests. Unable to hold the Peninsula or to
withdraw from it, he seemed at one time resolved
on conquest, at another disposed toward retreat.
In the autumn of 1808 both paths ran together, for
his credit required him to conquer before he could
honorably establish any dynasty on the throne; and
during the months of September and October he
marched new French armies across the Pyrenees and
massed an irresistible force behind the Ebro. A
year before, he had thought one hundred thousand
men enough to occupy all Spain and Portugal; but in
October, 1808, he held not less than two hundred and

fifty thousand men beyond the Pyrenees, ready to move at the moment of his arrival.

October 25, after his return from Germany, the Emperor pronounced a speech at the opening of his legislative chambers; and the embarrassment of his true position was evident under the words in which he covered it.

" Russia and Denmark," he said, " have united with me against England. The United States have preferred to renounce commerce and the sea rather than recognize their slavery. A part of my army marches against those that England has formed or disembarked in Spain. It is a special benefit of that Providence which has constantly protected our arms, that passion has so blinded English councils as to make them renounce the protection of the sea and at last present their armies on the Continent. I depart in a few days to place myself at the head of my army, and with God's aid to crown the King of Spain in Madrid, and plant my eagles on the forts of Lisbon."

He left Paris October 29, and ten days later, November 9, began the campaign which still attracts the admiration of military critics, but which did not result in planting his eagles on the forts of Lisbon. " To my great astonishment," he afterward said,[1] " I had to fight the battles of Tudela, Espinosa, Burgos, and Somo Sierra, to gain Madrid, which, in spite of my victories, refused me admission during two days." After disposing in rapid succession of all the Spanish armies, he occupied Madrid December 4, and found

[1] Correspondance de Napoléon, xxxii. 366.

himself at the end of his campaign. The conquest of Lisbon and Cadiz required more time, and led to less military result than suited his objects. At that moment he learned that an English army under Sir John Moore had ventured to march from Portugal into the north of Spain, and had already advanced so far toward Burgos as to make their capture possible. The destruction of an English army, however small, offered Napoleon the triumph he wanted. Rapidly collecting his forces, he hurried across the Guadarrama Mountains to cut off Moore's retreat; but for once he was out-generalled. Sir John Moore not only saved his own army, but also led the French a long and exhausting chase to the extreme northwestern shore of Spain, where the British fleet carried Moore's army out of their reach.

Napoleon would not have been the genius he was had he wasted his energies in following Moore to Corunna, or in trying to plant his eagles on the forts of Lisbon or Cadiz. A year earlier, Lisbon and Cadiz had been central points of his scheme; but in December, 1808, they were worth to him little more than any other seaports without fleets or colonies. For Spain and Portugal Napoleon showed that he had no further use. The moment he saw that Moore had escaped, which became clear when the Emperor reached Astorga, Jan. 2, 1809, throwing upon Soult the task of marching one hundred and fifty miles to Corunna after Moore and the British army, Napoleon

stopped short, turned about, and with rapidity unusual even for him, quitted Spain forever. "The
affairs of Spain are finished," he wrote January 16 ;[1]
although Joseph had the best reason to know and
much cause to tell how his brother left nothing
finished in Spain. "The circumstances of Europe
oblige me to go for three weeks to Paris," he wrote
to Joseph early in the morning of January 15; "if
nothing prevents, I shall be back again before the
end of February."[2] With characteristic mixture of
harshness and tenderness toward his elder brother, he
wrote at noon the same day another account, equally
deceptive, of his motives and intentions : —

"You must say everywhere, and make the army believe, that I shall return in three or four weeks. In fact,
my mere presence at Paris will make Austria shrink back
to her nullity ; and then, before the end of October, I
will be back here. I shall be in Paris in five days. I
shall go at full speed, day and night, as far as Bordeaux. Meanwhile everything will go on quieting itself
in Spain."[3]

Giving out that the conduct of Austria required his
presence at Paris, he succeeded in imposing this fiction upon Europe by the empire of his will. Europe
accepted the fable, which became history ; but although the Emperor soon disposed of Austria, and

[1] Napoleon to Jerome, 16 Janvier, 1809 ; Correspondance,
xviii. 237.

[2] Correspondance, xviii. 225.

[3] Correspondance, xviii. 227.

although Spain was a more difficult prcblem than
Austria ever was, Napoleon never kept his word to
Joseph, and never again ventured within sight of the
mistakes he could no longer correct.

Meanwhile Armstrong, disgusted with the disap-
pointments and annoyances of his residence at Paris,
had become anxious to escape without further loss of
credit. His letters to Madison, published by Congress, returned to terrify his French acquaintance,
and to close his sources of information. He could see
no hope of further usefulness. As early as Oct. 25,
1808, when the Emperor was addressing his legislative
chambers before setting out for Spain, Armstrong
wrote to Madison that no good could come from
keeping an American minister at Paris.[1] Yet in
the enforced idleness of the month when Napoleon
was in Spain, Armstrong found one ally whose aid
was well worth seeking. After the Czar Alexander
accepted, at Tilsit, the ascendency of Napoleon, he
appointed as his minister of foreign relations the
Count Nicholas Roumanzoff. The Czar was still a
young man in his thirty-first year, while Roumanzoff,
fifty-four years old, had the full powers of maturity.
Together they shaped a Russian policy, in the tradi-
tional direction of Russian interests, founded upon
jealousy of British maritime tyranny. Lord Howick's
and Spencer Perceval's Orders in Council served to
sharpen Russian as well as American antipathies, and

[1] Armstrong to Madison, Oct. 25, 1808 ; MSS. State Department Archives.

brought the two distant nations into a sympathy which was certainly not deep, but which England had reason to fear. In the autumn of 1808 Count Roumanzoff came to Paris to arrange with Champagny the details of their joint diplomacy; and at the same time, in the month of November, William Short arrived in Paris secretly accredited as minister plenipotentiary at St. Petersburg, but waiting confirmation by the Senate before going to his post. When Armstrong told Roumanzoff that an American minister would soon be on his way to St. Petersburg, the count was highly pleased, and promised at once to send a full minister to replace André Daschkoff, the chargé at Washington. " Ever since I came into office," he said to Armstrong,[1] " I have been desirous of producing this effect; for in dissolving our commercial connections with Great Britain it became necessary to seek some other power in whom we might find a substitute; and on looking round I could see none but the United States who were at all competent to this object." So far as concerned England, the alliance promised great advantages ; but Armstrong's chief anxiety affected France, and when he attempted to enlist Roumanzoff in resistance to Napoleon's robberies, he found no encouragement. Roumanzoff had already tried his influence with Napoleon on behalf of the Danes, who wanted compensation for their plundered commerce. " Give

[1] Armstrong to Madison, Nov. 24, 1808 ; MSS. State Department Archives.

them a civil answer," replied Napoleon,[1] "but of course one never pays for this sort of thing, — *On ne paye jamais ces choses-là, n'est-ce pas ?* " From Roumanzoff's refusal, Armstrong inferred that no change need be hoped in Napoleon's conduct.

" On the contrary," he wrote to Madison, the day when Napoleon abandoned the pursuit of Sir John Moore,[2] " their anti-neutral system is more rigidly observed ; the embargo on ships of the United States found here before the imperial decrees were issued is continued ; every ship of ours coming into a port of France or of her allies is immediately seized and sequestered ; cargoes regularly admitted to entry by the custom-houses are withheld from their owners ; ships most obviously exceptions to the operation of the Decrees have been recently condemned ; and — what in my view of the subject does not admit of aggravation — the burning of the ship ' Brutus ' on the high seas, so far from being disavowed, is substantially justified."

Had this been all, perhaps President Madison and Congress might have waited with courtesy, if not with hope, for Napoleon's pleasure ; but grievances equally serious ran back to the year 1803, and not one of them had been redressed by France.

" It is now three years since one of her admirals, on the principle of self-preservation, burnt four of our ships at sea, and the Emperor immediately acknowledged the debt and repeatedly promised to discharge it ; but not

[1] Gallatin's Writings, ii. 490.

[2] Armstrong to Madison, Jan. 2, 1809 ; MSS. State Department Archives.

a shilling has yet been paid, nor is it probable that a shilling ever will be paid. Besides this breach of justice in the first instance and of promise in the last, we have to complain that bills of exchange drawn to the order of citizens of the United States by the public functionaries of France, to the amount of many millions of dollars, and for articles of the first necessity, and drawn many years ago, are not only not paid, but are officially denounced as not payable."

Armstrong's temper, bad in the winter, became worse in the spring, until his letters to the Department of State seemed to leave no remedy but war for the grievances he described. The angry tone of his despatches was not counteracted by fair words in the instructions sent by Champagny to Turreau, which were calculated to irritate President Madison beyond patience.

" You cannot too much call attention to the grievances of the Americans against England in order to make them more sensibly felt," wrote Champagny to Turreau, after the Emperor went to Spain.[1] " The Americans would like France to grant them commercial privileges which no nation at present enjoys. . . . But . . . hitherto it has not seemed proper, in the execution of general measures, to introduce exceptions which would have really destroyed their effect. If the rules adopted against English commerce had not been made common, that commerce would continue through every opening left to it; England would preserve the same resources as before for

[1] Champagny to Turreau, Dec. 10, 1808 ; Archives des Aff. Étr. MSS.

supporting the war. A system of exception for one
people would turn the rule into an injustice toward all
others; all would have right to complain of a privilege
granted to the Federal government which themselves
would not enjoy."

Unanswerable as this reasoning was from the
Napoleonic standpoint, it was open to the objection
of placing Madison among the belligerents at war
with England, and of obliging him not only to accept the rules imposed by Napoleon on the allies
of France, but also to admit the corresponding
right of British retaliation, even to the point of war.
Until President Madison made up his mind to war
with England, he could hardly be induced by Napoleon's diplomacy to overlook his causes of war with
France.

Had Napoleon acted according to rules of ordinary
civilization, he would at least have softened the
harshness of his commercial policy toward America
by opening to the American President some vista of
compensation elsewhere. Florida seemed peculiarly
suited for this object, and no one so well as Napoleon knew the anxiety of the late Administration
to obtain that territory, which, for any legitimate
purpose, was useless and worthless to France. In
December, 1808, Napoleon could have retained little
or no hope of controlling the Spanish colonies by
force; yet he ordered the American government to
leave them alone, as he ordered it to adopt the
French system of commercial restraint. "I ven-

ture to presume," continued Champagny to Turreau,
"that if his Majesty has no reason to complain of
the disposition shown by the United States toward
him, he will show himself more and more inclined
to treat them favorably. What will most influence
his course will be the conduct pursued by the
United States toward the Spanish colonies, and the
care that shall be taken to do nothing in regard
to them which can contravene the rights of the
mother-country."

Thus from Turreau's attitude as well as from Armstrong's letters, the government at Washington was
advised that neither favor nor justice need be expected from Napoleon. This impression, strengthened by all the private advices which arrived from
France during the winter of 1808–1809, even though
partly balanced by the bulletins of the Emperor's
splendid Spanish campaign, had much to do with the
refusal of Congress to declare a double war, which,
however general in terms, must in effect be waged
against England alone. Anger with France affected
Republicans almost as strongly as fear of Napoleon
excited Federalists. When the final struggle took
place in Congress over the embargo, no small share
of the weakness shown by the Administration and
its followers was due to their consciousness that
the repeal of the embargo would relieve them from
appearing to obey an imperial mandate.

Turreau understood the repeal in no other light,
and was extremely irritated to see the decline of

his influence. Men who had given him pledge upon pledge that the embargo should be withdrawn only when war against England should be declared, could plead no better excuse for failing to keep their promise than that Napoleon had forfeited his claim to their support. March 19, two weeks after Congress rose, Turreau wrote from Baltimore to Champagny,[1] —

"You will have judged from my last despatches that the Embargo Law would be repealed. It has been so, in fact, despite my efforts to maintain it, and notwithstanding the promise of quite a large number of influential Representatives, especially among the senators, who had guaranteed to me its continuance till the next Congress, and who have voted against their political conscience. I had informed your Excellency of the disunion projects shown by some of the Northern States. Their avowed opposition to the continuance of the embargo, and their threats to resist its execution, terrified Congress to such a degree that the dominant party became divided, and the feebleness (*faiblesse*) of Mr. Jefferson sanctioned the last and the most shameful act of his Administration. . . . I say it with regret, — and perhaps I have said it too late, — I am convinced there is nothing to hope from these people."

Erskine, whose persistent efforts to conciliate had also something to do with the action of Congress, made Turreau's anger the subject of a despatch, doubtless hoping it might guide Canning's thoughts

[1] Turreau to Champagny, 19 March, 1809; Archives des Aff. Étr., MSS.

toward the wisdom of conciliation.[1] "The French minister it seems is so much offended at the Non-intercourse Law which has been lately passed, and is so little pleased with the general disposition, as he conceives it, of the new Administration of the United States toward France, that he has quitted this city, having previously given up his house and removed all his furniture, without calling either upon the new President or any of the members of the Administration, as was his uniform custom in former years, and as is always done by foreign ministers." Robert Smith informed Erskine that the Government would consider it to be their duty, which he was sure they would feel no disposition to shrink from, to recommend to the new Congress to enter upon immediate measures of hostility against France in the event of Great Britain giving way as to her Orders so far as to afford an opportunity to the United States to assert their rights against France.

During the month of March, Turreau watched the workings of the Non-intercourse Act, but found little encouragement. "Generally the ventures have not been so numerous as was to be expected from the well-known avidity of American merchants, and the privations they have suffered from the embargo." [2] Most of the outgoing vessels had cleared for the

[1] Erskine to Canning, March 17, 1809; MSS. British Archives.

[2] Turreau to Champagny, 15 April, 1809; Archives des Aff Étr. MSS.

West Indies or the Azores, " but the French government may rest assured that among a hundred ships leaving the ports of the Union for the high seas, ninety of them will have the real object of satisfying the wants and demands of England." Such a commerce was in his opinion fair prey. England had gained the upper-hand in America ; English superiority could no longer be contested ; and to France remained only the desperate chances of the political gambler.

" To-day not only is the separation of New England openly talked about, but the people of those five States wish for this separation, pronounce it, openly prepare it, will carry it out under British protection, and probably will meet with no resistance on the part of the other States. Yet this project, which is known and avowed ; the last proceedings of Congress, which are blamed ; the progress of the Federalists ; the alarms of commerce ; the feebleness of the highest authorities (*des premiers pouvoirs*), and the doubts regarding the capacity and the party views of the new President, — cause a ferment of public opinion ; and perhaps the moment has come for forming a party in favor of France in the Central and Southern States, whenever those of the North, having given themselves a separate government under the support of Great Britain, may threaten the independence of the rest." [1]

Turreau's speculations might show no great sagacity, but they opened a glimpse into his mind, and

[1] Turreau to Champagny, 20 April, 1809; Archives des Aff. Étr. MSS.

they were the chief information possessed by Napoleon to form his estimate of American character. Nothing could more irritate the Emperor than these laments from his minister at Washington over the victory of English interests in the United States. The effect of such reports on Napoleon was likely to be the more decided because Turreau saw everything in darker colors than the facts warranted. Deceived and defeated in the case of the embargo, he imagined himself also in danger on the other main point of his diplomacy, — the Spanish colonies. The old Spanish agents, consular and diplomatic, mostly patriots, were still officially recognized or privately received at Washington. Rumor said that troops were collecting at New Orleans to support a movement of independence in Florida; that General Wilkinson, on his way to take command in Louisiana, had stopped at Havana and Pensacola; that President Jefferson, on the eve of quitting the Presidency, had been heard to say, " We must have the Floridas and Cuba." Anonymous letters, believed by Turreau to be written by one of the clerks in the State Department, warned him against the intrigues of the Federal government in the Spanish colonies. So much was he troubled by these alarms, that April 15 he addressed an unofficial note on the subject to Robert Smith.[1]

The President, having no wish to quarrel with the

[1] Turreau to Champagny, 22 April, 1809; Archives des Aff. Étr., MSS.

French minister, and probably aware of his irritation, asked Gallatin, on his way northwards, to call on Turreau at Baltimore and make to him such soothing explanations as the case seemed to require. The interview took place during the last week of April, and Turreau's report threw another ray of light into the recesses of Jefferson's councils.[1]

"'I am specially charged,' said Gallatin, 'to assure you that whatever proceedings of General Wilkinson may seem to warrant your suspicions must not be attributed to the Executive, but solely to the vanity, the indiscretion, and the ordinary inconsistencies of that General, whom you know perhaps as well as we. . . . We are and we wish to be strangers to all that passes in the Floridas, in Mexico, and also in Cuba. You would be mistaken if you supposed that Mr. Madison wishes the possession of the Floridas. That was Mr. Jefferson's hobby (*marotte*), — it has never been the wish of his Cabinet; and Mr. Madison values to-day the possession of the Floridas only so far as they may be thought indispensable to prevent every kind of misunderstanding with Spain, and to secure an outlet for the produce of our Southern States. We have had no part in the meetings which have taken place in the Floridas, and we could not know that General Wilkinson has been ill received there.' (This is true.) 'As for the possession of Cuba, this was also a new idea of Mr. Jefferson which has not been approved by the Executive council; and I am authorized to protest to you that even if Cuba were

[1] Turreau to Champagny, 1 June, 1809; Archives des Aff. Étr., MSS. Cf. Madison to Jefferson, May 1, 1809; Writings, ii. 440.

offered us as a gift, we would not accept it. We are also opposed to every step which would tend, under the pretext of commerce, to involve us in the politics of France and Spain, and we shall see to it that any persons undertaking such enterprises are properly dealt with. I flatter myself therefore that you will believe the Cabinet to be firmly resolved carefully to avoid every disturbance of the good understanding between the United States and France.' "

Gallatin was a persistent enemy of the Florida intrigue, and doubtless believed that Madison held opinions like his own; but Madison's opinions on this subject, as on some others, were elusive, — perhaps no clearer to himself than to readers of his writings; and Gallatin had yet to learn that the instinct which coveted Florida could not be controlled by a decision of the Cabinet. Yet he said only what he seemed authorized to say; and his reference to the *marotte* of President Jefferson was significant. For the moment the weakness seemed cured. Gallatin gave Turreau to understand that President Madison would not intrigue in Florida or Cuba, and to that extent he was doubtless expressly authorized by the President. Perhaps only on his own authority he went a step further, by hinting that Napoleon need no longer dangle Florida before Madison's eyes.

A rupture with France seemed certain. Turreau expected it and hoped only to delay it. In his eyes the Emperor had suffered an indignity that could not be overlooked, although he asked that retaliation

should be delayed till autumn. " However dissatisfied the French government may be by the last
measures adopted by Congress, I believe it would be
well to await the result of the next session two
months hence before taking a severer course against
the Americans. This opinion, which I express only
with doubt, is yet warranted by advices which I have
received within a few days, and which have been
given me by men who know the Executive intentions,
and who at least till now have not deceived me."
Turreau believed that when the Emperor learned
what the late Congress had done, he would strike the
United States with the thunderbolt of his power.
Doubtless the same impression was general. Even
after Napoleon's character has been the favorite study
of biographers and historians for nearly a hundred
years, the shrewdest criticism might fail in the effort
to conjecture what shape the Emperor's resentment
took. This story has shown many of his processes
from the time when he met the resistance of the Hay-
tian negroes in 1803 to the time when he met the
uprising of the Spanish patriots in 1809; but even
with the advantage of his own writings as a guide,
neither friend nor enemy could test theories of his
character better than by attempting to divine the
conduct he was to pursue toward the United States
after their defiance of his wishes in the repeal of the
embargo.

As though to remove the last doubt of rupture with
Napoleon, the President startled the country by sud-

denly announcing a settlement of his disputes with England. April 7 Erskine received new instructions from London, and during the next two weeks he was closeted with the President and the Cabinet. April 21 the " National Intelligencer " announced the result of their labors.

CHAPTER III.

In Canning's note to Pinkney of Sept. 23, 1808, — the same paper which expressed his Majesty's regret for the embargo "as a measure of inconvenient restriction upon the American people," — a paragraph easily overlooked had been inserted to provide for future chances of fortune : —

"It is not improbable, indeed, that some alterations may be made in the Orders of Council as they are at present framed, — alterations calculated, not to abate their spirit or impair their principle, but to adapt them more exactly to the different state of things which has fortunately grown up in Europe, and to combine all practicable relief to neutrals with a more severe pressure upon the enemy. But of alterations to be made with this view only it would be uncandid to take any advantage in the present discussion, however it might be hoped that in their practical effect they might prove beneficial to America, provided the operation of the embargo were not to prevent her from reaping that benefit."

This intended change in the orders depended on the political change which converted Spain from an enemy into an ally. Spencer Perceval did not care

to press the cause of British commerce so far as to
tax American wheat and salt-fish on their way to
Spain and Portugal, where he must himself provide
money to pay for them after they were bought by the
army commissaries. Accordingly, in December, 1808,
a new Order in Council appeared, doing away with
the export duties lately imposed by Parliament on
foreign articles passing through England. Thenceforward American wheat might be shipped at Liverpool for the Spanish peninsula without paying ten
shillings a quarter to the British Treasury,[1] if only
the embargo did not prevent American wheat from
entering Liverpool at all.

In a short note, dated December 24, Canning enclosed to Pinkney a copy of the new order; and while
taking care to explain that this measure conceded
nothing in principle, he offered it as a step toward
removing the most offensive, if not the most oppressive, restraint imposed on American commerce by the
Orders of 1807 : —

" As I have more than once understood from you that
the part of the Orders in Council which this order goes to
mitigate is that which was felt most sorely by the United
States, I have great pleasure in being authorized to communicate it to you."

Pinkney was in no humor to bear more of what he
considered Canning's bad taste, and he could have
but one opinion of the measure which Canning an-

[1] Act of Geo. III. 1808 ; Cap. xxvi. American State Papers,
iii. 274.

nounced. "This order is a shadow," he wrote to Madison,[1] " and if meant to conciliate us, ridiculous." His reply to Canning verged for the first time on abruptness, as though the moment were near when he meant to speak another language.

" It is perfectly true," began Pinkney's acknowledgment of Dec. 28, 1808,[2] " as the concluding paragraph of your letter supposes me to believe, that the United States have viewed with great sensibility the pretension of this Government (which, as a pretension, the present order reasserts without much if at all modifying its practical effect) to levy imposts upon their commerce, outward and inward, which the Orders in Council of the last year were to constrain to pass through British ports. But it is equally true that my Government has constantly protested against the entire system with which that pretension was connected, and has in consequence required the repeal, not the modification, of the British Orders in Council."

This reception roused the temper of Canning, who could not understand, if Pinkney honestly wished harmony, why he should repel what might be taken as a kindness ; yet the same reasons which induced him to make the advance impelled him to bear with the American minister's roughness. The moment was ill adapted for more quarrels. Napoleon had occupied Madrid three weeks before, and was driving Sir John Moore's army in headlong flight back to England ; the dreams of midsummer had vanished ;

[1] Pinkney to Madison, Dec. 25, 1808 ; Wheaton's Pinkney.
[2] Pinkney to Canning, Dec. 28, 1808 ; State Papers, iii. 240.

the overthrow of France was no nearer than before the Spanish uprising; the United States were seriously discussing war, and however loudly a few interested Englishmen might at times talk, the people of England never wanted war with the United States. Canning found himself obliged to suppress his irritation, and so far from checking the spirit of concession to America, was drawn into new and more decided advances. Spencer Perceval felt the same impulse, and of his own accord proposed other steps to his colleague, after Pinkney's letter of December 28 had been read and considered by the Cabinet. With the impression of that letter fresh in the minds of both, Canning wrote to Perceval on the last day of the year : [1] —

" We have given quite proof enough of our determination to maintain our principle to enable us to relax, if in other respects advisable, without danger of being suspected of giving way. The paragraph in my letter to Pinkney, of September 23, prepares the world for any relaxations that we may think fit to make, provided they are coupled with increased severity against France ; and though this last consideration is something impaired by my last communication to Pinkney, yet the manner in which he has received that communication (with respect to which reception I partake of the fury which you describe as having been kindled in Hammond) leaves us quite at liberty to take any new steps without explanation, and exempts us from any hazard of seeing them too well received."

[1] Canning to Perceval, Dec. 31, 1808 ; Perceval MSS.

The year 1809 began with this new spirit of accommodation in British councils. The causes which produced it were notorious. From the moment Europe closed her ports, in the autumn of 1807, articles commonly supplied from the Continent rose to speculative prices, and after the American embargo the same effect followed with American produce. Flax, linseed, tallow, timber, Spanish wool, silk, hemp, American cotton doubled or trebled in price in the English markets during the years 1807 and 1808.[1] Colonial produce declined in the same proportion. Quantities of sugar and coffee overfilled the warehouses of London, while the same articles could not be bought at Amsterdam and Antwerp at prices three, four, and five times those asked on the Royal Exchange. Under the Orders in Council, the whole produce of the West Indies, shut from Europe by Napoleon and from the United States by the embargo, was brought to England, until mere plethora stopped accumulation.

Debarred from their natural outlets, English merchandise and manufactures were forced into every other market which seemed to offer a hope of sale or barter. When Portugal fell into Napoleon's hands, and the royal family took refuge in Brazil under British protection, English merchants glutted Brazil with their goods, until the beach at Rio Janeiro was covered with property, which perished for want of buyers and warehouses. The Spanish trade, thrown open soon afterward, resulted in similar losses. In

[1] Tooke's History of Prices, i. 274–279.

the effort to relieve the plethora at home, England gorged the few small channels of commerce that remained in her control.

These efforts coincided with a drain of specie on government account to support the Spanish patriots. The British armies sent to Spain required large sums in coin for their supplies, and the Spaniards required every kind of assistance. The process of paying money on every hand and receiving nothing but worthless produce could not long continue without turning the exchanges against London; yet a sudden call for specie threatened to shake the foundations of society. Never was credit so rotten. Speculation was rampant, and inflation accompanied it. None of the familiar signs of financial disaster were absent. Visionary joint-stock enterprises flourished. Discounts at long date, or without regard to proper security, could be obtained with ease from the private banks and bankers who were competing for business; and although the Bank of England followed its usual course, neither contracting nor expanding its loans and issues, suddenly, at the close of 1808, gold coin rose at a leap from a nominal rate of 103 to the alarming premium of 113. The exchanges had turned, and the inevitable crash was near.

The political outlook took the same sombre tone as the finances. The failure of the Spaniards and the evacuation of Spain by the British army after the loss of Sir John Moore at Corunna, January 16, destroyed confidence in all political hopes. Lord Castlereagh, as war-secretary, was most exposed to attack. Instead of defending him, Canning set the example of weakening his influence. Aware that the Administration had not the capacity to hold its own, Canning undertook to reform it. As early as October, 1808, he talked freely of Castlereagh's incompetence, and made no secret of his opinion that the Secretary for War must go out.[1] Whether his judgment of Castlereagh's abilities were right or wrong was a matter for English history to decide; but Americans might at least wonder that the Convention of Cintra and the campaign of Sir John Moore were not held to be achievements as respectable as the American diplomacy of Canning or the commercial experiments of Spencer Perceval. Canning himself agreed that Perceval was little, if at all, superior to Castlereagh, and he saw hope for England chiefly in his own elevation to the post of the Duke of Portland.

Although no one fully understood all that had been done by the Portland ministry, enough was known to render their fall certain; and Canning saw himself sinking with the rest. He made active efforts to secure his own safety and to rise above the misfortunes which threatened to overwhelm his colleagues. Among other annoyances, he felt the recoil of his American policy. The tone taken by Pinkney coin-

---

[1] Brougham to Grey, Nov. 25, 1809, Brougham's Memoirs, i. 417 ; Temple's Courts and Cabinets, iv. 276, 283 ; Canning to the Duke of Portland, March 24, 1809; Walpole's Spencer Perceval, i. 347, 350.

cided with the warlike threats reported by Erskine, and with the language of Campbell's Report to the House of Representatives. Erskine's despatch of November 26, in which Campbell's Report was enclosed, and his alarming despatches of December 3 and 4 were received by Canning about the middle of January,[1] at a time when the Ministry was sustained only by royal favor. The language and the threats of these advices were such as Canning could not with dignity overlook or with safety resent; but he overlooked them. January 18, at a diplomatic dinner given by him on the Queen's birthday, he took Pinkney aside to tell him that the Ministry were willing to consider the Resolutions proposed in Campbell's Report as putting an end to the difficulties which prevented a satisfactory arrangement.[2] Pinkney, surprised by Canning's "more than usual kindness and respect," suggested deferring the subject to a better occasion; and Canning readily acquiesced, appointing January 22 as the day for an interview.

The next morning, January 19, Parliament met, and American affairs were instantly made the subject of attack on ministers. In the Lords, Grenville declared that " the insulting and sophistical answer " returned by Canning to the American offer, persuaded him " that the intention of the King's government is

---

[1] Canning to Erskine, Jan. 23, 1809 ; Cobbett's Debates, xvii, cxix.

[2] Pinkney to Madison, Jan. 23, 1809 ; Wheaton's Pinkney, p. 420.

to drive things to extremity with America." Lord
Hawkesbury the Home Secretary, who had succeeded
his father as Earl of Liverpool, replied in the old
tone that ministers felt no disposition to irritate
America, but that national dignity and importance
were not to be sacrificed " at the very moment when
America seemed so blind to her own interest, and
betrayed so decided a partiality in favor of France." [1]
In the Commons, Whitbread and the other leaders
of opposition echoed the attack, but Canning did not
echo the reply.

" The same infatuation," said Whitbread,[2] " seems
now to prevail that existed in the time of the late
American war. There were the same taunts, the
same sarcasms, and the same assertions that America
cannot do without us." Only a few weeks earlier
or later, Canning would have met such criticisms
in his loftiest tone, and with more reason than in
1807 or in 1808. In his desk were Erskine's latest
despatches, announcing impending war in every accent of defiance and in many varieties of italics
and capital letters ; fresh in his memory was his
own official pledge that " no step which could even
mistakenly be construed into concession should be
taken " while a doubt existed whether America had
wholly abandoned her attempt at commercial restriction. Yet instead of maintaining England's authority at the moment when for the first time it was

[1] Cobbett's Debates, xii. 25.
[2] Cobbett's Debates, p. 69.

threatened by the United States, Canning became apologetic and yielding. Repeating the common-places of the newspapers that America had sided with France, and even going so far as to assert, what he best knew to be an error, that the Orders in Council had not been the cause of the embargo, and " it was now a notorious fact that no such ground had been laid for the embargo;" after declaring the exclusion of British war-vessels from American harbors to have been the chief obstacle to the compromise offered by America, — treading, with what seemed a very uncertain foot, among these slippery and ill-balanced stepping-stones, he reached the point where he meant to rest. The " Chesapeake " Proclamation, which excluded British war-ships from American harbors, being his chief grievance, any settlement which removed that grievance would be so far satisfactory; and for this reason the measures proposed in Campbell's Report, though clothed in hostile language, might, if made known to the British government in amicable terms, have led to the acceptance of the compromise proposed, since they excluded French as well as English ships of war from American ports.

Canning next turned to Pinkney to ascertain how much concession would be safe. The interview took place January 22; but Pinkney's powers had been withdrawn, and he neither could nor would furnish Canning with any assurance on which a concession could be offered with the certainty either that it would be accepted, or that it would be refused. Canning seemed particularly anxious to know how the embargo could be effectually enforced against commerce with France, after being removed in regard to England.[1] He "presumed that the government of the United States would not complain if the naval force of this country should assist in preventing such a commerce."[2] Pinkney felt many doubts of Canning's good faith,[3] and had every reason for avoiding committal of himself or of his Government. According to his own account, he declined to enter into the discussion of details, and confined himself to general encouragement of Canning's good disposition.[4]

After experimenting upon Pinkney, much as he had sounded Parliament, Canning lost not an hour in composing the new instructions to Erskine. Four in number, all bearing the same date of January 23, they dealt successively with each of the disputed points; but in order to understand the embroilment they caused, readers must carry in mind, even at some effort of memory, precisely what Canning ordered Erskine to do, and precisely what Erskine did.

The first instruction dealt with the " Chesapeake " affair, and the Proclamation occasioned by it. Ac-

[1] Pinkney to Madison, Jan. 23, 1809 ; Wheaton's Pinkney, p. 423.

[2] Brief Account, etc., Jan. 23, 1809 ; State Papers, iii. 299.

[3] Pinkney to Madison, Jan. 23, 1809 ; Wheaton's Pinkney, p. 424.

[4] Pinkney to R. Smith, June 6, 1809 ; State Papers, iii. 303.

cepting Gallatin's idea that the Proclamation being merged in the general non-intercourse would cease to exist as a special and separate provision of law, Canning instructed Erskine that if French ships of war should be excluded from American ports, and if the Proclamation should be tacitly withdrawn, he need no longer insist upon the formal recall. Further, Gallatin had suggested that Congress was about to exclude foreign seamen by law from national ships; and Canning admitted also this evasion of his demand that the United States should engage not to countenance desertions. Finally, he withdrew the demand for disavowals which had wrecked Rose's mission.

Evidently the British government wished to settle the "Chesapeake" affair. Had Canning in like manner swept away his old conditions precedent to withdrawal of the Orders in Council, his good faith would have been above suspicion; but he approached that subject in a different spirit, and imposed one condition after another while he adopted the unusual course of putting each new condition into the mouth of some American official. He drew from Erskine's despatches the inference that Madison, Smith, and Gallatin were willing to recognize in express terms the validity of the British " Rule of 1756." [1] For this misunderstanding Erskine was to blame,[2] but Can-

[1] Canning to Erskine, Jan. 23, 1809 ; American State Papers, iii. 300.

[2] Second Administration of Jefferson, vol. iv. pp. 388–389.

ning was alone responsible for the next remark, that
" Mr. Pinkney has recently, but for the first time,
expressed to me his opinion that there will be no
indisposition on the part of his Government to the
enforcement, by the naval power of Great Britain,"
of the Act of Congress declaring non-intercourse
with France. On the strength of these supposed expressions of William Pinkney, Madison, Smith, and
Gallatin, none of which was official or in writing,
Canning concluded : —

" I flatter myself that there will be no difficulty in
obtaining a distinct and official recognition of these conditions from the American government. For this purpose you are at liberty to communicate this despatch *in
extenso* to the American government."

The chief interest of these instructions lay in the
question whether Canning meant in good faith to
offer on any conditions a withdrawal of the Orders
in Council. The course of his own acts and of Perceval's measures, suggested that he did not intend
to offer any terms which the United States could
accept. His remark to Perceval three weeks before,
that they were quite at liberty to take new steps
without " any hazard of seeing them too well received," pointed in the same direction. Yet motives
were enigmas too obscure for search, and the motives
of Canning in this instance were more perplexing
than usual. If he was serious in hoping an agreement, how could he insist on requiring official recognition of the right of Great Britain to enforce the

municipal laws of the United States when he afterward admitted that such a claim "could not well
find its way into a stipulation; that he had never-
theless believed it proper to propose the condition
to the United States; that he should have been
satisfied with the rejection of it; and that the consequence would have been that they should have
intercepted the commerce to which it referred, if
any such commerce should be attempted"?[1] In the
instructions to Erskine he imposed the condition as
essential to the agreement, — the same condition
which he thought "could not well find its way into
a stipulation," and which "he should have been satisfied" to see rejected.

For two years Canning had lost no opportunity
of charging the American government with subser-
vience to Napoleon; even in these instructions he
alleged Jefferson's "manifest partiality" to France
as a reason why England could entertain no propositions coming from him. He had in his hands Madison's emphatic threats of war; how then could he
conceive of obtaining from Madison an express recognition of the British Rule of 1756, which Madison
had most deeply pledged himself to resist?

On the other hand, Canning showed forbearance
and a wish for peace, by leaving Erskine minister
at Washington as well as by passing unnoticed
Madison's threats of war; and he betrayed a singular incapacity to understand the bearing of his own

[1] Pinkney to R. Smith, June 23, 1809; State Papers, iii. 303.

demands when he directed Erskine to communicate his instructions *in extenso* to the American government. Had he intelligently acted in bad faith, he would not have given the President, whose attachment to France he suspected, the advantage of seeing these instructions, which required that America should become a subject State of England.

Perhaps a partial clew to these seeming contradictions might be found in the peculiar traits of Canning's character. He belonged to a class of men denied the faculty of realizing the sensibilities of others. At the moment when he took this tone of authority toward America, he gave mortal offence to his own colleague Lord Castlereagh, by assuming a like attitude toward him. He could not understand, and he could never train himself to regard, the rule that such an attitude between States as between gentlemen was not admitted among equals.

Whatever was the reason of Canning's conduct, its effect was that of creating the impression of bad faith by offering terms intended to be refused. The effect of bad faith was the more certain because the instructions closed by giving Erskine some latitude, not as to the conditions which were to be distinctly and officially recognized, but as to the form in which the recognition might be required : —

" Upon the receipt here of an official note containing an engagement for the adoption of the three conditions above specified, his Majesty will be prepared on the faith of such engagement, — either immediately, if the repeal shall have been immediate in America or on any day specified by the American government for that repeal, — reciprocally to recall the Orders in Council."

The form of the required engagement was left to Erskine's discretion; and in case Erskine failed, Canning would be still at liberty to claim, as he afterward did, that his conditions were not so rigorously meant as Erskine should have supposed them to be.

Meanwhile the Government of England was falling to pieces. Day by day the situation became more alarming. For months after these despatches were sent, the Commons passed their time in taking testimony and listening to speeches intended to prove or disprove that the Duke of York, commander-in-chief of the army, was in the habit of selling officers' commissions through the agency of his mistress, a certain Mrs. Clarke; and although the Duke protested his innocence, the scandal drove him from his office. The old King, blind and infirm, was quite unfit to bear the shame of his son's disgrace; while the Prince of Wales stood no better than the Duke of York either in his father's esteem or in public opinion. The Ministry was rent by faction; Perceval, Castlereagh, and Canning were at cross purposes, while the Whigs were so weak that they rather feared than hoped their rivals' fall. Whatever might be the factiousness of Congress or the weakness of government at Washington, the confusion in Parliament was worse, and threatened worse dangers.

" All power and influence of Perceval in the House is
quite gone by," wrote a Whig member, February 16.[1]
" He speaks without authority and without attention paid
to him ; and Canning has made two or three such rash
declarations that he is little attended to.   You may judge
the situation of the House, when I tell you we were last
night nearly three quarters of an hour debating about the
evidence of a drunken footman by Perceval suggesting
modes of ascertaining how to convict him of his drunken-
ness, — Charles Long [one of the Administration], near
whom I was sitting telling me at the time what a lamen-
table proof it was of the want of some man of sense and
judgment to lead the House.   There is no government
in the House of Commons, — you may be assured the
thing does not exist ; and whether they can ever recover
their tone of power remains to be proved.   At present
Mr. Croker, Mr. D. Brown, and Mr. Beresford are the
leaders. . . . The Cintra Convention, or the general
campaign, or the American question, are minor considerations, and indeed do not enter into the consideration
of any one."

The House of Lords maintained more appearance
of dignity ; and there, February 17, four-and-twenty
hours after Colonel Fremantle wrote this letter, Lord
Grenville began a debate on American affairs.   As
a test of Tory sincerity in view of what Erskine was
soon to do at Washington, the debate — as well as
all else that was said of American affairs during
the session — deserved more than ordinary notice, if

[1] W. H. Fremantle to the Marquis of Buckingham, Feb. 16,
1809 ; Courts and Cabinets of George III., iv. 318.

only in justice to the British ministry, whose language was to receive a commentary they did not expect.[1]

The most significant speech came from Lord Sidmouth. The conservatism of this peer stood above reproach, and compared closely with that of Spencer Perceval. Rather than abandon the "established principle" of the Rule of 1756, he far preferred an American war. He proved his stubborn Tory consistency too clearly, both before and after 1809, to warrant a suspicion of leanings toward liberal or American sympathies; but his speech of February 17 supporting Grenville, and charging ministers with bad faith, was long and earnest. He called attention to the scandal that while the Government professed in the speech from the Throne a persuasion "that in the result the enemy will be convinced of the impolicy of persevering in a system which retorts upon himself, in so much greater proportion, those evils which he endeavors to inflict," yet instead of retorting those evils, Perceval licensed the export and import both with France and Holland of the very articles which those countries wished to sell and buy, while Canning at the same moment rejected the American offers of trade because he thought it "important in the highest degree that the disappointment of the hopes of the enemy should not have been purchased by any concession."

Ministers might disregard Grenville's furious de-

[1] Cobbett's Debates, xii. 771–803.

nunciation of the orders as an act of the most egre-
gious folly and the most unexampled ignorance that
ever disgraced the councils of a State ; they might
even close their ears to Sidmouth's charge that the
folly and ignorance of the orders were surpassed by
their dishonesty, — but not even Spencer Perceval
could deny or forget that while a year before, Feb.
15, 1808, forty-eight peers voted against him, on
Feb. 17, 1809, seventy lords, in person or by proxy,
supported Grenville. While the opposition gained
twenty-two votes, the government gained only nine.

The impression of weakness in the ministry was
increased by the energy with which the authors of
the orders stood at bay in their defence. When
Whitbread in the House of Commons renewed the
attack, and the House, March 6, entered on the debate, James Stephen came forward as the champion
of his own cause. Stephen's speech,[1] published afterward as a pamphlet, was intended to be an official
as well as a final answer to attacks against the
orders, and was conclusive in regard to the scope
and motives of Perceval's scheme. Neither Canning
nor Liverpool spoke with personal knowledge to be
compared with that of Stephen. Canning in particular had nothing to do with the orders except as
a subject of diplomatic evasion. Stephen, Perceval,
and George Rose were the parents of commercial
restriction, and knew best their own objects. With
frankness creditable to him, but contrasting with

[1] Cobbett's Debates, xiii. App. no. 2, xxxi.

the double-toned language of Perceval and Canning, Stephen always placed in the foreground the commercial objects he wanted and expected to attain. His speech of March 6, 1809, once more asserted, in language as positive as possible, that the orders had no other purpose than to stop the American trade with France because it threatened to supplant British trade. The doctrine of retaliation, or the object of retorting evils on France, had nothing to do with Stephen's scheme. His words were clear, for like a true enthusiast he was wholly intent on the idea in which he thought safety depended.

Canning also planted himself on advanced ground. The question, he said, was between England and France ; not between England and America. On the principles of international law he had no defence to offer for the Orders in Council as between England and America. "He was willing to admit that it was not upon the poor pretence of the existing law of nations, but upon the extension of that law (an extension just and necessary), that his Majesty's ministers were to rely, in the present instance, for justification." This extension rested on the excuse that France had first discarded the law of nations ; and America, in attempting to give to Great Britain the priority in wrong, had incurred this censure, — "that she had brought a false charge, and persisted in it." In his opinion, the American offer to withdraw the embargo in favor of England and to enforce it against France, "was illusory ; he might add,

in the language of Mr. Madison, ' it was insulting.' "
Those who accused ministers of a disinclination to
adopt pacific measures respecting America had lost
sight of the facts. " We had rather gone too far
than done too little. We twice offered to negotiate;
yet the Non-importation Act was not revoked."

If this was Canning's true state of mind, his instructions to Erskine less than a month before, offering to abandon the Orders in Council, seemed to
admit no defence. Still less could be explained how
President Madison, after reading these speeches,
should have expected from Canning the approval of
any possible arrangement. Yet the irritation of Canning's tone showed him to be ill at ease, — he felt the
ground slipping under his feet. The public had become weary of him and his colleagues. The commercial system they had invented seemed to create the
evils it was made to counteract. The press began
to complain. As early as January 13 the " Times "
showed signs of deserting the orders, which it declared to be no " acts of retaliation," but " measures of counteraction," complicated by transit duties
doubtful either in expediency or justice. " If America will withdraw her Embargo and Non-importation
Acts as far as they relate to England, provided we
rescind the Orders in Council, we cannot consider
this as a disgraceful concession on our part." After
the debate of March 6, the " Times " renewed its
complaints. Every day increased the difficulties of
ministers, until mere change became relief.

At length, April 26, the reality of the weakness of
Perceval and Canning became clear. On that day
a new Order in Council[1] appeared, which roused
great interest because it seemed to abandon the
whole ground taken in the Orders of November,
1807, and to return within the admitted principles
of international law. The machinery of the old
orders was apparently discarded; the machinery
of blockade was restored in its place. The Order of
April 26, 1809, declared that the old orders were
revoked and annulled except so far as their objects
were to be attained by a general blockade of all ports
and places under the government of France. The
blockade thus declared was to extend northward as
far as Ems, and was to include on the south the
ports of northern Italy. Of course the new blockade
was not even claimed to be effective. No squadrons
were to enforce its provisions by their actual presence
before the blockaded ports. In that respect the Order
of April 26, 1809, was as illegal as that of Nov. 11,
1807; but the new arrangement opened to neutral
commerce all ports not actually ports of France,
even though the British flag should be excluded
from them, — retaliating upon France only the injury
which the French decrees attempted to inflict on
England.

Pinkney was greatly pleased, and wrote to Madison in excellent spirits[2] that the change gave all

---

[1] Order in Council of April 26, 1809; State Papers, iii. 241.

[2] Pinkney to Madison, May 3, 1809; Wheaton's Pinkney, p. 428.

the immediate benefits which could have arisen from
the arrangement proposed by him in the previous
August, except the right to demand from France the
recall of her edicts. " Our triumph is already considered as a signal one by everybody. The pretexts
with which ministers would conceal their motives for
a relinquishment of all which they prized in their
system are seen through, and it is universally viewed
as a concession to America. Our honor is now safe ;
and by management we may probably gain everything we have in view." Canning said to Pinkney :
" If these alterations did not do all that was expected, they at least narrowed extremely the field
of discussion, and gave great facilities and encouragement to reviving cordiality." [1]   Government took
pains to impress the idea that it had done much, and
wished to do more for conciliation ; yet the doubt
remained whether Government was acting in good
faith. Pinkney overestimated its concessions.   If
the British navy was to blockade Holland, France,
and northern Italy only in order that British commerce might be forced, through the blockade and
license system, into the place of neutral commerce,
the new system was only the old one in disguise.
Under a blockade, in good faith, licenses seemed to
have no place. In that case, the Order in Council
of April 26 might lead to a real settlement ; but
how was it possible that Perceval, George Rose, and

[1] Pinkney to R. Smith, May 1, 1809. MSS. State Dep.
Archives.

James Stephen should have given up what they believed to be the only hope for England's safety?

If one frank and straightforward man could be found among the ministerial ranks, James Stephen had a right to that distinction, and to his language one might hope to look with confidence for the truth; yet Stephen seemed for once not to understand himself. In publishing his speech of March 6, he added an appendix on the new order, and closed his remarks by a prayer that seemed meant to open the way for the full admission of American offers: —

" It is not strange that a measure so indulgent [as the new Order] should be generally approved by the American merchants and agents resident in England. The most eminent of the gentlemen of that description who opposed the Orders of November have openly professed their satisfaction at this important change. May the same sentiment prevail on notice of it beyond the Atlantic! Or, what would be still better, may an amicable arrangement there have already terminated all the differences between us and our American brethren on terms that will involve a complete revocation of our retaliatory orders, and impose on America herself, by her own consent, the duty of vindicating effectually the rights of neutrality against the aggressions of France!"

CHAPTER IV.

EARLY in February, when Congress refused to support Madison's war-policy, — the mere shadow of which brought Perceval and Canning almost to their senses, — Canning's instructions were despatched from the Foreign Office. April 7, more than a month after the Tenth Congress had expired, amidst political conditions altogether different from those imagined by Canning, the instructions reached Washington; and Erskine found himself required to carry them into effect.

A cautious diplomatist would have declined to act upon them. Under pretext of the change which had altered the situation he would have asked for new instructions, while pointing out the mischievous nature of the old. The instructions were evidently impossible to execute; the situation was less critical than ever before, and Great Britain was master of the field.

On the other hand, the instructions offered some appearance of an advance toward friendship. They proved Canning's ignorance, but not his bad faith; and if Canning in good faith wanted a settlement,

Erskine saw every reason for gratifying him. The arrogance of Canning's demands did not necessarily exclude further concession. The great governments of Europe from time immemorial had used a tone of authority insufferable to weaker Powers, and not agreeable to one another; yet their tone did not always imply the wish to quarrel, and England herself seldom resented manners as unpleasant as her own. Used to the rough exchange of blows, and hardened by centuries of toil and fighting, England was not sensitive when her interests were at stake. Her surliness was a trick rather than a design. Her diplomatic agents expected to enjoy reasonable liberty in softening the harshness and in supplying the ignorance of their chiefs of the Foreign Office; and if such latitude was ever allowed to a diplomatist, Erskine had the best right to use it in the case of instructions the motives of which he could not comprehend.

Finally, Erskine was the son of Lord Erskine, and owed his appointment to Charles James Fox. He was half Republican by education, half American by marriage; and probably, like all British liberals, he felt in secret an entire want of confidence in Canning and a positive antipathy to the Tory commercial system.

Going at once to Secretary Robert Smith, Erskine began on the "Chesapeake" affair, and quickly disposed of it. The President abandoned the American demand for a court-martial on Admiral Berkeley,

finding that it would not be entertained.[1] Erskine
then wrote a letter offering the stipulated redress for
the " Chesapeake " outrage, and Madison wrote a
letter accepting it, which Robert Smith signed, and
dated April 17.

Two points in Madison's " Chesapeake " letter attracted notice. Erskine began his official note [2] by
alluding to the Non-intercourse Act of March 1, as
having placed Great Britain on an equal footing with
the other belligerents, and warranting acknowledgment on that account. The idea was far-fetched, and
Madison's reply was ambiguous : —

" As it appears at the same time, that in making this
offer his Britannic Majesty derives a motive from the
equality now existing in the relations of the United
States with the two belligerent Powers, the President
owes it to the occasion and to himself to let it be understood that this equality is a result incident to a state of
things growing out of distinct considerations."

If Madison knew precisely what " distinct considerations " had led Congress and the country to that
state of things to which the Non-intercourse Act
was incident, he knew more than was known to Congress ; but even though he owed this statement to
himself, so important an official note might have expressed his ideas more exactly. " A result incident
to a state of things growing out of distinct considera-

[1] Erskine to Canning, April 18, 1809; Cobbett's Debates,
xvii. Appendix, cxlvii.

[2] Erskine to R. Smith, April 17, 1809; State Papers, iii. 295.

tions" was something unusual, and to say the least wanting in clearness, but seemed not intended to gratify Canning.

The second point challenged sharper criticism.

" With this explanation, as requisite as it is frank," Smith's note continued, " I am authorized to inform you that the President accepts the note delivered by you in the name and by the order of his Britannic Majesty, and will consider the same with the engagement therein, when fulfilled, as a satisfaction for the insult and injury of which he has complained. But I have it in express charge from the President to state that while he forbears to insist on the further punishment of the offending officer, he is not the less sensible of the justice and utility of such an example, nor the less persuaded that it would best comport with what is due from his Britannic Majesty to his own honor."

According to Robert Smith's subsequent account, the last sentence was added by Madison in opposition to his secretary's wishes.[1] One of Madison's peculiarities showed itself in these words, which endangered the success of all his efforts. If he wished a reconciliation, they were worse than useless; but if he wished a quarrel, he chose the right means. The President of the United States was charged with the duty of asserting in its full extent what was due to his own honor as representative of the Union; but he was not required, either by the laws of his country or by the custom of nations, to define the conduct which

---

[1] Robert Smith's Address to the People, 1811.

in his opinion best comported with what was due from his Britannic Majesty to the honor of England. That Erskine should have consented to receive such a note was matter for wonder, knowing as he did that Kings of England had never smiled on servants who allowed their sovereign's honor to be questioned; and the public surprise was not lessened by his excuse.

" It appeared to me," he said,[1] " that if any indecorum could justly be attributed to the expressions in the official notes of this Government, the censure due would fall upon them; and that the public opinion would condemn their bad taste or want of propriety in coldly and ungraciously giving up what they considered as a right, but which they were not in a condition to enforce."

Under the impression that no " intention whatever existed in the mind of the President of the United States to convey a disrespectful meaning toward his Majesty by these expressions," Erskine accepted them in silence, and Madison himself never understood that he had given cause of offence.

Having thus disposed of the " Chesapeake " grievance, Erskine took up the Orders in Council.[2] His instructions were emphatic, and he was in effect ordered to communicate these instructions *in extenso* to the President, for in such cases permission was

[1] Erskine to Canning, Aug. 3, 1809; Cobbett's Debates, xvii. clvi.

[2] Erskine to Canning, April 30, 1809; Aug. 7, 1809. Erskine to Robert Smith, Aug. 14, 1809. Cobbett's Debates, xvii. cli. clxx. State Papers, iii. 305.

equivalent to order. He disobeyed; in official sense
he did not communicate his instructions at all. " I
considered that it would be in vain," he afterward
said. This was his first exercise of discretion; and
his second was more serious. After reading Canning's repeated and positive orders to require from
the American government " a distinct and official
recognition " of three conditions, he decided to treat
these orders as irrelevant. He knew that the President had no Constitutional power to bind Congress,
even if Madison himself would patiently bear a single
reading of three such impossible requirements, and
that under these circumstances the negotiation had
better never begin than end abruptly in anger. Erskine would have done better not to begin it; but he
thought otherwise. Under more favorable circumstances, Monroe and Pinkney had made the same
experiment in 1806.

Canning offered to withdraw the Orders in Council,
on three conditions precedent: —

(1) That all interdicts on commerce should be revoked by the United States so far as they affected
England, while they were still to be enforced against
France. When Erskine submitted this condition to
Robert Smith, he was assured that the President would
comply with it, and that Congress would certainly assert the national rights against France, but that the
President had no power to pledge the government by
a formal act. Erskine decided to consider Canning's
condition fulfilled if the President, under the eleventh

section of the Non-intercourse Act, should issue a proclamation renewing trade with Great Britain, while retaining the prohibition against France. This settlement had the disadvantage of giving no guarantee to England, while it left open the trade with Holland, which was certainly a dependency of France.

(2) Canning further required that the United States should formally renounce the pretension to a colonial trade in war which was not permitted in time of peace. To this condition, which Erskine seems to have stated as applying only to the direct carrying-trade to Europe, Robert Smith replied that it could not be recognized except in a formal treaty ; but that it was practically unimportant, because this commerce, as well as every other with France or her dependencies, was prohibited by Act of Congress. Erskine accepted this reasoning, and left the abstract right untouched.

(3) Canning lastly demanded that the United States should recognize the right of Great Britain to capture such American vessels as should be found attempting to trade with any of the Powers acting under the French Decrees. To this suggestion Secretary Smith replied that the President could not so far degrade the national authority as to authorize Great Britain to execute American laws ; but that the point seemed to him immaterial, since no citizen could present to the United States government a claim founded on a violation of its own laws. Erskine once more acquiesced, although the trade with

Holland was not a violation of law, and would probably give rise to the very claims which Canning
meant to preclude.

Having thus disposed of the three conditions which
were to be distinctly and officially recognized, Erskine
exchanged notes with Robert Smith, bearing date
April 18 and 19, 1809, chiefly admirable for their
brevity, since they touched no principle. In his note
of April 18, Erskine said that the favorable change
produced by anticipation of the Non-intercourse Act
had encouraged his Government to send out a new
envoy with full powers; and that meanwhile his
Majesty would recall his Orders in Council if the
President would issue a Proclamation renewing intercourse with Great Britain. Secretary Smith replied
on the same day that the President would not fail in
doing so. April 19, Erskine in a few lines announced
himself " authorized to declare that his Majesty's
Orders in Council of January and November, 1807,
will have been withdrawn as respects the United
States on the 10th of June next." Secretary Smith
answered that the President would immediately issue
his Proclamation. Two days afterward the four
notes and the Proclamation itself were published in
the " National Intelligencer."

The United States heard with delight that friendship with England had been restored. Amid an outburst of joy commerce resumed its old paths, and
without waiting for June 10 hurried ships and merchandise to British ports. No complaints were

heard; not a voice was raised about impressments; no regret was expressed that war with France must follow reconciliation with England; no one found fault with Madison for following in 1809 the policy which had raised almost a revolution against President Washington only fourteen years before. Yet Madison strained the law, besides showing headlong haste, in acting upon Erskine's promises without waiting for their ratification, and without even asking to see the British negotiator's special powers or instructions. The haste was no accident or oversight. When Turreau remonstrated with Gallatin against such precipitate conduct contrary to diplomatic usage, Gallatin answered, —

" The offers could not be refused."

" But you have only promises," urged Turreau ; " and already twelve hundred vessels, twelve thousand sailors, and two hundred million [francs] of property have left your ports. May not the English take all this to serve as a guarantee for other conditions which their interest might care to impose?"

" We would like it!" replied the Secretary of the Treasury. " Perhaps our people may need such a lesson to cure them of British influence and the mania of British commerce." [1]

Impatient at the conduct of Congress and the people, Madison was glad to create a new situation, and preferred even hostilities to the Orders in Council. Erskine's conduct was unusual, yet Great Britain had

[1] Turreau to Champagny, 1 June, 1809; Archives des Aff. Étr. MSS.

shown no such regard for Madison's feelings that Madison should hesitate before the eccentricities of British diplomacy. Perplexed to account for Canning's sudden change, the President and his friends quieted their uneasiness by attributing their triumph to their own statesmanship. The Republican newspapers, the "National Intelligencer" at their head, announced that England had been conquered by the embargo, and taunted not only the Federalists but also the Northern Republicans with the triumph. While nothing could be more positive than the language thus encouraged by the Government, the error was partly redeemed by the tenderness with which it was used to soothe the wounded feelings of Jefferson.

"The bright day of judgment and retribution has at length arrived," said the "National Intelligencer" of April 26, "when a virtuous nation will not withhold the tribute of its warmest thanks from an Administration whose sole ambition has ever been to advance the happiness of its constituents, even at the sacrifice of its present popularity. Thanks to the sage who now so gloriously reposes in the shades of Monticello, and to those who shared his confidence! . . . It may be boldly alleged that the revocation of the British Orders is attributable to the embargo."

President Madison wrote to Jefferson somewhat more cautiously:[1] "The British Cabinet must have

[1] Madison to Jefferson, April 24, 1809; Madison's Writings, ii. 439.

changed its course under a full conviction that an
adjustment with this country had become essential."
Accepting quietly a turn of fortune that would have
bewildered the most astute diplomatist, Madison made
ready to meet the special session of Congress.

The Eleventh Congress differed little in character
from its predecessor, but that little difference was not
to its advantage. G. W. Campbell of Tennessee,
David R. Williams of South Carolina, Joseph Clay of
Pennsylvania, Joseph Story of Massachusetts, and
Wilson Cary Nicholas of Virginia disappeared from
the House, and no one of equal influence stepped into
their places. The mediocrity of the Tenth Congress
continued to mark the character of the Eleventh.
John W. Eppes became chairman of the Committee
of Ways and Means. Varnum was again chosen
Speaker, while Vice-President George Clinton still
presided over the deliberations of thirty-four men
whose abilities were certainly not greater than those
of any previous Senate.

May 23 President Madison's first Annual Message
was read. No objection could be made to its brief
recital of the steps which led to the arrangement
with Erskine; but the next paragraph not only provoked attack, it threatened the country also with
commercial wars to the end of time: —

" Whilst I take pleasure in doing justice to the councils of his Britannic Majesty which, no longer adhering to
the policy which made an abandonment by France of her
Decrees a prerequisite to the revocation of the British

Orders, have substituted the amicable course which has issued thus happily, I cannot do less than refer to the proposal heretofore made on the part of the United States, embracing a like restoration of the suspended commerce, as a proof of the spirit of accommodation which has at no time been intermitted, and to the result which now calls for our congratulations as corroborating the principles by which the public councils have been guided during a period of the most trying embarrassments."

When Madison spoke of the "principles by which the public councils have been guided," he meant to place at their head the principles of embargo and non-intercourse, — a result of Erskine's arrangement hardly more agreeable to commercial America than to despotic England; but however England might resent what Canning would certainly think an offence, Americans were in no humor for fault-finding, and they received Madison's allusions with little protest. The remainder of the Message contained nothing that called for dispute.

The Federalist minority — strong in numbers, flushed by victory over Jefferson, and full of contempt for the abilities of their opponents — found themselves suddenly deprived by Erskine and Madison of every grievance to stand upon. For once, no one charged that Madison's act was dictated from the Tuileries. The Federalist newspapers, like their Republican rivals, advanced the idea that their success was the natural result of their own statesmanship. Their

efforts against the embargo had opened the path for
Canning's good-will to show itself, and the removal
of Jefferson's sinister influence accounted for the
brilliancy of Madison's success. The attempt to approve Erskine's arrangement without approving Jefferson's system, required ingenuity as great as was
shown in the similar attempt of Madison to weigh
down Erskine's arrangement by coupling it with
the embargo. These party tactics would hardly deserve notice had not John Randolph, in drawing a
sharp line between Jefferson and Madison, enlivened
the monotony of debate by comments not without
interest.

" Without the slightest disposition to create unpleasant
sensations," said he, " to go back upon the footsteps of
the last four years, I do unequivocally say that I believe
the country will never see such another Administration as
the last. It had my hearty approbation for one half of
its career ; as for my opinion of the remainder of it, it
has been no secret. The lean kine of Pharaoh devoured
the fat kine ; the last four years, with the embargo in
their train, ate up the rich harvest of the first four ; and
if we had not had some Joseph to have stepped in and
changed the state of things, what would have been now
the condition of the country? I repeat it, — never has
there been any Administration which went out of office
and left the country in a state so deplorable and calami-
tous as the last."

Not satisfied with criticising Jefferson, Randolph
committed himself to the opinion that Canning had
been influenced by the same antipathy, and had been

withheld from earlier concessions only by Jefferson's conduct : —

" Mr. Canning obtained as good a bargain from us as he could have expected to obtain ; and those gentlemen who speak of his having heretofore had it in his power to have done the same, did not take into calculation the material difference between the situation in which we now stand and the situation in which we before stood."

In the virulence of temper with which Randolph blackened the Administration of Jefferson, he could not help committing himself to unqualified support of Madison ; and even Barent Gardenier, whose temper was at least as indiscreet as Randolph's, seemed to revel in the pleasure of depressing the departed President in order to elevate the actual Executive, whose eight years of coming power were more dangerous to the opposition than the eight years of Jefferson had ever been.

" I am pretty well satisfied," said Barent Gardenier,[1] " that when the secret history of the two last years is divulged, it will be found that while the former President was endeavoring to fan the flames of war, the Secretary of State . . . was smoothing the way for the happy discharge of his Presidential duties when he should come to the chair. I think it did him honor. . . . It is for the promptitude and frankness with which the President met the late overture that I thank him most cordially for my country. I approve it most heartily. . . . And it is now in proof before us, as I have said and contended, that nothing was wanting but a proper spirit of conciliation,

[1] Annals of Congress, 1809–1810, p. 210.

and fair and honorable dealing on the part of this
country, to bring to a happy issue all the fictitious differences between this country and Great Britain."

Political indiscretion could go no further. The
rule that in public life one could never safely speak
well of an opponent, was illustrated by the mistake
of the Federalists in praising Madison merely to
gratify their antipathy to Jefferson. Had they been
silent, or had they shown suspicion, they would have
been safe; but all admitted that French influence and
hostility to England had vanished with Jefferson; all
were positive that England had gained what she had
sought, and that Canning had every reason to be
satisfied. For the moment Madison was the most
popular President that ever had met Congress. At
no session since 1789 had such harmony prevailed
as during the five weeks of this political paradise,
although not one element had changed its character or position, and the harmony, like the discord,
was a play of imagination. Congress passed its
bills with unanimity altogether new. That which
restored relations of commerce with England passed
without discussion, except on the point whether
French ships of war should be admitted to American
ports. Somewhat to the alarm of the Eastern men,
Congress decided not to exclude French national
vessels, — a decision which threw some doubt on
Madison's wish to push matters to a head with Napoleon. Yet care was taken to avoid offence to Great
Britain. Little was said and nothing was done about

impressments. An attempt to increase the protective duties was defeated. Not a voice was raised on behalf of France; not a fear of Napoleon's revenge found tongue.

Although no one ventured to avow suspicion that Canning would refuse to ratify Erskine's act, news continued to arrive from England which seemed hard to reconcile with any immediate thought, in the British ministry, of giving up their restrictive system. June 10, the day when amid universal delight the new arrangement went into effect, the public pleasure was not a little disturbed by the arrival of news that on April 26 the British government had issued a very important Order in Council, revoking the order of Nov. 11, 1807, and establishing in its place a general blockade of Holland, France, and Italy. This step, though evidently a considerable concession, — which would have produced its intended effect in checking hostile feeling if Erskine had not intervened,— roused anxiety because of its remote resemblance to Erskine's arrangement, which it seemed to adopt by means that the United States could not admit as legal or consistent with the terms of Erskine's letters.

" The new Orders," wrote Madison to Jefferson,[1] . . . " present a curious feature in the conduct of the British Cabinet. It is explained by some at the expense of its sincerity. It is more probably ascribed, I think, to an

[1] Madison to Jefferson, June 12, 1809 ; Madison's Writings, ii. 443.

awkwardness in getting out of an awkward situation, and to the policy of withholding as long as possible from France the motive of its example to have advances on her part toward adjustment with us.   The crooked proceeding seems to be operating as a check to the extravagance of credit given to Great Britain for the late arrangement with us, and so far may be salutary."

Such reasoning was soon felt to be insufficient. The more the new order was studied, the less its motive was understood.   How could Canning in January have authorized Erskine to withdraw the orders of 1807 without reserve, when in April, without waiting to hear from Erskine, he himself withdrew those orders only to impose another that had every mark of permanence ?   How could Erskine, April 18, have been authorized to throw open the ports of Holland, when his Government, April 26, was engaged in imposing a new blockade upon them ?   So rapidly did the uneasiness of Congress increase that Erskine was obliged to interpose.   June 15 he wrote an official note to the Secretary of State, which the President sent the same day to Congress.[1]

" I have the honor," said Erskine, " to enclose a copy of an Order of his Majesty in Council issued on the 26th of April last.   In consequence of official communications sent to me from his Majesty's government since the adoption of that measure, I am enabled to assure you that it has no connection whatever with the overtures which I have been authorized to make to the government

[1] Message of June 15, 1809 ; State Papers, iii. 297.

of the United States; and that I am persuaded that the terms of the agreement so happily concluded by the recent negotiation will be strictly fulfilled on the part of his Majesty."

The expressions of this letter, if carefully read, still left cause for doubt; and Madison saw it, although he clung to what he thought he had gained. June 20 he wrote again to Jefferson:[1] —

"The 'Gazette' of yesterday contains the mode pursued for reanimating confidence in the pledge of the British government given by Mr. Erskine in his arrangement with this government. The puzzle created by the Order of April struck every one. Erskine assures us that his Government was under such impressions as to the views of this, that not the slightest expectation existed of our fairly meeting its overtures, and that the last order was considered as a seasonable mitigation of the tendency of a failure of the experiment. This explanation seems as extraordinary as the alternative it shows. The fresh declarations of Mr. Erskine seem to have quieted the distrust which was becoming very strong, but has not destroyed the effect of the ill grace stamped on the British retreat, and of the commercial rigor evinced by the new and insidious duties stated in the newspapers. It may be expected, I think, that the British government will fulfil what its minister has stipulated; and that if it means to be trickish, it will frustrate the proposed negotiation, and then say their orders were not permanently repealed but only withdrawn in the mean time."

[1] Madison to Jefferson, June 20, 1809; Madison's Writings, ii. 443.

Madison had chosen to precipitate a decision, with a view to profiting in either case, whether England consented or refused to have her hands thus forced. Indeed, if he had not himself been old in the ways of diplomacy, Turreau was on the spot to warn him, and lost no chance of lecturing the Administration on the folly of trusting Erskine's word.

Meanwhile Turreau so far lost his temper as to address to Secretary Smith a long letter complaining of the persistently unfriendly attitude of the United States government toward France.   So strong was the language of the letter that Turreau was obliged to withdraw it.[1] Robert Smith attempted to pacify him by assurances that the new Administration would respect the Spanish possessions more strictly than the old one had done.

" The Secretary of State did not deny that there might have been some attempt in that direction," reported Turreau, June 14,[2] " but at the same time, while himself alluding to the affair of Miranda, he attributed these events to causes independent of the actual Administration and anterior to its existence, and especially to the weakness and the indiscretions of Mr. Jefferson ; that he [Smith] was then in the Cabinet, and knew better than any one how much the want of vigor (*mollesse*), the uncertainty, and absence of plan in the Executive

[1] Turreau to Smith, June 14, 1809. John Graham to the editors of the Federal Republican, Aug. 31, 1813. Niles, v. 37–40.

[2] Turreau to Champagny, 14 June, 1809 ; Archives des Aff. Étr. MSS.

head had contributed to the false steps of the Federal government."

The new Administration meant to show vigor. Every act and expression implied that its path was to be direct to its ends. The President and Congress waited with composure for the outcome of Erskine's strange conduct.

No new measure was suggested, after June 10, to provide for the chance that Erskine's arrangement might fail, and that the Order in Council of April 26, 1809, might prove to be a permanent system. Congress seemed disposed to indulge the merchants to the utmost in their eagerness for trade. The nearest approach to suspicion was shown in the House by appropriating $750,000 for fortifications. Randolph, Macon, Eppes, and Richard M. Johnson tried to reduce the amount to $150,000. The larger appropriation was understood to mean an intention of preparing for attack, and eighty-four members sustained the policy against a minority of forty-seven; but notwithstanding this vote and the anxiety caused by the new Order in Council, Congress decided to stop enlistments for the army; and by an Act approved June 28 the President was authorized, " in the event of a favorable change in our foreign relations," to reduce the naval force, although the words of the Act implied doubt whether the favorable change would take place.

Nothing could be happier for Madison than this situation, where all parties were held in check not

only by his success but by his danger. So completely
was discipline restored, that June 27 he ventured to
send the name of J. Q. Adams a second time to the
Senate as minister to Russia; and nineteen Republicans confirmed the nomination, while but one ad
hered to the opinion that the mission was unnecessary.
The power of England over America was never more
strikingly shown than by the sudden calm which fell
on the country, in full prospect of war with France,
at a word from a British minister. As Canning
frowned or smiled, faction rose to frenzy or lay down
to slumber throughout the United States. No sooner
did the news of Erskine's arrangement reach Quebec
May 1, than Sir James Craig recalled his secret agent,
John Henry, from Boston, where he still lingered.
" I am cruelly out of spirits," wrote Secretary Ryland
to Henry,[1] " at the idea of Old England truckling to
such a debased and accursed government as that of
the United States ; " but since this was the case,
Henry's services could no longer be useful. He returned to Montreal early in June.

June 28 Congress adjourned, leaving the Executive,
for the first time in many years, almost without care,
until the fourth Monday in November.

---

[1] Ryland to Henry, May 1, 1809; State Papers, iii. 552.

CHAPTER V.

ERSKINE'S despatches were received by Canning May 22, and the "Morning Post" of the next day printed the news with approval: "Upon this pleasing event we sincerely congratulate the public." The "Times" of May 24 accepted the arrangement: "We shall not urge anything against the concessions." May 25, with "considerable pain though but little surprise," the same newspaper announced that Erskine was disavowed by the Government.

Canning's abrupt rejection of Erskine's arrangement without explanation must have seemed even to himself a high-handed course, at variance with some of his late professions, certain to injure or even to destroy British influence in America, and likely to end in war. To the settlement as a practical measure no objection could be alleged. No charge of bad faith could be supported. No shadow of law or reason could be devised for enforcing against America rights derived from retaliation upon France, when America enforced stronger measures of retaliation upon France than those imposed by the Orders in Council. Neither the Non-importation Act of 1806,

nor the " Chesapeake " proclamation of 1807, nor the
embargo, nor the Non-intercourse Act of March, 1809,
could be used to justify the rejection of an arrangement which evaded or removed every British grievance. Even the subject of impressments had been
suppressed by the American government. Madison
flung himself into Canning's arms, and to fling him
back was an effort of sheer violence.

Perhaps the effort gave to Canning's conduct an
air that he would not naturally have cared to be-
tray; for his manner was that of a man irritated
by finding himself obliged to be brutal. In the
want of a reason for rejecting the American arrangement, he was reduced to rejecting it without giving a reason. The process of disciplining Erskine
was simple, for Erskine had disregarded instructions
to an extent that no government could afford to
overlook; but President Madison was not in the employ of the British king, and had a right to such
consideration at least as one gentleman commonly
owes to another.

Canning addressed himself first to the simpler task.
May 22, a few hours after receiving the despatches
from Washington, he wrote a despatch to Erskine in
regard to the " Chesapeake " arrangement.[1] He re-
minded Erskine that his instructions had required
the formal exclusion of French war-vessels and the
formal withdrawal of the " Chesapeake " proclama-

[1] Canning to Erskine, May 22, 1809; Cobbett's Debates, xvii.
App. cxxvii.

tion before any arrangement should be concluded. Not only had these conditions been neglected, but two other less serious errors had been made.

Variations from the rigor of instructions might be ground for reproving Erskine, but could hardly excuse a disavowal of the compact; yet the compact was disavowed. An impression was general that the Ministry were disposed to ratify it, but were withheld by the paragraph in Robert Smith's letter defining what was due from his Britannic Majesty to his own honor. Milder Foreign Secretaries than George Canning would have found themselves obliged to take notice of such a reflection, and Canning appeared at his best when his adversaries gave him an excuse for the lofty tone he liked to assume.

"It remains for me," he continued, "to notice the expressions, so full of disrespect to his Majesty, with which that note concludes; and I am to signify to you the displeasure which his Majesty feels that any minister of his Majesty should have shown himself so far insensible of what is due to the dignity of his sovereign as to have consented to receive and transmit a note in which such expressions were contained."

Canning was hardly the proper person to criticise Robert Smith's disrespectful expressions, which, whatever their intention, failed to be nearly as offensive as many of his own; but this was a matter between himself and Erskine. Even after granting the propriety of his comment, diplomatic usage seemed to require that some demand of explanation or apology from the American government should precede the rejection of an engagement otherwise satisfactory; but no such step was in this case taken through Erskine. His settlement of the " Chesapeake " outrage was repudiated without more words, and the next day Canning repudiated the rest of the arrangement.

Nothing could be easier than to show that Erskine had violated his instructions more plainly in regard to the Orders in Council than in regard to the " Chesapeake " affair. Of the three conditions imposed by Canning, not one had been fulfilled. The first required the repeal of all Non-intercourse Acts against England, " leaving them in force with respect to France; " but Erskine had doubly failed to secure it : [1] —

" As the matter at present stands before the world in your official correspondence with Mr. Smith, the American government would be at liberty to-morrow to repeal the Non-intercourse Act altogether, without infringing the agreement which you have thought proper to enter into on behalf of his Majesty; and if such a clause was thought necessary to this condition at the time when my instructions were written, it was obviously become much more so when the Non-intercourse Act was passed for a limited time. You must also have been aware at the time of making the agreement that the American government had in fact formally exempted Holland, a Power which has unquestionably ' adopted and acted under the Decrees of France,' from the operation of the Non-intercourse

[1] Canning to Erskine, May 23, 1809; MSS. British Archives.

Act, — an exemption in direct contravention of the condition prescribed to you, and which of itself ought to have prevented you from coming to any agreement whatever."

Here, again, sufficient reasons were given for punishing Erskine; but these reasons were not equally good for repudiating the compact with the United States. No American vessels could enter a Dutch port so long as the British blockade lasted; therefore the exemption of Holland from the non-intercourse affected England only by giving to her navy another chance for booty, and to the Americans one more empty claim. Canning himself explained to Pinkney[1] " that the exemption of Holland from the effect of our embargo and non-intercourse would not have been much objected to by the British government" if the President had been willing to pledge himself to enforce the non-intercourse against France; but for aught that appeared to the contrary, " the embargo and non-intercourse laws might be suffered without any breach of faith to expire, or might even be repealed immediately, notwithstanding the perseverance of France in her Berlin and other edicts; and that Mr. Erskine had in truth secured nothing more, as the consideration of the recall of the Orders in Council, than the renewal of American intercourse with Great Britain."

Thus Canning justified the repudiation of Erskine's

[1] Pinkney to Robert Smith, June 23, 1809; State Papers, iii. 303.

arrangement by the single reason that the United States government could not be trusted long enough to prove its good faith. The explanation was difficult to express in courteous or diplomatic forms; but perhaps its most striking quality, next to its want of courtesy, was its evident want of candor. Had the American government evaded its obligation, the British government held the power of redress in its own hands. Clearly the true explanation was to be sought elsewhere, in some object which Canning could not put in diplomatic words, but which lay in the nature of Perceval's system. Even during the three days while the decision was supposed to be in doubt, alarmed merchants threw themselves in crowds on the Board of Trade, protesting that if American vessels with their cheaper sugar, cotton, and coffee were allowed to enter Amsterdam and Antwerp, British trade was at an end.[1] The mere expectation of their arrival would create such a fall in prices as to make worthless the accumulated mass of such merchandise with which the warehouses were filled, not only in London, but also in the little island of Heligoland at the mouth of the Elbe, where a system of licensed and unlicensed smuggling had been established under the patronage of the Board of Trade. Deputations of these merchants waited on Earl Bathurst to represent the danger of allowing even those American ships to enter Holland which might have already sailed from the United States on the faith

[1] The Courier, May 26, 1809.

of Erskine's arrangement. Somewhat unexpectedly ministers refused to gratify this prayer. An Order in Council of May 24, while announcing the Royal repudiation of Erskine's arrangement, declared that American vessels which should have cleared for Holland between April 19 and July 20 would not be molested in their voyage.

The chief objection to Erskine's arrangement, apart from its effect on British merchants, consisted in the danger that by its means America might compel France to withdraw her decrees affecting neutrals. The chance that Erskine's arrangement might involve America in war with Napoleon was not worth the equal chance of its producing in the end an amicable arrangement with Napoleon which would sacrifice the last defence of British commerce and manufactures. Had the British government given way, Napoleon, to whom the most solemn pledges cost nothing, would certainly persuade President Madison to lean once more toward France. The habit of balancing the belligerents — the first rule of American diplomacy — required the incessant see-saw of interest. So many unsettled questions remained open that British ministers could not flatter themselves with winning permanent American favor by partial concession.

To Canning's despatch repudiating the commercial arrangement, Erskine made a reply showing more keenness and skill than was to be found in Canning's criticism.

"It appears from the general tenor of your despatches," wrote Erskine [1] on receiving these letters of May 22 and 23, "that his Majesty's government were not willing to trust to assurances from the American government, but that official pledges were to have been required which could not be given for want of power, some of them also being of a nature which would prevent a formal recognition. Had I believed that his Majesty's government were determined to insist upon these conditions being complied with in one particular manner only, I should have adhered implicitly to my instructions; but as I collected from them that his Majesty was desirous of accomplishing his retaliatory system by such means as were most compatible with a good understanding with friendly and neutral Powers, I felt confident that his Majesty would approve of the arrangement I had concluded as one likely to lead to a cordial and complete understanding and co-operation on the part of the United States, which co-operation never could be obtained by previous stipulations either from the government of the United States, who have no power to accede to them, or from Congress, which would never acknowledge them as recognitions to guide their conduct."

This reply, respectful in form, placed Secretary Canning in the dilemma between the guilt of ignorance or that of bad faith; but the rejoinder of a dismissed diplomatist weighed little except in history, and long before it was made public Erskine and his arrangement had ceased to interest the world. Canning disposed of both forever by a third despatch,

[1] Erskine to Canning, Aug. 7, 1809; Cobbett's Debates, xvii. App. clx.–clxiii.

dated May 30, enclosing to Erskine an Order in
Council disavowing his arrangement and ordering
him back to England.

When the official disavowal appeared in the newspapers of May 25, Canning had an interview with
Pinkney.[1] At great length and with much detail he
read the instructions he had given to Erskine, and
commented on the points in which Erskine had violated them. He complained of unfriendly expressions
in the American notes; but he did not say why the
arrangement failed to satisfy all the legitimate objects
of England, nor did he suggest any improvement or
change which would make the arrangement, as it
existed, agreeable to him. On the other hand, he
announced that though Erskine would have to be recalled, his successor was already appointed and would
sail for America within a few days.

If Canning showed, by his indulgence to American
vessels and his haste to send out a new minister, the
wish to avoid a rupture with the United States, his
selection of an agent for that purpose was so singular
as to suggest that he relied on terror rather than
on conciliation. In case Erskine had obeyed his instructions, which ordered him merely to prepare the
way for negotiation, Canning had fixed upon George
Henry Rose as the negotiator.[2] Considering the im-

[1] Pinkney to R. Smith, May 28, 1809; MSS. State Department
Archives.

[2] Pinkney to Madison, Dec. 10, 1809; Wheaton's Pinkney,
p. 434.

pression left in America by Rose on his previous
mission, his appointment seemed almost the worst
that could have been made; but bad as the effect
of such a selection would have been, one man, and
perhaps only one, in England was certain to make a
worse; and him Canning chose. The new minister
was Francis James Jackson. Whatever good qualities Jackson possessed were overshadowed by the
reputation he had made for himself at Copenhagen.
His name was a threat of violence; his temper and
manners were notorious; and nothing but his rank
in the service marked him as suitable for the post.
Pinkney, whose self-control and tact in these difficult
circumstances could hardly be too much admired,
listened in silence to Canning's announcement, and
rather than risk making the situation worse, reported
that Jackson was, he believed, "a worthy man, and
although completely attached to all those British
principles and doctrines which sometimes give us
trouble will, *I should hope*, give satisfaction." The
English press was not so forbearing. The "Morning
Chronicle" of May 29 said that the appointment had
excited general surprise, owing to "the character of
the individual;" and Pinkney himself, in a later
despatch, warned his Government that "it is rather
a prevailing notion here that this gentleman's conduct will not and cannot be what we all wish, and
that a better choice might have been made." [1]

[1] Pinkney to R. Smith, June 23, 1809; MSS. State Department
Archives.

Jackson himself sought the position, knowing its difficulties. May 23, the day of his appointment, he wrote privately to his brother in Spain: " I am about to enter upon a most delicate — I *hope* not desperate — enterprise." [1]   At a later time, embittered by want of support from home, he complained that Canning had sent him on an errand which he knew to be impossible to perform.[2] So well understood between Canning and Jackson was the nature of the service, that Jackson asked and received as a condition of his acceptance the promise that his employment should last not less than twelve months.[3] The delicate enterprise of which he spoke could have been nothing more than that of preventing a rupture between England and America; but until he studied his instructions, he could hardly have known in its full extent how desperate this undertaking would be.

Canning made no haste. Nearly two months elapsed before Jackson sailed. After correcting Erskine's mistake and replacing the United States in their position under the Orders in Council of April 26, Canning, June 13, made a statement to the House of Commons. Declining to touch questions of general policy for the reason that negotiations were pending, he contented himself with satisfying the House

[1] Bath Archives; Diaries and Letters of Sir George Jackson, ii. 447.

[2] Bath Archives; Diaries and Letters of Sir George Jackson, Second Series, i. 109.

[3] Bath Archives; Diaries and Letters of Sir George Jackson, Second Series, i. 24, 46.

that Erskine had acted contrary to instructions and deserved recall. James Stephen showed more clearly the spirit of Government by avowing the opinion " that America in all her proceedings had no wish to promote an impartial course with respect to France and this country." The Whigs knew little or nothing of the true facts ; Erskine's conduct could not be defended ; no one cared to point out that Canning left to America no dignified course but war, and public interest was once more concentrated with painful anxiety on the continent of Europe. America dropped from sight, and Canning's last and worst acts toward the United States escaped notice or knowledge.

The session of Parliament ended June 21, a week before the special session of Congress came to an end ; and while England waited impatiently for news from Vienna, where Napoleon was making ready for the battle of Wagram, Canning drew up the instructions to Jackson, — the last of the series of papers by which, through the peculiar qualities of his style even more than by the violence of his acts, he embittered to a point that seemed altogether contrary to their nature a whole nation of Americans against the nation that gave them birth. If the famous phrase of Canning was ever in any sense true, — that he called a new world into existence to redress the balance of the old, — it was most nearly true in the sense that his instructions and letters forced the United States into a nationality of character which the war of the Revolution itself had failed to give them.

The instructions to Jackson [1] — five in number — were dated July 1, and require careful attention if the train of events which brought the United States to the level of war with England is to be understood.

The first instruction began by complaint of Erskine's conduct, passing quickly to a charge of bad faith against the American government, founded on " the publicity so unwarrantably given " to Erskine's arrangement : —

" The premature publication of the correspondence by the American government so effectually precluded any middle course of explanation and accommodation that it is hardly possible to suppose that it must not have been resorted to in a great measure with that view.

" The American government cannot have believed that such an arrangement as Mr. Erskine consented to accept was conformable to his instructions. If Mr. Erskine availed himself of the liberty allowed to him of communicating those instructions on the affair of the Orders in Council, they must have known that it was not so ; but even without such communication they cannot by possibility have believed that without any new motive, and without any apparent change in the dispositions of the enemy, the British government could have been disposed at once and unconditionally to give up the system on which they have been acting, and which they had so recently refused to relinquish, even in return for consid-

---

[1] Canning to F. J. Jackson, Nos. 1-5, July 1, 1809; MSS. British Archives, America, vol. xcv.

erations which though far from being satisfactory were yet infinitely more so than anything which can be supposed to have been gained by Mr. Erskine's arrangement."

Canning attributed this conduct to a hope held by President Madison that the British government would feel itself compelled, however reluctantly, to sanction an agreement which it had not authorized. In this case the American government had only itself to blame for the consequences : —

" So far, therefore, from the American government having any reason to complain of the non-ratification of Mr. Erskine's unauthorized agreement, his Majesty has on his part just ground of complaint for that share of the inconvenience from the publication which may have fallen upon his Majesty's subjects, so far as their interests may have been involved in the renewed speculations of their American correspondents ; and his Majesty cannot but think any complaint, if any should be made on this occasion in America, the more unreasonable, as the government of the United States is that government which perhaps of all others has most freely exercised the right of withholding its ratification from even the authorized acts of its own diplomatic agents."

In this spirit Jackson was to meet any " preliminary discussion" which might arise before he could proceed to negotiation. Canning did not touch on the probability that if Jackson met preliminary discussion in such a spirit as this, he would run something more than a risk of never reaching negotiation at all; or if Canning considered this point, he treated it orally.

The other written instructions given to Jackson dealt at once with negotiation.

The "Chesapeake" affair came first in order, and was quickly dismissed. Jackson was to require from the President a written acknowledgment that the interdict on British ships was annulled before any settlement could be made. The Orders in Council came next, and were the subject of a long instruction, full of interest and marked by many of Canning's peculiarities. Once more he explained that Erskine had inverted the relation of things by appearing to recall the orders as an inducement to the renewal of trade, — "as if in any arrangement, whether commercial or political, his Majesty could condescend to barter objects of national policy and dignity for permission to trade with another country. The character even more than the stipulations of such a compact must under any circumstances have put out of question the possibility of his Majesty's consenting to confirm it." He related the history of the orders, which he called "defensive retaliation," and explained why Erskine's arrangement failed to effect the object of that system : —

"In the arrangement agreed to by Mr. Erskine the incidental consequence is mistaken for the object of the negotiation. His Majesty is made by his minister to concede the whole point in dispute by the total and unconditional recall of the Orders in Council ; and nothing is done by the United States in return except to permit their citizens to renew their commercial intercourse with

Great Britain.   Whereas, before his Majesty's consent to
withdraw or even to modify the Orders in Council was
declared, the United States should have taken upon themselves to execute in substance the objects of the Orders
in Council by effectually prohibiting all trade between
their citizens and France, or the Powers acting under her
decrees, and by engaging for the continuance of that
prohibition so long as those decrees should continue
unrepealed."

As in the " Chesapeake " affair, so in regard to the
orders, — Canning's objection to Erskine's arrangement was stated as one of form.   That the " Chesapeake" proclamation was no longer in force ; that
Congress had effectually prohibited trade with France ;
and that the President had engaged as far as he
could to continue that prohibition till the French
Decrees were repealed, — these were matters of notoriety.   England took the ground that the United
States were liable to the operation of the British retaliatory orders against France, even though Congress should have declared war upon France, unless
the declaration of war was regularly made known to
the British minister at Washington, and unless " the
United States should have taken upon themselves,"
by treaty with England, to continue the war till
France repealed her decrees.

Canning was happy in the phrase he employed in
Parliament, March 6, to justify the course of ministers
toward America.   " Extension of the law of nations "
described well the Orders in Council themselves ; but

the instruction to Jackson was remarkable as a pro-
digious extension of the extended orders. The last
legal plea was abandoned by these instructions, and
the subject would have been the clearer for that
abandonment were it not that owing to the rapidity
of events the new extravagance was never known ;
with Canning himself the subject slipped from public
view, and only the mystery remained of Canning's
objects and expectations.

Another man would have temporized, and would
have offered some suggestion toward breaking the
force of such a blow at a friendly people. Not only
did Canning make no new suggestion, but he even
withdrew that which he had made in February. He
told Jackson to propose nothing whatever : —

" You are to inform the American Secretary of State
that in the event of the government of the United States
being desirous now to adopt this proposal, you are authorized to renew the negotiation and to conclude it on
the terms of my instructions to Mr. Erskine ; but that
you are not instructed to press upon the acceptance of
the American government an arrangement which they
have so recently declined, especially as the arrangement
itself is become less important, and the terms of it less
applicable to the state of things now existing."

The remainder of this despatch was devoted to
proving that the late order of April 26 had so modified that of November, 1807, as to remove the most
serious American objections ; and although the blockade was more restrictive than the old orders as con-

cerned French and Dutch colonies, yet the recent
surrender of Martinique had reduced the practical
hardship of this restriction so considerably that it
was fairly offset by the opening of the Baltic.   America had the less inducement to a further arrangement which could little increase the extent of her
commerce, while England was indifferent provided
she obtained her indispensable objects : —

" I am therefore not to direct you to propose to the
American government any formal agreement to be substituted for that which his Majesty has been under the
necessity of disavowing.   You are, however, at liberty
to receive for reference home any proposal which the
American government may tender to you ; but it is
only in the case of that proposal comprehending all the
three conditions which Mr. Erskine was instructed to
require."

The fourth instruction prescribed the forms in
which such an arrangement, if made, must be framed.
The fifth dealt with another branch of the subject, —
the Rule of 1756.   Canning declined to accept a mere
understanding in regard to this rule.   Great Britain
would insist on her right to prohibit neutral trade
with enemies' colonies, " of which she has permitted
the exercise only by indulgence ; . . . but the indulgence which was granted for peculiar and temporary
reasons being now withdrawn, the question is merely
whether the rule from which such an indulgence was
a deviation shall be established by the admission of
America or enforced as heretofore by the naval power

of Great Britain." As a matter of courtesy the British government had no objection to allowing the United States to sanction by treaty the British right, so that legal condemnations should be made under the authority of the treaty instead of an Order in Council; "but either authority is sufficient. No offence is taken at the refusal of the United States to make this matter subject of compact. The result is that it must be the subject of an Order in Council."

The result was that it became the subject of a much higher tribunal than his Majesty's Council, and that the British people, and Canning himself, took great offence at the refusal of the United States to make it a subject of one-sided compact; but with this concluding touch Canning's official irony toward America ended, and he laid down his pen. About the middle of June, Jackson with three well-defined *casus belli* in his portfolio, and another — that of impressments — awaiting his arrival, set sail for America on the errand which he strangely hoped might not be desperate. With his departure Canning's control of American relations ceased. At the moment when he challenged for the last time an instant declaration of war from a people who had no warmer wish than to be permitted to remain his friends, the career of the Administration to which he belonged came to an end in scandalous disaster.

Hardly had the Duke of York stopped one source of libel, by resigning May 16 his office of commander-in-chief, when fresh troubles from many directions assailed ministers. As early as April 4, Canning had satisfied the Duke of Portland that he must dismiss Castlereagh for incompetence, and every Cabinet minister except Castlereagh himself was acquainted with this decision; but contrary to Canning's wishes no action was taken, and the conduct of the war was left at a critical moment in the hands of a man whose removal for incompetence had been decreed by his own colleagues. The summer campaign was then fought. April 9 Austria had begun another war with Napoleon. At Essling, May 21, she nearly won a great victory; at Wagram, July 6, she lost a battle, and soon afterward entered on negotiations which ended, October 20, in the treaty of Vienna. While this great campaign went on, Sir Arthur Wellesley drove Soult out of Portugal much as Napoleon had driven Sir John Moore out of Spain; and then marching up the valley of the Tagus scared Joseph a second time from Madrid, and fought, July 28, the desperate battle of Talavera. In any case the result of the Austrian war would have obliged him to retreat; but the concentration of the French forces in his front quickly drove the British army back toward Lisbon, and ended all hope of immediate success in the Peninsula. A third great effort against Napoleon was directed from London toward the Scheldt and Meuse. The Cabinet, June 14, decided that Castlereagh should attempt this experiment; for raids of the kind had charms for a naval power, and although

success could affect the war but little, it might assist
smuggling and destroy a naval depot of Napoleon.
Castlereagh sent to the Scheldt forty thousand soldiers who were grievously wanted on the Tagus.
July 28, while Wellington fought the battle of Talavera, Lord Chatham's expedition started from the
Downs, and reaching the mouth of the Scheldt occupied itself until August 15 with the capture of Flushing. In gaining this success the army was worn out;
nearly half its number were suffering from typhoid,
and September 2 the Cabinet unanimously voted to
recall the expedition.

Talavera and Flushing closed Castlereagh's career
in the War Office, as Jackson's mission closed that
of Canning in American diplomacy. Defeat abroad,
ruin at home, disgrace and disaster everywhere were
the results of two years of Tory administration.
August 11 the Duke of Portland was struck by
paralysis; and deprived of its chief, the Cabinet went
to pieces. September 7 Castlereagh was gently forced
to resign. Canning, refusing to serve under Perceval
or under any one whom Perceval suggested, tendered
his own resignation. In the course of the complicated negotiations that followed, Perceval showed to
Castlereagh letters in which for a year past Canning
had pressed Castlereagh's removal from office. Then
at last Castlereagh discovered, as he conceived, that
Canning was not a gentleman or a man of honor, and
having called him out, September 21, in a duel on
Putney Heath shot him through the thigh.

Such an outcome was a natural result of such an Administration; but as concerned the United States Canning had already done all the harm possible, and more than three generations could wholly repair.

CHAPTER VI.

The news of Erskine's disavowal reached America so slowly that merchants enjoyed three months of unrestricted trade, and shipped to England or elsewhere the accumulations of nearly two years' produce. From April 21 till July 21 this process of depletion continued without an anxiety; and when July 21 news arrived that the arrangement had been repudiated, merchants still had time to hurry their last cargoes to sea before the government could again interpose.

The first effect of Canning's disavowal seemed bewilderment. No one in the United States, whether enemy or friend of England, could for a time understand why Canning had taken so perplexing a course. Very few of England's friends could believe that her conduct rested on the motives she avowed; they sought for some noble, or at least some respectable, object behind her acts. For several months the Federalist newspapers were at a loss for words, and groped in the dark for an English hand to help them; while the Republican press broke into anger, which expressed the common popular feeling. "The late conduct of the British ministry," said the "National

Intelligencer " of July 26, " has capped the climax
of atrocity toward this country." Every hope of
reconciliation or even of peace with England seemed
almost extinguished; yet the country was still far
from a rupture. Not until popular feeling could
express itself in a new election would the national
will be felt; and the next election was still more
than a year away, while the Congress to be then
chosen would meet only in December, 1811. Until
then war was improbable, perhaps impossible, except
by the act of England.

When the news arrived, President Madison was
at his Virginia plantation. During his absence
Gallatin was in charge of matters at Washington,
and on the instant wrote that he thought the President should return. In a letter of July 27, three
days after the news reached Washington, Gallatin
gave his own view of the situation : [1] —

" I will not waste time in conjectures respecting the
true cause of the conduct of the British government,
nor can we, until we are better informed, lay any permanent plan of conduct for ourselves. I will only observe that we are not so well prepared for resistance as
we were one year ago. Then all or almost all our mercantile wealth was safe at home, our resources entire, and
our finances sufficient to carry us through during the first
year of the contest. Our property is now all afloat;
England relieved by our relaxations might stand two
years of privations with ease. We have wasted our

[1] Gallatin to Montgomery, July 27, 1809 ; Adams's Gallatin,
p. 395.

resources without any national utility; and our treasury being exhausted, we must begin our plan of resistance with considerable and therefore unpopular loans."

The immediate crisis called first for attention. Gallatin held that the Non-intercourse Act necessarily revived from the moment the supposed fact on which alone its suspension rested was shown not to have taken place. The remoter problem of Jackson's mission seemed to the secretary simpler than the question of law:[1] —

"If we are too weak or too prudent to resist England in the direct and proper manner, I hope at least that we shall not make a single voluntary concession inconsistent with our rights and interest. If Mr. Jackson has any compromise to offer which would not be burdened with such, I shall be very agreeably disappointed. But judging by what is said to have been the substance of Mr. Erskine's instructions, what can we expect but dishonorable and inadmissible proposals? He is probably sent out like Mr. Rose to amuse and to divide; and we shall, I trust, by coming at once to the point, bring his negotiation to an immediate close."

The President heard the news with as much perplexity as anger, and even tried to persuade himself that Canning would be less severe than he threatened. Madison still clung to hope when he first replied to Gallatin's summons:[2] —

[1] Gallatin to Montgomery, July 27, 1809; Adams's Gallatin, p. 395.

[2] Madison to Gallatin, July 28, 1809; Gallatin's Works, i. 454.

" The conduct of the British government in protesting
the arrangement of its minister surprises one in spite of
all their examples of folly.   If it be not their plan, now
that they have filled their magazines with our supplies
and ascertained our want of firmness in withholding them,
to adopt openly a system of monopoly and piracy, it
may be hoped that they will not persist in the scandalous
course in which they have set out.   Supposing Erskine
to have misunderstood or overstrained his instructions,
can the difference between our trading directly and indirectly with Holland account for the violent remedy applied to the case?   Is it not more probable that they
have yielded to the clamors of the London smugglers in
sugar and coffee, whose numbers and impudence are dis-
played in the scandalous and successful demand from
their government that it should strangle the lawful trade
of a friendly nation lest it should interfere with their
avowed purpose of carrying on a smuggling trade with
their enemies?   Such an outrage on all decency was
never before heard of even on the shores of Africa."

Madison exaggerated.   The outrage on decency
committed by the British government in May, 1809,
was on the whole not so great as that of Sir William
Scott's decision in the case of the " Essex " in July,
1805; or that of the blockade of New York and the
killing of Pierce in April, 1806; or that of Lord
Howick's Order in Council of January, 1807, when
the signatures to Monroe's treaty were hardly dry;
or that of Spencer Perceval's Orders in November,
1807, and the speeches made in their defence; or
the mission of George Henry Rose in the winter of

1807-1808; or Erskine's letter of February 23, or Canning's letters of September 23, 1808, — for all these left the United States in a worse position than that created by the disavowal of Erskine. Indeed, except for the disgrace of submitting to acts of illegal force, the United States stood in a comparatively easy attitude after the orders of April 26, 1809, so long as Napoleon himself enforced within his empire a more rigid exclusion of neutral commerce than any that could be effected by a British blockade.

" Still, I cannot but hope," continued Madison, " on the supposition that there be no predetermined hostility against our commerce and navigation, that things may take another turn under the influence of the obvious and striking considerations which advise it."

The hope vanished when Erskine's instructions became known, and was succeeded by consternation when the public read the reports made by Erskine and Canning of the language used by Madison, Gallatin, and Pinkney. For the first time in this contest, Englishmen and Americans could no longer understand each other's meaning. Erskine had so confused every detail with his own ideas, and Canning's course on one side the Atlantic seemed so little to accord with his tactics on the other, that neither party could longer believe in the other's good faith. Americans were convinced that Canning had offered terms which he intended them to refuse. Englishmen were sure that Madison had precipitated a settlement which he knew could not be carried out.

Madison credited Canning with fraud as freely as Canning charged Madison with connivance.

"I find myself under the mortifying necessity of setting out to-morrow morning for Washington," wrote Madison to Jefferson, August 3.[1] "The intricate state of our affairs with England produced by the mixture of fraud and folly in her late conduct, and the important questions to be decided as to the legal effect of the failure of the arrangement of April on our commercial relations with her are thought by the heads of departments to require that I should join them. . . . You will see by the instructions to Erskine, as published by Canning, that the latter was as much determined that there should be no adjustment as the former was that there should be one."

The President remained three days in Washington in order to sign, August 9, a Proclamation reviving the Non-intercourse Act against Great Britain. On the same day the Secretary of the Treasury enclosed this Proclamation to the Collectors of Customs in a circular, with instructions not to enforce the penalties of the law against vessels entering American ports on the faith of Erskine's arrangement. This done, Madison returned to Montpelier, August 10, leaving Erskine to exchange apologetic but very unsatisfactory explanations with Robert Smith and Gallatin.

The Proclamation of August 9 was sharply criticised, and with reason ; for Congress had given

[1] Madison to Jefferson, Aug. 3, 1809; Madison's Works, ii. 449.

the President no express authority to revive the
Non-intercourse Act, and he had clearly exceeded
his powers, if not in the Proclamation which revived
the Act, then certainly in the original Proclamation
of April 19, which set it aside. Even this stretch of
authority hardly equalled Gallatin's assumption of
the power to admit what vessels he pleased without
regard to the Non-intercourse Act. Yet right or
wrong the President had no choice but to use all
the powers he needed. Evidently his original mistake in opening intercourse was a greater stretch
of authority than any subsequent act could be, except that of leaving it open after the mistake was
admitted. Sullenly and awkwardly the Government
restored some degree of order to its system, and
then President and Cabinet scattered once more,
leaving the village of Washington to the solitude
of August and September.

A month passed without further change, until
September 5 Jackson landed at Annapolis, whence
he reached Washington September 8. He came with
his wife — a fashionable Prussian baroness with a toi-
lette — and young children, for whose health a Washington September was ill suited; he came too with
a carriage and liveries, coachmen and servants, and
the outfit of a long residence, as though neither he
nor Canning doubted his welcome.

Francis James Jackson had many good qualities,
and was on the whole the only English minister of
his time so severely treated by the American gov-

ernment as to warrant almost a feeling of sympathy. He was probably suffering from some or-
ganic disease which made his temper irritable, while
his instructions were such as to leave him no room
to show his best capacities in his profession. In
ordinary times a man of his experience, intelligence,
and marked character might have succeeded in winning at Washington a name for ability and straight-
forwardness; but he was ill fitted for the special
task he had undertaken, and had no clear idea of
the dangers to which he was exposed. Gallatin expressed the feeling of the Administration when he
advised coming at once to the point with Jackson,
and bringing his negotiation to an immediate close.
Madison could not have wished to repeat his experience with Rose, or to allow a British minister to
reside at Washington for the sole purpose of dividing
American counsels and intriguing with Senator Pickering. Had Jackson been quick in his perceptions,
he would have seen early that nothing but mortification could be in store for him; but he had the
dogged courage and self-confidence of his time, and
undertook to deal single-handed with a government and people he did not trouble himself to
understand.

The President was not in Washington when the
British minister drove into that " famous city," as
he called it, which " resembles more nearly Hamp-
stead Heath than any other place I ever saw." [1]

[1] Bath Archives ; Second Series, i. 9.

Robert Smith apologized for the incivility of leaving him without the usual public recognition, and explained that the risk of fever and the fatigue of four days' journey made the President extremely unwilling to return before October 1, the day fixed for Jackson's reception. Indirectly Smith suggested that Jackson might visit the President at Montpelier, or even begin negotiation before being officially received; but the minister replied that he would cheerfully wait. Gallatin wrote to the President, September 11, —

"I do not think that there is any necessity to hurry yourself beyond your convenience in returning here. It will be as well the 10th as the 1st of October, for I am sure, although I have not seen Mr. Jackson and can judge only from what has passed between him and Mr. Smith, that he has nothing to say of importance, or pleasant."[1]

Madison replied, proposing to set out for Washington about the 29th, but agreeing with Gallatin that in view of "Jackson's apparent patience and reserve," his disclosures "would not be either operative or agreeable."[2]

Whether Jackson showed patience or activity, he could not avoid giving offence; and perhaps he did wisely to gain all the time he could, even if he gained nothing else. Unlike some of his predecessors, he understood how to make the best of his situation.

[1] Gallatin to Madison, Sept. 11, 1809; Works i. 461.
[2] Gallatin's Works, i. 462.

He found amusement for a month of idleness, even though the month was September and the place was Washington.   He took the house which Merry and Erskine had occupied, — a house that stood amid fields looking over Rock Creek to Georgetown :

" Erskine had let it go to such a state of ruin and dirt that it will be several weeks before we can attempt to move into it.   A Scotchman with an American wife who would be a fine lady, are not the best people to succeed on such an occasion.

" It is but justice to say that I have met with nothing but the utmost civility, and with none of those hardships and difficulties of which the Merrys so bitterly complained.   The travelling is not worse than much that I have met with before in my life, and the accommodations are better than many I have thought supportable. The expense is about the same as in England, and must be considered most exorbitant when the inferiority of their arrangements to ours and the greater cheapness of provisions are taken into account." [1]

As the season advanced, Jackson began to enjoy his autumn picnic on the heath of Washington.   He had an eye for the details which gave interest to travel.   " I put up a covey of partridge," he wrote October 7, " about three hundred yards from the House of Congress, yclept the Capitol."   He had the merit of being first to discover what few men of his time had the taste to feel,— that Washington was beautiful : —

[1] F. J. Jackson to Mrs. Jackson, Oct. 7, 1809 ; Bath Archives, Second Series, i. 17.

" I have procured two very good saddle-horses, and Elizabeth and I have been riding in all directions round this place whenever the weather has been cool enough. The country has a beautifully picturesque appearance, and I have nowhere seen finer scenery than is composed by the Potomac and the woods and hills about it ; yet it has a wild and desolate air from being so scantily and rudely cultivated, and from the want of population. . . . So you see we are not fallen into a wilderness, — so far from it that I am surprised no one should before have mentioned the great beauty of the neighborhood. The natives trouble themselves but little about it ; their thoughts are chiefly of tobacco, flour, shingles, and the news of the day. The Merrys, I suppose, never got a mile out of Washington, except on their way to Philadelphia."

Part of Jackson's leisure was employed in reading Erskine's correspondence, although he would have done better had he neglected this customary duty, and had he brought to his diplomacy no more preju- dices than such as belonged to his nature and train- ing. His disgust with Erskine only added to his antipathy for Erskine's objects, methods, and friends.

" My visitors," he wrote, " are a different set from Erskine's, I perceive ; many of them he says he never saw. Per contra, many of the Democrats who were his intimates never come to me, and I am well pleased and somewhat flattered by the distinction. . . . Erskine is really a greater fool than I could have thought it possible to be, and it is charity to give him *that* name. . . . Now that I have gone through all his correspondence, more than ever am I at a loss to comprehend how he could have been allowed to remain here for the last two years. . . . To be obliged to wade through such a mass of folly and stupidity, and to observe how our country has been made, through Erskine's means, the instrument of these people's cunning, is not the least part of my annoyance. Between them our cause is vilified indeed. The tone which Erskine had accustomed them to use with him, and to use without any notice whatever being taken of it, is another great difficulty I have had to overcome. Every third word was a declaration of war."

The month passed only too soon for Jackson's comfort, and October 1, punctual to his word, the President arrived. The next day Erskine had his farewell audience, and October 3 Jackson was officially received. Merry's experience had not been without advantage to both sides; and Jackson, who seemed to feel more contempt for his own predecessors — Merry and Erskine — than for his American antagonists, accepted everything in good part.

" Madison, the President, is a plain and rather mean-looking little man, of great simplicity of manners, and an inveterate enemy to form and ceremony; so much so that I was officially informed that my introduction to him was to be considered as nothing more than the reception of one gentleman by another, and that no particular dress was to be worn on the occasion, — all which I was very willing to acquiesce in. Accordingly I went in an afternoon frock, and found the President in similar attire. Smith, the Secretary of State, who had walked from his office to join me, had on a pair of dusty boots, and his round hat in his hand. When he had introduced us he retired, and the President then asked me to take a chair. While we were talking, a negro servant brought in some glasses of punch and a seed-cake. The former, as I had been in conference the whole morning, served very agreeably to wet, or whet, my whistle, and still more strongly to contrast this audience with others I had had with most of the sovereigns of Europe."

Perhaps this passing allusion to previous acquaintance with " most of the sovereigns of Europe" threw a light, somewhat too searching, into the recesses of Jackson's character. The weakness was pardonable, and not specially unsuited to success in his career, but showed itself in private as a form of self-deception which promised ill for his coming struggle. Madison's civility quite misled him.

" I do not know," he wrote October 24, " that I had ever more civility and attention shown me than at a dinner at the President's yesterday, where I was treated with a distinction not lately accorded to a British minister in this country. A foolish question of precedence, which ever since Merry's time has been unsettled, and has occasioned some heart-burnings among the ladies, was also decided then by the President departing from his customary indifference to ceremony and etiquette, and taking Elizabeth in to dinner, while I conducted Mrs. Madison."

Evidently this deference pleased the British minister, who saw nothing behind it but a social triumph for himself and his wife; yet he had already been forced to protest against the ceremonial forms with which Madison studiously surrounded him, and had he read Shakspeare rather than Erskine's writings, he might have learned from Julius Cæsar the general diplomatic law that " when love begins to sicken and decay, it useth ever an enforced ceremony." A man of tact would have seen that from the moment Madison became formal he was dangerous. The dinner of October 23 at the White House came at a moment when Jackson had been so carefully handled and so effectually disarmed as to stand at Madison's mercy ; and although he was allowed to please himself by taking Mrs. Madison to dinner, the " mean-looking little man " at the head of the table, was engaged only in thinking by what stroke the British minister's official life should be most quickly and quietly ended.

Jackson's interviews with Robert Smith began immediately after the President's arrival in Washington. The first conversation was reported by the British minister to his Government in language so lifelike, but showing such astonishment on both sides at the attitude of each, as to give it place among the most natural sketches in American diplomatic history. After some fencing on the subject of Erskine's responsibility, Jackson passed to the subject of his own instructions, and remarked that he was ordered to wait for propositions from the President.

" Here the American minister," reported Jackson,[1] " exhibited signs of the utmost surprise and disappointment. He seemed to be so little prepared for this close

[1] Jackson to Canning, Oct. 17, 1809 ; MSS. British Archives.

of my conversation that he was some time before he could recollect himself sufficiently to give me any answer at all. Expecting to meet suggestions of a totally different nature, and finding that what he had ready to say to them did not suit the occasion, he seemed to require some time and reflection to new arrange his thoughts. Accordingly a considerable pause in our conversation took place, which at length he broke in upon by saying: 'Then, sir, you have no proposal to make to us, — no explanation to give? How shall we be able to get rid of the Non-intercourse Act?'"

Robert Smith was a wearisome burden to Madison, and his incompetence made no agreeable object of study; but his apparent bewilderment at Jackson's audacity was almost as instructive as the sincere astonishment of the Englishman at the effect of his own words. The game of cross-purposes could not be more naturally played. Robert Smith had been requested by Madison to ascertain precisely what Jackson's instructions were; and both at the first and at a second interview he pressed this point, always trying to discover what Jackson had to offer, while the Englishman always declined to offer anything whatever. Two conversations satisfied the President that Jackson's hands were fast tied, and that he could open no door of escape. Then Madison gently set the Secretary of State aside, and, as openly as the office of Chief Magistrate permitted, undertook to deal with the British minister.

October 9 the Secretary of State sent to the British

Legation a formal letter, written, like all Robert Smith's important papers, by the President.[1]   After recapitulating the negative results reached in the two interviews, Jackson was asked whether he had been rightly understood ; and the letter ended by saying, that, "to avoid the misconceptions incident to oral proceeding, I have also the honor to intimate that it is thought expedient that our further discussions on the present occasion be in the written form."[2]

Jackson saw a challenge in this change of attitude, and undertook to meet it by vigorous resistance.   He had no mind to be thrown on the defensive ; as he wrote to Canning, he wished to teach the American government not to presume on his patience.

"On connecting all these circumstances," he reported,[3] — "the manner in which Mr. Smith had conducted our conferences ; the abruptness, especially, with which he had put an end to them ; and the style in which he announces to me, without leaving any choice or alternative, but as the absolute decision of his Government, 'that it is thought expedient that our future discussions on the present occasion' (i. e., the only occasion of doing away existing differences) 'should be in the written form,' — it occurred to me to be necessary to put the matter on such a footing as to preclude, in limine, the idea that every species of indirect obloquy was to be patiently submitted to by his Majesty's minister in this country."

[1] Madison's Works, ii. 499.

[2] Secretary of State to Mr. Jackson, Oct. 9, 1809 ; State Papers, iii. 308.

[3] Jackson to Canning, Oct. 18, 1809 ; MSS. British Archives.

In this temper Jackson wrote a long letter, dated
October 11, for the purpose, as he reported to Canning,[1] of checking " that spirit which can never lead
to conciliation, by which America thinks herself entitled to make her will and her view of things the
criterion by which they are to be generally approved or condemned." Beginning with the assertion that " there does not exist in the annals of
diplomacy a precedent " for stopping verbal communication within so few days after the delivery of
credentials, he rehearsed the story of Erskine's arrangement, and justified his refusal of apology or
explanation. In doing so, he allowed himself to
insinuate what Canning expressly asserted in his
instructions, that Robert Smith had connived at
Erskine's misconduct : —

" It was not known when I left England whether Mr.
Erskine had, according to the liberty allowed him, communicated to you *in extenso* his original instructions. It
now appears that he did not. But . . . I find . . .
that he has submitted to your consideration the three
conditions specified in those instructions as the ground-
work of an arrangement. . . . Mr. Erskine reports,
verbatim et seriatim, your observations upon each of the
three conditions, and the reasons which induced you to
think that others might be substituted in lieu of them.
It may have been concluded between you that these
latter were an equivalent for the original conditions ;
but the very act of substitution evidently shows that
those original conditions were in fact very explicitly

[1] Jackson to Canning, Oct. 18, 1809; MSS. British Archives.

communicated to you, and by you, of course, laid before
the President for his consideration."

After justifying the disavowal of Erskine on the
admitted ground that he had disobeyed instructions,
Jackson came to the point of his own powers. "His
Majesty has authorized me," he said, "notwithstanding the ungracious manner in which his former offer
of satisfaction for the affair of the 'Chesapeake' was
received, to renew that which Mr. Erskine was instructed to make." As for the Orders in Council,
these had been so far modified by the blockade of
April 26 as to make any formal agreement on that
subject seem unnecessary, and he reserved his proposals until he should hear those of the President.

Two days after this letter was despatched, Robert
Smith sent a civil message that there had been no
intention to stop personal intercourse; "he should be
most happy to see me whenever I would call upon
him; we might converse upon indifferent subjects;
but that his memory was so incorrect that it was on
his account necessary that in making his reports to
the President he should have some written document
to assist him." [1] With this excuse for the secretary's
sudden withdrawal from the field the British minister
contented himself until October 19, when he received
an official letter, signed as usual by Robert Smith, but
written with ability such as that good-natured but
illiterate Secretary of State never imagined himself
to possess.

[1] Jackson to Canning, Oct. 18, 1809; MSS. British Archives.

The American note of October 19, far too long to quote or even to abridge, was perhaps the best and keenest paper Madison ever wrote. His faults of style and vagueness of thought almost wholly disappeared in the heat of controversy ; his defence was cool, his attack keen, as though his sixty years weighed lightly the day when he first got his young antagonist at his mercy. He dealt Jackson a fatal blow at the outset, by reminding him that in July, 1808, only the previous year, Canning had put an end to oral communication after two interviews with Pinkney on the subjects under negotiation. He then made three points, well stated and easily remembered : (1) That when a government refuses to fulfil a pledge, it owes a formal and frank disclosure of its reasons. (2) That, in the actual situation, Mr. Erskine's successor was the proper channel for that disclosure. (3) That since Mr. Jackson disclaimed authority to make either explanations or proposals, the President could do no more than express his willingness to favor any honorable mode of settling the matters in dispute.

In enlarging on the subjects touched by Jackson's letter, the President made more than one remark of the kind that most exasperated the British minister. Since no settlement of the dispute was possible or even desired by Jackson, such flashes of Madison's temper were neither harmful nor inappropriate, yet they were certainly on the verge of insult. He told Jackson plainly that Great Britain, by retaining her

so-called retaliation after admitting that it no longer
retaliated, was guilty of deception : —

" You cannot but be sensible that a perseverance under
such circumstances in a system which cannot longer be
explained by its avowed object would force an explanation by some object not avowed. What object might be
considered as best explaining it is an inquiry into which
I do not permit myself to enter, further than to remark
that in relation to the United States it must be an
illegitimate object."

On the other hand, Madison seemed not to resent,
as warmly as he might have done, the intimation that
he had induced Erskine to violate instructions.   The
President either affected not to see, or failed fully to
grasp at first, the serious scope of this charge :

" The stress you have laid on what you have been
pleased to state as the substitution of the terms finally
agreed on for the terms first proposed, has excited no
small degree of surprise.   Certain it is that your predecessor did present for my consideration the three conditions which now appear on the printed document ; that
he was disposed to urge them more than the nature of
two of them (both palpably inadmissible, and one more
than merely inadmissible) could permit ; and that on
finding his first proposals unsuccessful, the more reasonable terms . . . were adopted.   And what, sir, is there
in this to countenance the conclusion you have drawn in
favor of the right of his Britannic Majesty to disavow
the proceeding?   Is anything more common in public
negotiations than to begin with a higher demand, and
that failing, to descend to a lower? "

Contenting himself with the remark that he had for the first time learned, from Jackson's note, the restrictions on Erskine's authority, the President passed to other points as though unaware that his good faith was in question.

The letter of October 19 forced Jackson one step backward, and drove him nearly to the wall. Obliged to choose between the avowal that he had no proposal to make, or the assertion that he had both explanations and proposals, he yielded, somewhat surlily, to the weakness of offering explanations, such as they were, and of inviting proposals eventually to be embodied in a convention. In a note dated October 23 he answered the American note of October 19.[1] If Madison had doubted his own advantage, his doubts must have vanished in reading Jackson's second note, which shuffled and evaded the issues in a manner peculiar to disconcerted men; but the most convincing proof of Jackson's weakness appeared in the want of judgment he showed in exposing himself to attack at the moment when he was seeking safety. He committed the blunder of repeating the charge that Madison was responsible for Erskine's violation of instructions : —

"These instructions . . . were at the time, in substance, made known to you. . . . So far from the terms which he was actually induced to accept having been contemplated in that instruction, he himself states that

[1] Jackson to the Secretary of State, Oct. 23, 1809; State Papers, iii. 315.

they were substituted by you in lieu of those originally proposed."

Jackson's folly in thus tempting his fate was the more flagrant because his private letters proved that he knew something of his true position. "Madison is now as obstinate as a mule," he wrote October 26.[1] "Until he gets [the absolute surrender of the Orders in Council] he will not even accept any satisfaction for the affair of the 'Chesapeake,' which has been now for the third time offered to him in vain;" and he added: "There is already a great and growing fermentation in the United States, which shows itself in a manner highly prejudicial to the amity and good understanding which doubtless our ministers wish to see established between the two countries."

A few days after writing this evidence of his own uneasiness, the British minister received from the Department of State a third note, dated November 1, which left no doubt that the President meant to push his antagonist to extremes. After accepting the explanations at last made in regard to the Orders in Council, and pointing out that they did not apply to the case of the "Chesapeake," Madison requested Jackson to show his full powers, as an "indispensable preliminary to further negotiation." The letter was short, and ended with a stern warning: —

"I abstain, sir, from making any particular animadversions on several irrelevant and improper allusions in

[1] Bath Archives, Second Series, i. 28.

your letter, not at all comporting with the professed disposition to adjust, in an amicable manner, the differences
unhappily subsisting between the two countries ; but it
would be improper to conclude the few observations to
which I purposely limit myself, without adverting to your
repetition of a language implying a knowledge on the
part of this Government that the instructions of your predecessor did not authorize the arrangement formed by
him.   After the explicit and peremptory asseveration that
this Government had no such knowledge, and that with
such a knowledge no such arrangement would have been
entered into, the view which you have again presented
of the subject makes it my duty to apprise you that such
insinuations are inadmissible in the intercourse of a
foreign minister with a Government that understands
what it owes to itself."

This letter placed Jackson in a position which he
could not defend, and from which he thought, perhaps with reason, that he could not without disgrace
retreat.   The insinuations he had made were but a
cautious expression of the views he was expressly
ordered to take.   November 4 he replied, with more
ability than he had hitherto shown, to the letter of
November 1 ; but he gave himself, for a mere point
of temper, into Madison's hands.

"I am concerned, sir, to be obliged, a second time, to
appeal to those principles of public law, under the sanction and protection of which I was sent to this country.
. . . You will find that in my correspondence with you
I have carefully avoided drawing conclusions that did
not necessarily follow from the premises advanced by me,
and least of all should I think of uttering an insinuation

where I was unable to substantiate a fact. To facts, such as I have become acquainted with them, I have scrupulously adhered; and in so doing I must continue, whenever the good faith of his Majesty's government is called in question, to vindicate its honor and dignity in the manner that appears to me best calculated for that purpose."

When Jackson was sent to Copenhagen with a message whose general tenor resembled that which he brought to the United States, he was fortunate enough to be accompanied by twenty ships of the line, forty frigates, and thirty thousand regular troops. Even with this support, if court gossip could be believed, King George expressed to him surprise that he had escaped being kicked downstairs. At Washington he had no other force on his side than such as his footman or his groom could render, and the destiny that King George predicted for him could not, by any diplomatic weapons, be longer escaped. November 8, Secretary Smith sent to the Legation one more note, which closed Jackson's diplomatic career: —

"Sir, — . . . Finding that in your reply of the 4th instant you have used a language which cannot be understood but as reiterating and even aggravating the same gross insinuation, it only remains, in order to preclude opportunities which are thus abused, to inform you that no further communications will be received from you. . . ."

CHAPTER VII.

THE effect of American conciliation upon Canning was immediate and simple; but the effect of American defiance upon Napoleon will be understood only by those who forget the fatigue of details in their interest for Napoleon's character. The Emperor's steps in 1809 are not easily followed. He was overburdened with labor; his motives and policy shifted as circumstances changed; and among second-rate interests he lost more habitually than ever the thread of his own labyrinth.

Travelling day and night from Spain in January, 1809, with the same haste and with something of the same motive as when four years afterward he posted back to Paris from his Russian disaster, Napoleon appeared unexpectedly at his capital January 24. The moment was one of crisis, but a crisis of his own making. He had suffered a political check in Spain, which he had but partially disguised by a useless campaign. The same spirit of universal dominion which grasped at Spain and required the conquest of England, roused resistance elsewhere almost as desperate as that of the Spaniards and English. Even the American Congress repealed its embargo and poured its commerce through so-called neutral ports into the lap of England, while at the same moment Austria, driven to desperation, prepared to fight for a fourth time. Napoleon had strong reasons for choosing that moment to force Austria wholly into his system. Germany stood at his control. Russia alone could have made the result doubtful; but the Czar was wholly French. " M. Romanzoff," wrote Armstrong to the State Department,[1] " with the fatalism of the Turk, shakes his head at Austria, and asks what has hitherto been got by opposition; calls to mind the fate of Prussia, and closes by a pious admonition not to resist the will of God."

Toward Austria the Emperor directed all his attention, and rapidly drove her government into an attitude of resistance the most spirited and the most desperate taken by any people of Europe except Spain. Although Austria never wearied of fighting Napoleon, and rarely fought without credit, her effort to face, in 1809, a Power controlling the military resources of France, Italy, and Germany, with the moral support of Russia behind them, had an heroic quality higher than was shown at any time by any other government in Europe. April 9 the Austrian army crossed the Inn, and began the war. April 13 Napoleon left Paris for the Danube, and during the next three months his hands were full. Austria

---

[1] Armstrong to R. Smith, Feb. 16, 1809; MSS. State Department Archives.

fought with an energy which put Germany and Russia to shame.

Such a moment was ill suited for inviting negotiation on American affairs ; but Armstrong received instructions a few days after Napoleon left Paris, and with these instructions came a copy of the Nonintercourse Act of March 1, which, while apparently forbidding intercourse with England and France, notified Napoleon that the United States would no longer obey his wishes, or keep their industries from seeking a British market through indirect channels. Armstrong communicated this Act to the French government in the terms of his instructions : [1] —

" The undersigned is instructed to add that any interpretation of the Imperial Decrees of Nov. 21, 1806, and Dec. 17, 1807, which shall have the effect of leaving unimpaired the maritime rights of the Union, will be instantaneously followed by a revocation of the present Act [as regards France] and a re-establishment of the ordinary commercial intercourse between the two countries."

May 17 Champagny, then at Munich, having received Armstrong's letter of April 29, notified the Minister of Marine,[2] —

" The news of this measure having received an official character by the communication made to me by the

[1] Armstrong to Champagny, April 29, 1809; State Papers, iii. 324.

[2] Champagny to Decrès, 17 May, 1809; Archives des Aff. Étr. MSS.

United States minister on the part of his Government,
I think it my duty to transmit to your Excellency a
copy of the law which he has addressed to me."

Armstrong informed Secretary Robert Smith [1] that
nothing need be expected from this step, unless it
were perhaps his own summary expulsion from
France as a result of offence given either by the
Non-intercourse Act or by the language of Armstrong's despatches surreptitiously published. Bitterly as Armstrong detested Napoleon, he understood
but little the mind and methods of that unusual
character. Never in his career had the Emperor
been busier than when Armstrong wrote this note to
Champagny, but it caught his attention at once. He
had fought one battle after another, and in five days
had captured forty thousand men and a hundred
pieces of cannon; he had entered Vienna May 10,
and had taken his quarters at Schönbrunn, the
favorite palace of the Austrian emperor. There he
was in a position of no little difficulty, in spite of his
military successes, when his courier brought him
despatches from Paris containing news that the
United States, March 1, had repealed the embargo,
and that the British government, April 26, had withdrawn the Orders in Council of November, 1807, and
had substituted a mere blockade of Holland, France,
and Italy. The effect of these two events was
greatly increased by their coming together.

[1] Armstrong to R. Smith, April 27, 1809; MSS. State Department Archives.

At first Napoleon seemed to feel no occasion for altering his course. After reading Armstrong's letter, he dictated May 18 a reply which was to serve as the legal argument to justify his refusal of concessions. His decrees were founded on eternal principles, and could not be revoked : —

" The seas belong to all nations. Every vessel sailing under the flag of any nation whatever, recognized and avowed by it, ought to be on the ocean as if it were in its own ports. The flag flying from the mast of a merchantman ought to be respected as though it were on the top of a village steeple. . . . To insult a merchant-vessel carrying the flag of any Power is to make an incursion into a village or a colony belonging to that Power. His Majesty declares that he considers the vessels of all nations as floating colonies belonging to the said nations. In result of this principle, the sovereignty and independence of one nation are a property of its neighbors." [1]

The conclusion that the sovereignty and independence of every nation were the property of France, and that a floating colony denationalized by the visit of a foreign officer became the property of Napoleon, involved results too extreme for general acceptance. Arbitrary as the Emperor was, he could act only through agents, and could not broach such doctrines without meeting remonstrance. His dissertation on the principles of the *jus gentium* was sent May 18 to Champagny. Four days afterward, May 22, Napoleon fought the battle of Essling, in which he lost fifteen

[1] Correspondance, xix. 21.

or twenty thousand men and suffered a serious re-
pulse. Even this absorbing labor, and the critical
situation that followed, did not long interrupt his
attention to American business. May 26, Champagny
made to the Emperor a report[1] on American affairs,
taking ground altogether different from that chosen
by Napoleon. After narrating the story of the various orders, decrees, blockades, embargoes, and non-
intercourse measures, Champagny discussed them in
their practical effect on the interests and industries
of France : —

" The fact cannot be disguised ; the interruption of
neutral commerce which has done much harm to England
has been also a cause of loss to France. The staple
products of our territory have ceased to be sold. Those
that were formerly exported are lost, or are stored
away, leaving impoverished both the owner who produced them and the dealer who put them on the market.
One of our chief sources of prosperity is dried up. Our
interest therefore leads us toward America, whose commerce would still furnish an ample outlet for several of
our products, and would bring us either materials of
prime necessity for our manufactures, or produce the
use of which has become almost a necessity, and which
we would rather not owe to our enemies."

For these reasons Champagny urged the Emperor
not to persist in punishing America, but to charge
M. d'Hauterive, the acting Minister of Foreign Rela-

[1] Champagny to Napoleon, May 26, 1809; Archives des
Aff. Étr. MSS.

tions at Paris, with the duty of discussing with General Armstrong the details of an arrangement. Champagny supported his advice by urging that England had made advances to America, had revoked her orders of November, 1807, and seemed about to turn the French Decrees against France. " It will always be in your Majesty's power to evade this result. A great step to this end will be taken when Mr. Armstrong is made aware that your Majesty is disposed to interpret your commercial decrees favorably for the Americans, provided measures be taken that no tribute shall be paid to England, and that their efficacy shall be assured. Such will be the object of M. d'Hauterive's mission."

Napoleon, impressed by Champagny's reasoning, fortified by the news that Erskine had settled the commercial disputes between England and America, sent to Champagny the draft of a new decree,[1] which declared that inasmuch as the United States by their firm resistance to the arbitrary measures of England had obtained the revocation of the British Orders of November, 1807, and were no longer obliged to pay imposts to the British government, therefore the Milan Decree of Dec. 17, 1807, should be withdrawn, and neutral commerce should be replaced where it stood under the Berlin Decree of Nov. 21, 1806.

This curious paper was sent June 10 to Paris for

[1] Napoleon to Champagny, June 10, 1809; Correspondance, xix. 95.

a report from the Treasury as to its probable effects. June 13 Champagny sent instructions to Hauterive [1] directing him to begin negotiation with Armstrong. Far from overlooking either the intention or the effect of the Non-intercourse Act, Champagny complained that it was unfair to France and "almost an act of violence;" but he did not resent it. "The Emperor is not checked by this consideration; he feels neither prejudice nor resentment against the Americans, but he remains firm in his projects of resisting British pretensions. The measures taken by England will chiefly decide his measures." Champagny explained that the Emperor hesitated to issue the new decree already forwarded for the inspection of the customs authorities, not because any change had taken place in the reasons given for its policy, but because the arrangement of Erskine was said to be disavowed.

"What has prevented the Emperor till now from coming to a decision in this respect is the news contained in the English journals of an arrangement between England and America, and announced by a Proclamation of the President of the United States, April 19, 1806. If from this act should result the certainty that the English renounce their principle of blockade, then the Emperor would revoke the whole of his measures relative to neutral commerce. But the 'Gazette de France' of June 5, for I have no other authority, pretends that the British ministry refuse to sanction the arrangement

[1] Champagny to Hauterive, June 13, 1809; Archives des Aff. Étr. MSS.

concluded in America; and the result of all this is an extreme uncertainty, which prevents a decision as to the course proper to be taken."

This was the situation of the American dispute June 13, 1809, at Vienna, at the moment Canning's disavowal of Erskine became certain. Thus far Napoleon's mind had passed through two changes, — the first, in consequence of the British Order in Council of April 26, which led him to decide on withdrawing the Milan Decree; the second, in consequence of Erskine's arrangement, which led him to promise America everything she asked. The news of Canning's refusal to carry out the arrangement stopped Napoleon short in his career of concession; he left the American affair untouched until after the battle of Wagram, July 6, which was followed by the submission of Austria, July 12. The battle of Wagram placed him in a position to defy resistance. Immediately afterward he sent orders to Paris to stop Hauterive's negotiation. About the middle of July Hauterive told the American minister "that a change had taken place in the views of the Emperor; and in particular that a decree prepared by his orders as a substitute for those of November, 1806, and December, 1807, and which would have been a very material step toward accommodation, had been laid aside." [1]

In the heat and fury of the battle of Wagram this

[1] Armstrong to R. Smith, July 22, 1809; MSS. State Department Archives.

order must have been given, for it was known at Paris only one week afterward, and Armstrong reported the message, July 24, as a notice that unless America resisted the British doctrines of search and blockade she need expect no relaxation on the part of Napoleon; while this notice was supported by a menace that until the Emperor knew the President's decision he would take no step to make matters worse than they already were.[1]

If Armstrong put trust in this last promise or menace, he showed once more his want of sympathy with the Emperor's character. Quick to yield before an evident disaster, Napoleon was equally quick to exhaust the fruits of an evident victory; and the advantage he had obtained over the United States was as decided, if not as extensive, as that which he had gained over Austria. In one way or another America must pay for rebellion, and she could be made to pay only by the usual process of seizing her commerce.

June 7, while the Emperor was still hesitating or leaning to concession, Decrès, his Minister of Marine, wrote to him that an American schooner with a cargo of colonial produce had arrived at San Sebastian May 20, and that more such vessels must be expected to arrive, since the Non-intercourse Act had opened the trade to Spanish ports. What should be done with them? The French Decrees denationalized every vessel which went to England, or wished

[1] Armstrong to R. Smith, July 24, 1809; MSS. State Department Archives.

to go there, or had been visited by an English cruiser, or had violated the laws of the United States, or had incurred suspicion of fraud; but the schooner in question was under no suspicion of fraud, — she had not been to England, nor had she ever thought of going there; she had not been stopped by any cruiser; she was in a Spanish port, nominally outside of French jurisdiction, and she was authorized in going there by the law of the United States. Here was an unforeseen case, and Decrès properly referred it to the Emperor.[1]

Decrès' letter reached Vienna about June 13, the day when Champagny described the Emperor as vexed by an extreme uncertainty on American affairs. The subject was referred to the Minister of Finance. No decision seems to have been reached until August. Then Maret, the Secretary of State in personal attendance on the Emperor, created Duc de Bassano a few days later, enclosed to Champagny, August 4, the draft of a new decree,[2] which was never published, but furnished the clew to most of the intricate movements of Napoleon for the following year: —

"Napoleon, etc., — considering that the American Congress by its Act of March 1, 1809, has forbidden the entrance of its ports to all French vessels under penalty of confiscation of ships and cargo, — on the re-

[1] Rapport a l'Empereur par le Ministre de la Marine, 7 Juin, 1809. Archives des Aff. Étr. MSS.

[2] Décret Impérial; Archives des Aff. Étr. MSS. vol. lxii. (États Unis), pièce 166.

port of our Minister of Finance have decreed and decree
what follows : —

"Art. 1. The American schooner loaded with colonial
produce and entered at San Sebastian the 20th May,
1809, will be seized and confiscated.

"Art. 2. The merchandise composing the cargo of
the vessel will be conveyed to Bayonne, there to be
sold, and the produce of the sale paid into the *caisse de
l'amortissement* (sinking-fund).

"Art. 3. Every American ship which shall enter the
ports of France, Spain, or Italy will be equally seized
and confiscated, as long as the same measure shall continue to be executed in regard to French vessels in the
harbors of the United States."

Probably the ministers united in objecting to a
general confiscation founded on the phrase of a
penalty which the customs laws of every country
necessarily contained. Whatever the reason, this
draft rested in the files of the office over which
Champagny presided, and the Emperor seemed to
forget it ; but its advantages from his standpoint
were too great to be lost, and its principle was
thenceforward his guide.

Not even Armstrong, suspicious as he was of Napoleon's intentions, penetrated the projected policy ;
yet Armstrong was by no means an ordinary minister,
and his information was usually good. At the moment when he received what he supposed to be the
promise that Napoleon would not make matters
worse until he heard what the President had to
say, Armstrong warned his Government that this

assurance was intended as a menace rather than as
a pledge : [1] —

" What will satisfy him on even these points, particularly the former, is not distinctly explained. Our creed
on this subject is one thing ; that of the British government another ; and the French doctrine of visit, a
third. When we speak of illegal search, we mean that
which claims the right of impressment also ; but according to the imperial decrees and their commentators, the
offence is equally great whatever may be the object of
the visit, — whether it be to demand half your crew, or
to ascertain only the port from which you sailed, the
nature of your cargo, or the character of your flag.
This is pushing things to a point whither we cannot
follow them, and which, if I do not mistake, is selected
because it is a point of that description."

Before the month of August, Napoleon reverted
more energetically than ever to his old practice and
policy. Within Armstrong's reach remained only
one influence strong enough to offer a momentary
resistance to imperial orders, and thither he turned.
The kingdom of Holland was still nominally independent, and its trade an object of interest. While
England shaped her policy to favor the licensed or
smuggling trade with Dutch ports, the United States
risked their relations with England and France by
treating Holland as an independent neutral. Yet
the nominal independence of Holland was due only
to the accident that had made Louis its king, as it

[1] Armstrong to R. Smith, July 24, 1809 ; MSS. State Department Archives.

had made his brother Joseph king of Spain, — not wholly with a view to please them, but also to secure obedience to Napoleon's orders and energy to his system. No one would willingly deprive any member of Napoleon's family of virtues which the world allowed them; yet none but a Bonaparte thoroughly understood a Bonaparte, and Napoleon's opinion of his brothers, as their opinions of him, stand highest in authority. Napoleon was often generous and sometimes forbearing with his brothers, and left them no small freedom to seek popularity at his expense; but they were nothing except as they represented him, and their ideas of independence or of philanthropy showed entire misunderstanding of their situation. Of all Napoleon's brothers, Louis was the one with whom he was most reasonably offended. Lucien at least did not wait to be made a king before he rebelled; but Louis accepted the throne, and then intrigued persistently against the Emperor's orders. From the moment he went to Holland he assumed to be an independent monarch, devoted to winning popularity. He would not execute the Berlin Decree until Napoleon threatened to march an army upon him; he connived at its evasion; he issued licenses and admitted cargoes as he pleased; and he did this with such systematic disregard of remonstrance that Napoleon became at last angry.

July 17, some days after the battle of Wagram, the Emperor wrote from Vienna to Louis,[1] —

[1] Correspondance, xix. 261.

" You complain of a newspaper article ; it is France that has a right to complain of the bad spirit which reigns with you. . . . It may not be your fault, but it is none the less true that Holland is an English province."

At the same time he ordered Champagny to notify the Dutch government officially that if it did not of its own accord place itself on the same footing with France, it would be in danger of war.[1]

While this correspondence was still going on, Armstrong imagined that he might obtain some advantage by visiting Holland. He amused himself during the idle August by a journey to Amsterdam, where he obtained, August 19, a private interview with King Louis. Three days before, Flushing had capitulated to the English expedition which was supposed to be threatening Antwerp. At Vienna Napoleon was negotiating for peace, and between the obstinacy of Austria and the British attacks on Madrid and Antwerp he found himself ill at ease. President Madison had just issued his Proclamation of August 9 reviving the Non-intercourse Act, which kept open the American trade with Holland. Everywhere the situation was confused, irritable, and hard to understand. A general system of cross-purposes seemed to govern the political movements of the world.

King Louis told Armstrong that he was quarrelling seriously with the Emperor on account of the Ameri-

[1] Correspondance, xix. 261.

can trade, but was bent on protecting it at all haz-
ards.   This declaration to a foreign minister accredited not to himself but to his brother, showed
Louis attempting with the aid of foreign nations
a systematic opposition to Napoleon's will.   He denounced his brother's system as " the triumph of im-
morality over justice. . . . The system is bad, — so
bad that it cannot last; but in the mean time we
are the sufferers."   Even the British expedition to
Walcheren troubled Louis chiefly because it forced
him under his brother's despotism.   " It is an erring
policy, and will have no solid or lasting effect but
that of drawing upon us a French army which will
extinguish all that is left of ancient Holland.   Can
it be wisdom in England to see this country a province of France ? "

With such comfort as Armstrong could draw
from the knowledge that Napoleon's brothers were
as hostile as President Madison to the imperial
system, he returned to Paris, September 6, to wait
the further development of the Emperor's plans.   He
found on his arrival two notes from Champagny at
Vienna.   One of these despatches expressed a civil
hope, hardly felt by the Emperor,[1] that Armstrong
would not for the present carry out his project
of returning to America.   The other, dated August
22, was nothing less than a revised and permanent
form of the Emperor's essay on the *jus gentium*,

[1] Napoleon to Champagny, 21 August, 1809; Correspondance,
xix. 375.

which Champagny since May 18 had kept in his portfolio.[1]

In Champagny's hands Napoleon's views lost freshness without gaining legality. The " village steeple " disappeared, but with some modification the " floating colony " remained, and the principle of free seas was carried to its extreme results : —

" A merchant-vessel sailing with all the necessary papers (*avec les expéditions*) from its government is a floating colony. To do violence to such a vessel by visits, by searches, and by other acts of an arbitrary authority is to violate the territory of a colony ; this is to infringe on the independence of its government. . . . The right, or rather the pretension, of blockading by a proclamation rivers and coasts, is as monstrous (*révoltante*) as it is absurd. A right cannot be derived from the will or the caprice of one of the interested parties, but ought to be derived from the nature of things themselves. A place is not truly blockaded until it is invested by land and sea."

Every one could understand that to assert such principles was an impossibility for neutrals, and was so meant by Napoleon. He had no thought of making demands which England could accept. The destruction of her naval power was his favorite object after the year 1805. The battle of Wagram confirmed him in his plan, and Louis' oppposition counted for even less than Armstrong's diplomacy in checking the energy of his will. As he ordered

[1] Correspondance de Napoléon, xix. 374 ; State Papers, iii. 325.

Louis, so he ordered Madison, to obey; and thanks to the obstinacy of Spencer Perceval, both had no choice but to assist his scheme. As an answer to the American offer expressed in the Non-intercourse Act, Champagny's despatch of August 22 was final; but to preclude a doubt, it closed by saying that the ports of Holland, of the Elbe and the Weser, of Italy and of Spain, would not be allowed to enjoy privileges of which French ports were deprived, and that whenever England should revoke her blockades and Orders in Council, France would revoke her retali· atory decrees.

Without suicide, England could hardly accept the principles required by this note; nor had she reason to suppose that her acceptance would satisfy Napoleon's demands. As though to encourage her in obstinacy, the note was printed in the "Moniteur" of October 6, by the Emperor's order, before it could have reached America. This unusual step served no purpose except to give public notice that France would support England in restricting American rights; it strengthened the hands of Spencer Perceval and took away the last chance of American diplomacy, if a chance still existed. Yet neither this stroke nor the severity foreshadowed by the secret Decree of Vienna was the only punishment inflicted by Napoleon on the United States for the Non-intercourse Act and Erskine's arrangement.

The principle of the Vienna Decree required confiscation of American commerce in retaliation for penalties imposed on French ships that should knowingly violate the Non-intercourse Act. Although this rule and the Bayonne Decree seemed to cover all ordinary objects of confiscation, the Emperor adopted the supplementary rule that American merchandise was English property in disguise. In the month of November a cotton-spinner near Paris, the head of a very large establishment, petitioned for leave to import about six hundred bales of American cotton. His petition was returned to him with the indorsement: " Rejected, as the cotton belongs to American commerce." The severity of the refusal surprised every one the more because the alternative was to use Portuguese — that is to say English — cotton, or to encourage the consumption of fabrics made wholly in England, of English materials.[1] Having decided to seize all American merchandise that should arrive in France on private account, and having taken into his own hands the business of selling this property as well as of admitting other merchandise by license, Napoleon protected what became henceforward his personal interests, by shutting the door to competition.[2] Armstrong caught glimpses of this stratagem even before it had taken its finished shape.

" I am privately informed," wrote Armstrong December 10, " that General Loison has left Paris charged to take hold of all British property, or property suspected

[1] Armstrong to R. Smith, Nov. 18, 1809 ; MSS. State Department Archives.

[2] Mémoires de Mollien, iii. 133–135.

of being such in the ports of Bilbao, San Sebastian, Pasages, etc. The latter part of the rule is no doubt expressly intended to reach American property. With the General goes a mercantile man who will be known in the market as his friend and protégé, and who of course will be the exclusive purchaser of the merchandise which shall be seized and sold as British. This is a specimen at once of the violence and corruption which enter into the present system ; and of a piece with this is the whole business of licenses, to which, I am sorry to add, our countrymen lend themselves with great facility."

Under such conditions commerce between the United States and France seemed impossible. One prohibition crowded upon another. First came the Berlin Decree of Nov. 21, 1806, which turned away or confiscated every American vessel voluntarily entering a British port after that date. Second, followed the Milan Decree of Nov. 11, 1807, which denationalized and converted into English property every American ship visited by a British cruiser or sent into a British port, or which had paid any tax to the British government. Third, the Bayonne Decree of April 5, 1808, sequestered all American vessels arriving in France subsequent to the embargo, as being presumably British property. Fourth, the American Non-intercourse Act of March 1, 1809, prohibited all commerce with France or her dependencies. Fifth, the British Orders in Council of April 26, 1809, established a blockade of the whole coast of France. Sixth, the secret Decree of Vienna, of August, 1809, enforced in principle, sequestered

every American vessel arriving within the Emperor's
military control, in reprisal for the Non-intercourse
Act which threatened French ships with confiscation.
Yet with all this, and greatly to General Armstrong's
displeasure, American ships in considerable numbers
entered the ports of France, and, what was still more
incomprehensible, were even allowed to leave them.

CHAPTER VIII.

UNDER these circumstances President Madison was to meet Congress; but bad as his situation was in foreign affairs, his real troubles lay not abroad but at home. France never counted with him as more than an instrument to act on England. Erskine and Canning, by their united efforts, had so mismanaged English affairs that Madison derived from their mismanagement all the strength he possessed. The mission of Jackson to Washington retrieved a situation that offered no other advantage.

Jackson lost no occasion to give the President popularity. Comprehending at last that his high tone had only helped his opponent to carry out a predetermined course, Jackson lost self-confidence without gaining tact. At first he sustained himself by faith in Canning; but within a short time he heard with alarm the news from England that Canning was no longer in office or in credit. For a few days after the rupture he had a right to hope that the quarrel would not be pressed to a scandal; but November 13, the " National Intelligencer published an official statement which embarrassed Jackson to the last point of endurance.

" I came prepared to treat with a regular government," he wrote to his brother,[1] " and have had to do with a mob, and mob leaders. That I did not show an equal facility with Erskine to be duped by them has been my great crime."

That Jackson should be angry was natural, and if he was abusive, he received an ample equivalent in abuse ; but his merits as a diplomatist were supposed to be his courage and his truth, and these he could not afford to compromise. He had neither said nor done more than stood in his express orders. Canning's instructions charged Madison with fraud :

" The American government cannot have believed that such an arrangement as Mr. Erskine consented to accept was conformable to his instructions. . . . They cannot by possibility have believed that without any new motive, and without any apparent change in the dispositions of the enemy, the British government could have been disposed at once and unconditionally to give up the system ou which they had been acting."

This ground Jackson had been ordered to take in any " preliminary discussion " which might " in all probability " arise before he could enter on the details of his negotiation. In obedience to these instructions, and well within their limits, Jackson had gone as near as he dared to telling the President that he alone was to blame for the disavowal of Erskine, because Erskine's instructions " were at the time in substance made known " to him. In subsequently

---

[1] Bath Archives, Second Series, i. 44.

affirming that he made no insinuation which he could
not substantiate, Jackson still kept to what he believed
the truth ; and he reiterated in private what he insinuated officially, that Erskine had been " duped " by
the American government. November 16 he wrote
officially to the Foreign Office that without the slightest doubt the President had full and entire knowledge of Erskine's instruction No. 2.[1]   These views
were consistent and not unreasonable, but no man
could suppose them to be complimentary to President
Madison ; yet November 13 Jackson caused his secretary, Oakeley, to send in his name an official note
to the Secretary of State, complaining of the rupture
and rehearsing the charges, with the conclusion that
" in stating these facts, and in adhering to them, as
his duty imperiously enjoined him to do, Mr. Jackson
could not imagine that offence would be taken at it
by the American government, as most certainly none
could be intended on his part." [2]   He then addressed
the same counter-statement as a circular to the various British consuls in the United States, and caused
it to be printed in the newspapers,[3] — thus making
an appeal to the people against their own Government, not unlike the more famous appeal which
the French Minister Genet made in 1793 against
President Washington.

[1] Jackson to Bathurst. Nov. 16, 1809 ; MSS. British Archives.

[2] Mr. Oakeley to the Secretary of State, Nov. 13, 1809 ; State
Papers, iii. 319.

[3] National Intelligencer, Nov. 22, 1809.

In extremely bad temper Jackson quitted the capital. His wife wrote to her friends in joy at the prospect of shortening her stay in a country which could offer her only the tribute of ignorant admiration; but even she showed a degree of bitterness in her pleasure, and her comments on American society had more value than many official documents in explaining the attitude of England toward the United States : —

" Francis, being accustomed to treat with the civilized courts and governments of Europe, and not with savage Democrats, half of them sold to France, has not succeeded in his negotiation." [1]

At Washington she had seen few ladies besides Mrs. Madison, " une bonne, grosse femme, de la classe bourgeoise, . . . sans distinction," and also, to do her justice, " sans prétensions ; " who did the British minister's wife the honor to copy her toilettes. Immediately after the rupture Mrs. Jackson went to Baltimore, where she was received with enthusiasm by society ; but Baltimore satisfied her little better than Washington : " Between ourselves their cuisine is detestable ; coarse table-linen, no claret, champagne and madeira indifferent." Only as the relative refinement of New York and Boston was reached, with the flattery lavished upon the British minister by the Federalist society of the commercial cities, did Mrs. Jackson and her husband in some degree recover their composure and their sense of admitted superiority.

[1] Bath Archives, i. 56.

Incredible as the folly of a political party was apt to be, the folly of the Federalists in taking up Jackson's quarrel passed the limits of understanding. After waiting to receive their tone from England, the Federalist newspapers turned on their own path and raised the cry that Madison had deceived Erskine, and had knowingly entered into an arrangement which England could not carry out. The same newspapers which in April agreed with John Randolph that Canning had obtained through Erskine all he had ever asked or had a right to expect, averred in October that Erskine surrendered everything and got nothing in return. No political majority, still less a minority, could survive a somersault so violent as this; and the Federalists found that all their late recruits, and many friends hitherto stanch, deserted them in the autumn elections. Throughout the country the Administration was encouraged by great changes in the popular vote, even before the rupture with Jackson. With confidence, Madison might expect the more important spring elections to sweep opposition from his path. Although a whole year, and in some cases eighteen months, must pass before a new Congress could be chosen, the people were already near the war point.

Vermont chose a Republican governor and a legislature Republican in both branches. In Rhode Island, Connecticut, and New Jersey the Administration recovered more than the ground lost by the embargo. In Maryland the feud between Samuel Smith and his opponents was ended by a Republican majority so large that nothing could prevent Smith's return to the Senate, although every one knew that he would carry on a system of personal opposition, if he dared, and that a moderate Federalist would be less dangerous to the Administration. In the general return of deserters to the ranks, the party would not be too strict in its punishments ; and the President set the example by clemency to the worst offender, except John Randolph, of all the trusted lieutenants in the party service. He held out a hand to Monroe.

Madison's reasons for winning Monroe were strong. The more he had to do with Robert Smith, the more intolerable became the incubus of Smith's incompetence. He had been obliged to take the negotiations with Erskine and Jackson wholly on his own shoulders. The papers drafted by Smith were, as Madison declared,[1] brought from the Department of State in a condition " almost always so crude and inadequate that I was, in the more important cases, generally obliged to write them anew myself, under the disadvantage sometimes of retaining through delicacy some mixture of his draft." Smith had not even the virtue of dulness. He could not be silent, but talked openly, and criticised freely the measures of Government, especially those of commercial restriction.

Complicated with this incessant annoyance was Gallatin's feud. The combination of the Smiths with Giles, Leib, and Duane's " Aurora " against Gallatin

[1] Works, ii. 499.

had its counterpart in the Clintonian faction which
made Madison its target; and whenever these two
forces acted together, they made, with the Federalists,
a majority of the Senate.   Gallatin saw the necessity
of breaking down this combination of intrigue which
had already done incalculable harm by forcing Robert
Smith into the State Department.   He foresaw the
effects of its influence in weakening the Treasury in
order to expel himself.   On a visit to Monticello in
August he spoke plainly to Jefferson and Madison,
and pointed out the probability that he should be
forced to resign.   Jefferson reflected six weeks on
this communication, and then wrote entreating him
to stand firm.[1]   November 8, the day of the rupture
with Jackson, Gallatin answered Jefferson's appeal
in a long and outspoken letter evidently meant for
communication to Madison: —

"It has seemed to me from various circumstances that
those who thought they had injured were disposed to destroy, and that they were sufficiently skilful and formidable to effect their object.   As I may not, however,
perhaps, see their actions with an unprejudiced eye,
nothing but irresistible evidence both of the intention
and success will make me yield to that consideration.
. . . I do not ask that in the present situation of our
foreign relations the debt be reduced, but only that it
shall not be increased so long as we are not at war.   I
do not pretend to step out of my own sphere and to control the internal management of other departments; but
it seems to me that as Secretary of the Treasury I may

[1] Jefferson to Gallatin, Oct. 11, 1809; Works, v. 477.

ask, that, while peace continues, the aggregate of the expenditure of those departments be kept within bounds such as will preserve the equilibrium between the national revenue and expenditure without recurrence to loans. I cannot consent to act the part of a mere financier, to become a contriver of taxes, a dealer of loans, a seeker of resources for the purpose of supporting useless baubles, of increasing the number of idle and dissipated members of the community, of fattening contractors, pursers, and agents, and of introducing in all its ramifications that system of patronage, corruption, and rottenness which you so justly execrate."

From this avowal Madison's difficulties could be understood and his course foreseen. Very slow to move, he was certain at last to quarrel with the senatorial faction that annoyed him. He could not but protect Gallatin, and dismiss Smith. At the end of the vista, however far the distance, stood the inevitable figure of Monroe. Scarcely another man in public life could fill precisely the gap, and none except Armstrong could give strength to the President by joining him. Perhaps Littleton Tazewell, another distinguished Virginian of the same school, would have answered the President's purpose as well as Monroe ; but probably Tazewell would have declined to accept a seat in the Cabinet of a President whose election he had opposed.[1] Madison decided to take the first step. He had reason to think that Monroe repented his course, at least to the extent of wishing reconciliation. He authorized Jefferson to

[1] Grigsby's Tazewell, p. 87.

act as mediator; and the Ex-President, who spared no
effort for harmony, hastened to tell Monroe that the
government of Louisiana was still at his disposal.[1]
Monroe declined the office as being beneath his previous positions, but said that he would have accepted
the first place in Madison's Cabinet, and was sincere
in his desire for the success of the Administration;
he even pledged his support, and intimated that he
had lost favor with John Randolph owing to his
exertions for Madison.   When Jefferson reported
the result of this interview, the President replied:[2]
"The state of Colonel Monroe's mind is very nearly
what I had supposed; his willingness to have taken
a seat in the Cabinet is what I had not supposed."
Considering the state of Monroe's mind in 1808,
Madison might be excused for failing to see that
Monroe would accept the State Department in February, 1809.   Indeed, the suddenness of the change
would have startled Monroe's best friends; and
even in December, 1809, he would have fared ill
had his remarks to Jefferson been brought to John
Randolph's ears.

Monroe's adhesion having been thus attested,
Madison made no immediate use of the recruit, but
held him in reserve until events should make action
necessary.   Perhaps this delay was one of Madison's

[1] Jefferson to Madison, Nov. 30, 1809; Works, v. 481.   Cf.
Monroe to Colonel Taylor, Feb. 25, 1810; Monroe MSS. State
Department Archives.

[2] Madison to Jefferson, Dec. 11, 1809; Works, ii. 460.

constitutional mistakes, and possibly a prompt removal of Robert Smith might have saved some of
the worst disasters that befell the Government; but
in truth Madison's embarrassments rose from causes
that only time could cure, and were inherent in
American society itself. A less competent adminis-
trative system seldom drifted, by reason of its incompetence, into war with a superior enemy. No
department of the government was fit for its necessary work.

Of the State Department, its chief, and its long
series of mortifying disasters, enough has been said.
In November, 1809, it stood helpless in the face of
intolerable insults from all the European belligerents.
Neither the diplomatic nor the consular system was
better than a makeshift, and precisely where the
Government felt most need of ministers, — at Copenhagen, Stockholm, Berlin, and St. Petersburg, — it
had no diplomatic and but few consular agents, even
these often of foreign allegiance.

The Treasury, hitherto the only successful Executive department, showed signs of impending collapse,
not to be avoided without sacrifices and efforts which
no one was willing to make. The accounts for the
year ending September 30 showed that while the
receipts had amounted to $9,300,000, the actual
expenses had exceeded $10,600,000. The deficit of
$1,300,000, as well as reimbursements of debt to the
amount of $6,730,000, had been made good from the
balance in the Treasury. The new fiscal year began

with a balance of only $5,000,000; so that without
a considerable curtailment of expenses, a loan or
increased taxation, or both, could not be avoided.
Increased taxation was the terror of parties. Curtailment of expense could be effected only on the
principle that as the government did nothing well,
it might as well do nothing. Any intelligent expenditure, no matter how large or how small, would have
returned a thousand-fold interest to the country,
whatever had been the financial cost; but the waste
of money on gunboats and useless cruisers, or upon
an army so badly organized and commanded as to be
a hindrance in war, was an expense that might perhaps be curtailed, though only by admitting political
incapacity.

Naturally Gallatin threatened to resign. Even by
submitting to the Smiths, Duanes, Gileses, and Leibs,
and allowing them to cut off the sources or waste
the supplies of public revenue until the government
became an habitual beggar, he could promise himself
no advantage. Never had the chance of finding an
end to the public embarrassments seemed so remote.
The position in which the government stood could
not be maintained, but could be abandoned only by
creating still greater difficulties. Intended merely
as a makeshift, the Non-intercourse Act of March 1,
1809, had already proved more mischievous to America than to the countries it purported to punish.
While the three great commercial nations — France,
England, and the United States — were forcing trade

into strange channels or trying to dam its course, trade took care of itself in defiance of war and prohibitions. As one coast after another was closed or opened to commerce, countries whose names could hardly be found on the map — Papenburg, Kniphausen, Tönningen — became famous as neutrals, and their flags covered the sea, because England and France found them convenient for purposes of illegitimate trade.   The United States had also their Papenburg. Amelia Island and the St. Mary's River, which divided Florida from Georgia, half Spanish and half American waters, became the scene of a trade that New York envied. While the shore was strewn with American cotton and other produce waiting shipment in foreign vessels, scores of British ships were discharging merchandise to be smuggled into the United States, or were taking on board heavy freights of cotton or naval stores on American account. To the United States this manner of trading caused twofold loss. Not only were the goods charged with a double voyage and all the costly incidents of a smuggling business, and not only did the American shipowner lose the freight on this American merchandise, both outward and inward, but the United States government collected no duties on the British goods smuggled from Amelia Island, Bermuda, and Halifax. The Non-intercourse Act prohibited French and British merchandise; but in disregard of the prohibition such goods were freely sold in every shop. Erskine's arrangement, short as it was, brought in a fresh and large supply; custom-house oaths were cheap; custom-house officials did not inquire closely whether cloth was made in England, France, Holland, or Germany, or whether rum, sugar, and coffee came from St. Kitt's or St. Bart's. Some sorts of English goods, such as low-priced woollens, were necessities; and the most patriotic citizen could hardly pay so much respect to the laws of his country as to dispense with their use by his family, whatever he did on his own account. Finally, a law which in the eyes of a community was not respectable was not respected. The community had no other defence against bad legislation; and in a democracy the spirit of personal freedom deserved cultivation to the full as much as that of respect for bad law. The Non-intercourse Act was not only a bad law, — the result of admitted legislative imbecility, — but it had few or no defenders even among those who obeyed it.

Ingenuity could hardly have invented a system less advantageous for the government and people who maintained it. The government lost its revenue, the shipping lost much of its freight, the people paid double prices on imports and received half-prices for their produce; industry was checked, speculation and fraud were stimulated, while certain portions of the country were grievously wronged. Especially in the Southern States all articles produced for exchange were depressed to the lowest possible value, while all articles imported for consumption were raised

to extravagant rates.   Elisha Potter, a Congressman
from Rhode Island, complained with reason that the
system made the rich more rich and the poor more
poor.[1]   In a crowded or in a highly organized society such a system would probably have created a
revolution ; but America had not yet reached such
a stage of growth or decay, and the worst effect of
her legislation was to impoverish the government
which adopted and the class of planters who chiefly
sustained it.

Gallatin best knew how much the Non-intercourse
Act or any other system of commercial restriction
weakened the Treasury.   He knew that neither the
President nor Congress offered the germ of a better
plan.   He faced an indefinite future of weakness and
waste, with a prospect of war at the end ; but this
was not the worst.   His enemies who were disposed
to destroy, were skilful enough to invent the means of
destruction.   They might deprive him of the United
States Bank, his only efficient ally ; they might reject
every plan, and let the Treasury slowly sink into
ruin ; they might force the country into a war for no
other object than to gratify their personal jealousies.
Gallatin believed them capable of all this, and Madison seemed to share the belief.   The Treasury
which had till that time sustained the Republican
party through all its troubles, stood on the verge of
disaster.

From the military and naval departments nothing

[1] Annals of Congress, 1809–1810, p. 1263.

had ever been expected; but their condition was worse than their own chiefs understood. The machinery of both broke down as Madison took control. The navy consisted of a few cruisers and a large force of gunboats. Neither were of immediate use; but a considerable proportion of both were in active service, if service could be called active which chiefly consisted in lying in harbor or fitting for harbor defence when no enemy was expected. No sooner had Paul Hamilton succeeded Robert Smith at the navy department than the new secretary became aware that his predecessor had wasted a very large sum of money.[1] Hamilton made no concealment of his opinion that gunboats were expensive beyond relation to their value.[2] He intimated that the life of gunboats hardly exceeded one year, and that their value depended on the correct answer to the inquiry whether war was a defensive or aggressive operation. This hint that gunboats could do no harm to their enemies seemed to gain force from the suggestion that they had yet to prove their uses for their friends; but if Jefferson's gunboat system should prove to be a failure, nothing would be left of the navy except a few frigates and sloops which could hardly keep the sea in the event of war with England. The navy was a sink of money.

The army was something worse. At least the navy

[1] *Infra*, chap. x.

[2] Secretary Hamilton to Joseph Anderson, June 6, 1809; State Papers, Naval Affairs, p. 194.

contained as good officers and seamen as the world
could show, and no cruisers of their class were likely
to be more efficient than the frigates commanded by
Rodgers, Bainbridge, and Decatur, provided they could
escape a more numerous enemy ; but the army was
worthless throughout, and its deficiency in equipment
was a trifling evil compared with the effects of political influence on its organization.   The first attempt
to raise the army to efficiency ended in scandalous
failure within a few months.   Among a thousand obstacles to any satisfactory reform in the military service, the most conspicuous if not the most fatal was
General Wilkinson, whom President Jefferson could
not and would not sacrifice, but whose character and
temper divided the army into two hostile camps.
Wade Hampton, the next general officer in rank,
regarded Wilkinson with extreme contempt, and most
of the younger officers who were not partisans of
Jefferson shared Hampton's prejudice ; but July 4,
1808, a military court of inquiry formally acquitted
Wilkinson of being a Spanish pensioner.   President
Jefferson had already saved him from court-martial
on account of his relations with Burr, and Secretary
Dearborn restored him to command over an army
whose interests required an officer of other qualities.

When Madison and Gallatin in December, 1808,
looked to a declaration of war, their first anxiety concerned New Orleans and West Florida.   December 2,
1808, Secretary Dearborn gave Wilkinson, then at
Washington, orders to direct the new levies of troops

toward New Orleans, and to be ready to take command there in person as soon as practicable. In
pursuance of these orders, two thousand raw soldiers
were directed upon New Orleans from different quarters, and in the midst of war preparations, Jan. 24,
1809, Wilkinson himself embarked from Baltimore.[1]
Stopping at Annapolis, Norfolk, and Charleston, he
passed six weeks on the Atlantic coast. After the
overthrow of the war policy and the close of the
session he sailed March 12 from Charleston, and in
his mysterious way stopped at Havana and then at
Pensacola, " under a special mission from the Executive of the United States."   April 19 he re-entered
New Orleans, the scene of his exploits three years
before ; and he returned as a victor, triumphant over
Daniel Clark and the Burr conspirators, as well as
over Governor Claiborne, Wade Hampton, and all
ill-wishers in the subordinate ranks of the army, of
whom Captain Winfield Scott was one.

Wilkinson found at New Orleans, in his own
words,[2] —

" A body of two thousand undisciplined recruits, men
and officers with a few exceptions sunk in indolence and
dissipation ; without subordination, discipline, or police,
and nearly one third of them sick ; . . . without land or
water transport for a single company ; medical assistance for two thousand men dependent on two surgeons
and two mates, one of the former confined to his bed ; a

[1] Wilkinson's Memoirs, ii. 344.
[2] Wilkinson's Memoirs, ii. 346.

majority of the corps without paymasters; the men deserting by squads; the military agent representing the quartermaster's department without a cent in his chest, his bills protested, and he on the eve of shutting up his office; a great deficiency of camp equipage; not a haversack in store; the medicine and hospital stores scarcely sufficient for a private practitioner."

The General decided that, first of all, the troops must be removed from the city and sent into camp; but rains made encampment impossible until the river should fall, and May 12 nothing had been done excepting to notify the Secretary of War that in the course of the following week the General meant to select an encampment which would be so placed as to meet an attack from every hostile quarter.[1] His decision was made known to the Secretary of War in a letter dated May 29 : —

"With the general voice of American and Creole in favor of it, I have selected a piece of ground on the left bank of the Mississippi, below this city about four leagues, which I find perfectly dry at this moment, although the surface of the river, restrained by its dykes, is in general three feet above the level of the country. You will put your finger on the spot, at the head of the English turn, just where the road to the settlements on the Terre aux Boeufs leaves the river."[2]

June 10 the main body of troops moved down the river to the new camp. More than five hundred sick were transported with the rest, suffering chiefly from

[1] Wilkinson's Memoirs, ii. 351.
[2] Wilkinson's Memoirs, ii. 358.

chronic diarrhœa, bilious or intermittent fevers, and scurvy.

Secretary Eustis, who in March succeeded Dearborn at the War Department, being an army-surgeon by profession, noticed, before Wilkinson's arrival at New Orleans, the excessive proportion of troops on the sick-list. Quickly taking alarm, he wrote April 30 directing Wilkinson to disregard Dearborn's previous instructions, and after leaving a garrison of old troops at New Orleans, to transport the rest up the river to the high ground in the rear of Fort Adams, or Natchez. The orders were peremptory and pressing.[1]

This letter, dated April 30, should have gone, and was believed to have gone, by the post which left Washington May 6, and reached New Orleans May 25; another post followed a week later, and still another arrived June 8, two days before the troops moved to Terre aux Boeufs. According to Wilkinson the letter did not arrive by any of these mails, but came only by the fourth post, which reached New Orleans June 14, after he and his troops were fixed in camp. The cost of a bad character was felt at such moments. No one believed Wilkinson; his reputation for falsehood warranted suspicion that he had suppressed the orders in the belief that he knew best what the troops required. Such insubordination was no new thing on his part. Instead of expressing regret, he wrote to Eustis that even had

[1] State Papers, Military Affairs, i. 269.

he received the orders of April 30 in time, he should
still "have not sought the position you recommended," because the labor of ascending the river would
have diseased nine tenths of the men, the expense
would have exceeded twelve thousand dollars, and
the position of Fort Adams was ill-suited for the protection of New Orleans.[1]

On the troops the first effect of their encampment
was good ; but after the middle of June rains began,
generally several showers on the same day, and the
camp was deep in mud. The number of sick made
proper sanitary care impossible. The police officer's
report of July 12 [2] gave a revolting picture of the
sanitary conditions : "The whole camp abounds with
filth and nastiness of almost every kind." The sick-
list rose to six hundred and sixty in a force of
sixteen hundred and eighty-nine non-commissioned
officers and men ; in August it rose to nine hundred
and sixty-three in a total force of fifteen hundred and
seventy-four. The camp was a fever hospital, the
suffering beyond experience. Food, medicine, shel-
ter, clothing, and care were all wanting either to the
sick or to the well : [3] —

"The sick and the well lived in the same tents ; they
generally subsisted on the same provisions, were equally
exposed to the constant and incessant torrents of rain,
to the scorching heat of the sun, and during the night

[1] State Papers, Military Affairs, i. 269.

[2] Wilkinson's Memoirs, ii. Appendix cvii.

[3] Deposition of John Darrington, Captain Third Infantry ;
State Papers, Military Affairs, i. 282.

to the attacks of numberless mosquitoes. They mani-
fested the pains and sufferings they experienced by
shrieks and groans which during the silence of the night
were distinctly to be heard from one end of the line to
the other. It is my candid belief the mosquitoes produced more mischief than any other cause. In the night
the air was filled with them, and not a man was provided
with anything like a bar or net. Thus situated, the
sufferings of the unfortunate sick can perhaps better be
imagined than described."

Before the army had been a month in camp, the
officers petitioned the General for removal. He could
not but refuse. He had no means of escape, and to
do him justice, he bore with courage the consequences
of his own mistake. He did whatever occurred to
him to protect his men. Secretary Eustis took the
matter less calmly. No sooner did the secretary
learn, through Wilkinson's letters written in May,
that he seriously meant to encamp the troops at
Terre aux Boeufs, than official orders, admitting no
discretion, were despatched as early as June 22 from
the Department, directing that the whole force should
be instantly embarked for Natchez and Fort Adams.

The letter arrived July 19. Wilkinson dared not
again disobey, although he might be right in thinking
that the risks of removal were greater than those of
remaining. Every resource of the army and navy
was put at Wilkinson's command, and every man at
Terre aux Boeufs was eager to escape; yet week after
week passed without movement. The orders which
arrived July 19 were not made public till the end of

August, and only September 14 was the camp evacu-
ated. The effective force was then about six hundred
men in charge of nine hundred invalids. The
strength of all had been reduced, until they were
unequal to the fatigues of travel. Only one hundred
and twenty-seven men died at Terre aux Boeufs
between June 10 and September 14 ; but two hundred and fifty died on their way up the river, before
October 31, and altogether seven hundred and sixty-
four, out of two thousand soldiers sent to New
Orleans, died within their first year of service. The
total loss by death and desertion was nine hundred
and thirty-one.

Wilkinson himself was attacked by fever in passing
New Orleans, September 19, and on proceeding to
Natchez soon received a summons to Washington
to answer for his conduct. Brigadier-General Wade
Hampton succeeded him in command of what troops
were still alive at New Orleans. The misfortune was
compensated only by the advantage of affording one
more chance to relieve the army and the government
of a general who brought nothing but disaster.

With the four departments of Executive government in this state of helplessness, President Madison
met Congress, the least efficient body of all.

CHAPTER IX.

The President's Annual Message, read November 29 before Congress, threw no light on the situation. If Madison's fame as a statesman rested on what he wrote as President, he would be thought not only among the weakest of Executives, but also among the dullest of men, whose liveliest sally of feeling exhausted itself in an epithet, and whose keenest sympathy centred in the tobacco crop; but no statesman suffered more than Madison from the constraints of official dress. The Message of 1809 hinted that England had no right to disavow her minister's engagement, and that Jackson's instructions as well as his conduct betrayed a settled intent to prevent an understanding; but these complaints led to no corrective measures. The President professed himself still willing to listen with ready attention to communications from the British government through any new channel, and he seemed to fall back on Jefferson's " painful alternatives " of the year before, rather than on any settled plan of his own : —

" In the state which has been presented of our affairs with the parties to a disastrous and protracted war, carried on in a mode equally injurious and unjust to the

United States as a neutral nation, the wisdom of the national Legislature will be again summoned to the important decision on the alternatives before them. That these will be met in a spirit worthy of the councils of a nation conscious both of its rectitude and of its rights, and careful as well of its honor as of its peace, I have an entire confidence. And that the result will be stamped by a unanimity becoming the occasion, and be supported by every portion of our citizens with a patriotism enlightened and invigorated by experience, ought as little to be doubted."

Such political formulas, conventional as a Chinese compliment, probably had value, since they were current in every government known to man; but that President Madison felt entire confidence in the spirit of the Eleventh Congress could not be wholly believed. John Randolph best described Madison's paper in a letter to Judge Nicholson, a few days afterward : [1]

" I have glanced over the President's Message, and to say the truth it is more to my taste than Jefferson's productions on the same occasions. There is some cant to be sure ; but politicians, priests, and even judges, saving your honor's presence, must cant, ' more or less.' "

Probably the colorless character of the Message was intended to disarm criticism, and to prevent Randolph and the Federalists from rousing again the passions of 1808 ; but sooner or later some policy must be adopted, and although the Message suggested no opinion as to the proper course, it warned Congress that the crisis was at hand : " The insecurity

[1] Randolph to Nicholoson, Dec. 4, 1809; Nicholson MSS.

of our commerce and the consequent diminution of
the public revenue will probably produce a deficiency
in the receipts of the ensuing year." The moment
when a Republican administration should begin to
borrow money for ordinary expenses in time of peace
would mark a revolution in the public mind.

Upon Gallatin, as usual, the brunt of unpopular
responsibility fell. His annual Report, sent to the
House December 8, announced that a loan, probably
of four million dollars, would be required for the
service of 1810; that the Non-intercourse Law, as it
stood, was "inefficient and altogether inapplicable
to existing circumstances;" and finally that "either
the system of restriction, partially abandoned, must
be reinstated in all its parts, and with all the provisions necessary for its strict and complete execution, or all the restrictions, so far at least as they
affect the commerce and navigation of citizens of
the United States, ought to be removed." This subject, said Gallatin, required immediate attention;
but in regard to the wider question of war or peace
he contented himself with a reference to his two
preceding reports.

Congress showed more than usual unwillingness to
face its difficulties. The episodes of Erskine and
Jackson supplied excuse for long and purposeless
debates. In the Senate, December 5, Giles reported
from a special committee the draft of a Resolution
denouncing Jackson's conduct as indecorous, insolent,
affronting, insidious, false, outrageous, and premedi-

tated, — epithets which seemed to make superfluous the approval of Madison's course or the pledge of support with which the Resolution ended.   Giles reviewed the conduct of Jackson and Canning, entreating the Senate to banish irritation and to restore harmony and mutual good-will, " the most fervent prayer of one who in the present delicate, interesting crisis of the nation feels a devotion for his country beyond everything else on this side of heaven." [1] The experience of many years warranted Giles's hearers in suspecting that when he professed a wish for harmony, the hope of harmony must be desperate, for his genius lay in quite another direction ; and when he laid aside partisanship, his party had reason to look for some motive still narrower.   His course quickly proved the sense in which he understood these phrases.

January 3, 1810, the President recommended by message the enlistment for a short period of a volunteer force of twenty thousand men, and a reorganization of the militia ; adding that it would rest with Congress also "to determine how far further provision may be expedient for putting into actual service, if necessary, any part of the naval armament not now employed."   No one knew what this language meant. Crawford of Georgia, with his usual bluntness, said : [2] " This Message, in point of obscurity, comes nearer my ideas of a Delphic oracle than any state paper

[1] Annals of Congress, 1809–1810, p. 509.
[2] Annals of Congress, 1809–1810, p. 544.

which has come under my inspection. It is so cautiously expressed that every man puts what construction on it he pleases." Giles pleased to put upon it a warlike construction. January 10 he reported a bill for fitting out the frigates ; January 13 he supported this bill in a speech which surprised Federalists and Republicans alike, if they could be still surprised at the varieties of Giles's political philosophy.

" The visionary theory of energy," said he, " was the fatal error of the Federal party, and that error deprived it of the power of the nation. The government being thus placed in the hands of the Republicans, while heated by the zeal of opposition to the Federal doctrines and flushed with their recent triumph, it was natural for them, with the best intentions, to run into the opposite extreme ; to go too far in the relaxations of the powers of the government, and to indulge themselves in the delightful visions of extending the range of individual liberty. . . . It was natural that in the vibration of the political pendulum, it should go from one extreme to another ; and that this has been too much the case with the Republican administration, he regretted to say, he feared would be demonstrated by a very superficial review of the events of the last two or three years."

Energy was a fatal mistake in the Federalists ; relaxation was an equally fatal mistake in the Republicans, — and the remedy was a show of energy where energy did not exist. Giles won no confidence by thus trimming between party principles ; but when Samuel Smith argued for Giles's bill on grounds of economy, friends of the Administration felt little doubt of the motives that guided both senators. Had they declared for war, or for peace ; had they proposed to build more frigates or ships-of-the-line, or to lay up those in active service, — had they committed themselves to a decided policy of any kind, their motives would have offered some explanation consistent with a public interest ; but they proposed merely to fit out the frigates while giving them nothing to do, and the Republican party, as a whole, drew the inference that they wished to waste the public money, either for the personal motive of driving Madison and Gallatin from office, or for the public advantage of aiding the Federalists to weaken the Treasury and paralyze the nation.

Crawford replied to Giles with some asperity ; but although Crawford was known to represent the Treasury, so completely had the Senate fallen under the control of the various cabals represented by Vice-President Clinton, Giles, Smith, and Michael Leib of Pennsylvania, with their Federalist associates, that Crawford found himself almost alone. Twenty-five senators supported the bill ; only six voted against it.

Giles impressed the least agreeable qualities of his peculiar character on this Senate, — a body of men easily impressed by such traits. By a vote of twenty-four to four, they passed the Resolution in which Giles showed energy in throwing epithets at the British government, as they passed the bill for employing frigates to pretend energy that was not in their intentions. No episode in the national history was less encouraging than the conduct of Congress in regard to Giles's Resolution. From December 18 to January 4, the House wasted its time and strength in proving the helplessness of Executive, Congress, parties, and people in the grasp of Europe. With painful iteration every Republican proved that the nation had been insulted by the British minister; while every Federalist protested his inability to discern the insult, and his conviction that no insult was intended. Except as preliminary to measures of force, Giles's Resolution showed neither dignity nor object; yet the Republicans embarrassed themselves with denials of the Federalist charge that such language toward a foreign government must have a warlike motive, while the Federalists insisted that their interests required peace.

If the Resolution[1] was correct in affirming as it did that the United States had suffered " outrageous and premeditated insults " from Jackson, Congress could not improve the situation by affirming the insult without showing even the wish to resent it by means that would prevent its repetition; but the majority saw the matter in another light, and when the Federalists resorted to technical delays, the Republicans after a session of nineteen hours passed the Resolution by a vote of seventy-two to forty-one. Macon, Stanford, and the old Republicans voted with the

[1] Resolution approved Jan. 12, 1810; Annals of Congress, 1809–1810, p. 2590.

Federalists in the minority, while Randolph was ill and absent throughout the debate.

The Resolution marked the highest energy reached by the Eleventh Congress. Giles's bill for fitting out the frigates was allowed to slumber in committee; and a bill for taking forty thousand volunteers for one year into government service never came to a vote in the Senate. Congress was influenced by news from England to lay aside measures mischievous except as a prelude to hostilities. The change of Administration in London opened the way to new negotiations, and every fresh negotiation consumed a fresh year.

No course would have pleased Congress so much as to do nothing at all; but this wish could not be fully gratified. The Non-intercourse Act of March 1, 1809, was to expire by limitation with the actual session. As early as December 1 the House referred the matter to a committee with Macon for its head. Macon probably went to the Treasury for instructions. A plan drawn by Gallatin, and accepted without opposition by the Cabinet, was reported December 19 to the House in the form of a bill which had less the character of a Non-intercourse than of a Navigation Act; for while it closed American ports to every British or French vessel public and private, it admitted British and French merchandise when imported directly from their place of origin in vessels wholly American. The measure was as mild a protest as human skill could devise if compared with the outrages it retaliated, but it had the merit of striking at the British shipping interest which was chiefly to blame for the conduct of the British government. Under the provisions of the bill, American shipping would gain a monopoly of American trade. Not a British vessel of any kind could enter an American port.

Macon's bill came before the House Jan. 8, 1810, for discussion, which lasted three weeks. The opposition objected to the new policy for the double reason that it was too strong and too weak. St. Loe Livermore, a Massachusetts Federalist, began by treating the measure as so extreme that England and France would resent it by shutting their ports to all American ships; while Sawyer of North Carolina denounced it as evaporating the national spirit in mere commercial regulations, when no measure short of war would meet the evil. According as commerce or passion weighed with the reasoners, the bill was too violent or disgracefully feeble. Throughout the winter, these contradictory arguments were pressed in alternation by speaker after speaker. Macon reflected only the views of Madison and Gallatin when he replied that if England and France should retaliate by excluding American shipping from their ports, they would do what America wanted; for they must then enforce the non-intercourse which the United States had found impossible to enforce without their aid. He agreed with the war-members that the bill showed none too much energy, but he argued that the nation was less prepared for war than in 1808 and 1809; while as for Jackson's quarrels, he declined to admit that they changed the affair one iota.

Although the two extremes still stood so far apart that their arguments bore no relation to each other, the violence of temper which marked the embargo dispute, and which was to mark any step toward actual measures of force, did not appear at this session. Indeed, the Federalists themselves were not unanimous; some of the most extreme, like Barent Gardenier and Philip Barton Key, supported Macon's plan, while some of the extremists on the other side, like Troup of Georgia, voted against it. January 29, by a vote of seventy-three to fifty-two, the House passed the bill. The Senate soon afterward took it up; and then, as was to be expected, the factions broke loose. February 21, at the motion of Senator Samuel Smith, by a vote of sixteen to eleven the Senate struck everything from the bill except the enacting clause and the exclusion of belligerent war-vessels from United States' harbors.

An Administration measure could not without rousing angry feelings be so abruptly mutilated by a knot of Administration senators. Samuel Smith's motives, given in his own words, were entitled to proper attention; but President Madison's opinion on the subject, whether correct or mistaken, had even more effect on what was to follow. Madison believed that the rejection of the bill was an intrigue of the

Smiths for selfish or personal objects. He recorded
the language which he felt himself obliged to use
on the subject, twelve months afterward, to Robert
Smith's face : [1] —

" For examples in which he had counteracted what he
had not himself disapproved in the Cabinet, I referred
to the bills called Macon's bills, and the Non-intercourse
Bill, on the consultation on which he appeared to concur
in their expediency ; that he well knew the former, in its
outline at least, had originated in the difficulty of finding
measures that would prevent what Congress had solemnly protested against, — to wit, a complete submission
to the belligerent edicts ; that the measure was considered as better than nothing, which seemed to be the
alternative, and as part only of whatever else might in
the progress of the business be found attainable ; and that
he neither objected to what was done in the Cabinet (the
time and place for the purpose), nor offered anything in
the place of it, yet it was well understood that his conversations and conduct out of doors had been entirely
of a counteracting nature ; that it was generally believed
that he was in an unfriendly disposition personally and
officially ; and that although in conversations with different individuals he might not hold the same unfavorable language, yet with those of a certain temper it
was no secret that he was very free in the use of it,
and had gone so far as to avow a disapprobation of
the whole policy of commercial restrictions from the
embargo throughout."

Robert Smith, doubtless believing that all his
actions had been above question or reproach, pro-

[1] Madison's Works, ii. 498.

tested warmly against these charges of unfriendliness and intrigue; but Madison, with a feminine faculty for pressing a sensitive point, insinuated that in his opinion both the Smiths were little better than they should be. "With respect to his motives for dissatisfaction I acknowledged that I had been, for the reasons given by him, much puzzled to divine any natural ones without looking deeper into human nature than I was willing to do." The meaning of the innuendo was explained by Joel Barlow the following year in the "National Intelligencer," where he acted as Madison's mouthpiece in defending the Administration from Robert Smith's attacks. One of Smith's complaints rested upon Macon's bill. Barlow asked, "What gives Mr. Smith a right at this day to proclaim himself in opposition to that bill? Was it ever laid before the Cabinet and opinions taken? Did he there oppose it? Did he not rather approve it, and give his vote for every article? Did he ever utter a syllable against it till his more acute brother discovered the commercial bearing that it would have upon the house [of Smith and Buchanan], and concluded that their interest required its rejection?"

Perhaps this explanation, however offensive to the Smiths, injured them less than the other suspicion which had as much vogue as the first, — that their conduct toward Macon's bill was a part of their feud against Gallatin, and proved their determination to oppose everything he suggested. At the moment

when Samuel Smith revolted against Macon's measure, Washington was filled with tales of quarrels in
the Cabinet. In truth, these reports were greatly
exaggerated. Robert Smith had not the capacity
to develop or to pursue a difficult line of argument
even without opposition. Against Gallatin he could
not, and as Madison testified did not, open his mouth,
nor did Gallatin or Madison ever complain except
of Smith's silence in the Cabinet; but he talked
freely in society, and every one heard of battles supposed to be raging. Walter Jones, one of the most
respectable Virginia members, wrote to Jefferson,
February 19, imploring him to intervene : [1] —

"Before you quitted this place you knew that causes
of dissension subsisted in the Executive departments.
So ominous an event has not failed to be an object of
my continued and anxious attention, and I am now fully
persuaded that these unfriendly feelings are fast approaching to a degree of animosity that must end in
open rupture, with its very injurious consequences to
the Republican cause. . . . This break of harmony in
the Executive departments, added to the extreme points
of difference in opinion among the majority in Congress
in relation to the great questions of peace and war, ren-
ders the apathy and inaction of the Republicans here
extremely mortifying. I never knew them more discon-
nected in sentiment and system, as probably may have
been made manifest to you by the desultory and incon-
clusive work of nearly three months. . . . You will
recollect that at the close of the last Congress the ap-

[1] Walter Jones to Jefferson, Feb. 19, 1810 ; Jefferson MSS.

pearance of umbrage was confined to Mr. Gallatin and
Mr. R. Smith; indeed, excepting themselves there were
no other secretaries effectively in office.   It is now
supposed, and I believe with truth, that the former
stands alone against the more or less unfriendly dispositions of all the rest.   Their *main abettors* of last
spring have abated nothing of their strong and inde-
cent zeal."

Upon feelings so irritable and at a moment when
schism was imminent, as Walter Jones described,
the action of Samuel Smith and Michael Leib with
six or eight more Republican senators, in emascu-
lating Macon's bill, left small chance of reconciliation.   Giles, having declared himself in favor of
energy, did not vote at all.   The debate being for
the most part not reported, the arguments of the
dissenting senators have been lost.   One speaker
alone broke the monotony of the discussion by an
address that marked the beginning of an epoch.

Henry Clay had been barely two weeks a senator,
when, February 22, he rose to move that the bill
as amended by Samuel Smith be recommitted; and
this motion he supported by a war speech of no great
length, but full of Western patriotism.

" The conquest of Canada is in your power," he said.
" I trust I shall not be deemed presumptuous when I
state that I verily believe that the militia of Kentucky
are alone competent to place Montreal and Upper Canada at your feet. . . . The withered arm and wrinkled
brow of the illustrious founders of our freedom are
melancholy indications that they will shortly be removed

from us. Their deeds of glory and renown will then be
felt only through the cold medium of the historic page ;
we shall want the presence and living example of a new
race of heroes to supply their places. and to animate us
to preserve inviolate what they achieved. . . . I call
upon the members of this House to maintain its character for vigor. I beseech them not to forfeit the esteem of the country. Will you set the base example to
the other House of an ignominious surrender of our
rights after they have been reproached for imbecility
and you extolled for your energy ! But, sir, if we could
be so forgetful of ourselves, I trust we shall spare you
[Vice-President George Clinton] the disgrace of signing,
with those hands so instrumental in the Revolution, a
bill abandoning some of the most precious rights which
it then secured.''

Other members both of the House and of the
Senate had made war speeches, and in Clay's harangue no idea could be called original; yet apart
from the energy and courage which showed a new
and needed habit of command, these sentences of
Clay's maiden speech marked the appearance of a
school which was for fifty years to express the national ideals of statesmanship, drawing elevation of
character from confidence in itself, and from devotion to ideas of nationality and union, which redeemed
every mistake committed in their names. In Clay's
speech almost for the first time the two rhetorical
marks of his generation made their appearance, and
during the next half century the Union and the
Fathers were rarely omitted from any popular har-

angue. The ideas became in the end fetiches and phrases ; but they were at least more easily under-stood than the fetiches and phrases of Jeffersonian republicanism which preceded them. Federalists used the name of Washington in the same rhetorical manner, but they used it for party purposes to re-buke Washington's successors. The Union and the Fathers belonged to no party, and might be used with equal advantage by orators of every section. Clay enjoyed almost alone for years the advantage of winning popularity by this simple means ; but in 1810, at least along the Atlantic coast, such appeals had little popular success. Least of all had they weight in the Senate, which listened unmoved to Clay's oratory, and replied to it immediately on the same day by passing the "ignominious surrender" of national rights by a vote of twenty-six to seven. Giles did not vote. Samuel Smith, Leib, and even Crawford were in the majority.

Macon's bill came back to the House as a law for the exclusion of British and French war-vessels from American harbors. The House resented the treat-ment, and after another long debate, March 5, refused to concur in the Senate's amendments. By a vote of sixty-seven to forty-seven the bill was sent back to the Senate in its original form. A long wrangle ensued ; a committee of conference failed to agree, and March 16 the Senate was obliged to decide whether it would yield to the House, or allow the bill to fail.

On that question Samuel Smith made a speech,[1] which he afterward printed, and which demanded attention because it forced President Madison into a course that exposed him to severe and perhaps deserved criticism. The Senate was equally balanced. Samuel Smith's voice and vote decided the result. His reasons were such as no one could misunderstand.

" I found in it," said he, criticising Macon's bill, " or believed I did, that which would be ruinous to the commerce of the United States, and therefore felt myself bound by the duty I owe to my constituents to remove the veil and leave the measure open to public view. . . . Is there no danger, Mr. President, to be apprehended from the Emperor if the bill should pass with this provision [that any British or French ship hereafter arriving in an American harbor should with its cargo be seized and condemned]? His character for decision is well known. Might we not fear that he would retort our own measure upon us by causing all the property of our merchants now under sequestration (amounting to at least three millions of dollars) to be condemned? . . . But what will England do should this law pass? Will the King and Council retaliate our measure? I confess, Mr. President, that I think they will. . . . What will be the consequence? Ruin to your merchants and destruction to the party which now governs this country. . . . But I have been told that if England should retaliate, her retaliation would operate as a complete nonintercourse between the two countries, and in a way that would be effectual; and that as I had always ap-

[1] Annals of Congress, 1809–1810, p. 602.

proved those measures, this view of the subject must meet my approbation, — that it would precisely create that which I have said was a powerful measure against Great Britain : to wit, an embargo. I never will agree, Mr. President, in this side-way to carry into execution a great national measure."

The speech excited surprise that Samuel Smith, a man accounted shrewd, should suppose such arguments to be decent, much less convincing. From Federalists, who conscientiously wished submission to British policy, Smith's reasoning would have seemed natural; but Smith protested against submission, and favored arming merchant-ships and providing them with convoy, — a measure useless except to bring on war in a "side-way." Congress preferred to choose its own time for fighting, and declined listening to Smith's advice, although the Senate sustained him in rejecting Macon's bill. On this occasion Giles appeared, and voted with the Administration; but sixteen senators followed Smith, while only fifteen could be found to act in concert with the House and the Executive.

After the Senate had thus put an end to Macon's bill, the House after much hesitation, March 31, put an end to Smith's bill. After five months of discussion Congress found itself, April 1, where it had been in the previous November.

Rather than resume friendly relations with both belligerents without even expressing a wish for the recovery of national self-respect, the House made one more effort.   April 7 Macon reported a new bill, which was naturally nicknamed Macon's bill No. 2. This measure also seems to have had the assent of the Cabinet, but Macon himself neither framed nor favored it. " I am at a loss to guess what we shall do on the subject of foreign relations," he wrote to his friend Judge Nicholson, three days later.[1] " The bill in the enclosed paper, called Macon's No. 2, is not really Macon's, though he reports it as chairman. It is in truth Taylor's. This I only mention to you, because when it comes to be debated I shall not act the part of a father, but of a step-father." The Taylor who took this responsibility was a member from South Carolina, whose career offered no other great distinction than the measure which produced a war with England.

Macon's bill No. 2 was the last of the annual legislative measures taken by Congress to counteract by commercial interest the encroachments of France and Great Britain. The first was the Partial Non-intercourse Act of April, 1806 ; the second was the Embargo Act with its supplements, dating from Dec. 22, 1807 ; the third was the Total Non-intercourse Act of March 1, 1809 ; and the fourth was Macon's bill No. 2. Each year produced a new experiment ; but the difference could be easily remembered, for after the climax of the embargo each successive annual enactment showed weakening faith in the policy, until Macon's bill No. 2 marked the last stage toward the admitted

[1] Nicholson MSS.

failure of commercial restrictions as a substitute for war. Abandoning the pretence of direct resistance to France and England, this measure repealed the Non-intercourse Act of March 1, 1809, leaving commercial relations with all the world as free as ever before, but authorizing the President " in case either Great Britain or France shall, before the 3d day of March next, so revoke or modify her edicts as that they shall cease to violate the neutral commerce of the United States," to prohibit intercourse with the nation which had not revoked its edicts.

The objections to the bill were overpowering, for its effect was equivalent to alliance with England. Had the United States taken active part in the war against France, they could have done Napoleon no greater injury than by the passage of this Act, which invited Great Britain to control American commerce for her military purposes. On the other hand the bill conferred on the President a discretion dangerous, unconstitutional, and unnecessary, — a power once before conferred by the Non-intercourse Act of March 1, 1809, and then resulting in the mistakes of Erskine's arrangement, which seemed warning enough against repeating the same risk.

These objections were well understood and forcibly pointed out, while the arguments in support of the bill were melancholy in their admissions. The records of Congress could hardly parallel the disregard of dignity with which Taylor defended his bill in a tone that could have been endured only by an assembly lost to the habits of self-respect. His denunciation of war expressed party doctrine, and he harmed no one by repeating the time-worn moral drawn from Greece and Rome, the Persian millions, Philip of Macedon, Syracuse and Carthage,—as though the fate of warlike nations proved that they should have submitted to foreign outrage, or as though the world could show either arts or liberty except such as had sprung from the cradle of war; but feeling perhaps that classical authority proved too little or too much, he told the House frankly why those members who like himself opposed war found themselves unable to maintain the pledge of resistance they had given in imposing the embargo:—

" But concerning the breaking down of the embargo! Let the truth come out! Neither this plea nor the other miserable one of the fear of insurrections, and what not, will do. . . . The embargo repealed itself. The wants created by it to foreigners, and the accidental failure of crops in England had reduced the thing in one article to plain calculation. The vote of this House to repeal the law gave from four to five dollars rise on each barrel of flour. This was the weight that pulled us down."

The admission could not inspire enthusiasm or raise the moral standard of Congress; but the House accepted it, and amended the bill only by adding fifty per cent to the existing duties on all products of Great Britain and France. The amendment was also a business speculation, for it was intended to protect and encourage American manufactures; but it did not come directly from the manufacturers. Richard M. Johnson of Kentucky moved the amendment. "Kentucky, Pennsylvania, New Jersey, and the New England Republicans," wrote Macon,[1] "are full of manufacturing. To these may be added some of the Virginia Republicans. This plan is said to be a Cabinet project; if so, it satisfies me that the Cabinet is hard pushed for a plan."

April 19 the bill passed the House by a vote of sixty-one to forty. The Senate referred it to a select committee with Samuel Smith at its head, — a committee made for Smith to control. As before, he reported the measure with its only effective provision — the additional duty — struck out, and with the addition of a convoy-clause. The Senate, by nineteen votes to eight, sustained Smith; nor did one New England senator, Federalist or Republican, vote for the protection offered by Kentucky and Virginia. The bill went to a third reading by a vote of twenty-one to seven, and April 28, having passed the Senate as Smith reported it without a division, was sent back to the House for concurrence.

Irritated though the House was by the Senate's hostility to every measure which had support from the Treasury or was calculated to give it support, the members were for the most part anxious only to see the session ended. No one cared greatly for Macon's bill No. 2 in any shape. The House refused to accept the Senate's amendments, and found itself May 1

[1] Macon to Nicholson, April 21, 1810; Nicholson MSS.

within a few hours of adjournment, and within the same time of seeing the Non-intercourse Act expire, without having made provision for the commercial relations that were to follow.   Perhaps Congress might have shown wisdom by doing nothing; but the instinct to do something was strong, and party feeling mixed with the sense of responsibility.   At five o'clock in the afternoon committees of conference were appointed, and at the evening session, Samuel Smith having abandoned his convoy-clause, the House gave up its extra duties and the bill came to its passage.   All the Federalists voted against it with Macon, Randolph, and Matthew Lyon, — a minority of twenty-seven.   Sixty-four Republicans recorded themselves in its favor, and made the bill a law.

CHAPTER X.

RANDOLPH, who had been ill at home during the winter of 1809–1810, appeared in public affairs only after the debates were mostly ended. March 22 he moved a Resolution that the military and naval establishments ought to be reduced. He wished to bring Madison's administration back to the point where Jefferson's administration eight years before had begun; and in truth the country could choose only between the practices of 1801 and those of 1798. Randolph, who shunned no assumption of fact which suited his object, asked the House whether any one " seriously thought of war, or believed it a relation in which we could be placed " : —

" With respect to war we have — thank God ! — in the Atlantic a fosse wide and deep enough to keep off any immediate danger to our territory. The belligerents of Europe know as well as we feel that war is out of the question. No, sir! if our preparation was for battle, the State physicians have mistaken the state of the patient. We have been embargoed and non-intercoursed almost into a consumption, and this is not the time for battle."

Randolph easily proved the need of retrenchment. His statements were not to be denied. President Washington, with a gross income of fifty-eight million dollars in eight years, spent eleven millions and a quarter on the army and navy. John Adams in four years spent eighteen millions, and was supposed to have been driven from office for extravagance. President Jefferson in his first four years cut down these expenses to eight million, six hundred thousand dollars; in his second term he raised them again to sixteen millions, or nearly to the point reached by John Adams at a time of actual hostilities with France, — although President Jefferson relied not on armaments, but on peaceable coercion, which cost very large sums besides. At last the country had reached a point where, after refusing either to fight its enemies or resent its injuries, it had begun to run in debt for armaments it would not use. This waste needed to be stopped.

Three fourths of the Republican party and all the Federalists were of the same mind with Randolph, — that an army led by Wilkinson and a navy of gunboats, when the country refused to fight under any provocation, were not worth maintaining; and when Eppes of Virginia, April 14, brought forward the budget for the coming year, he started by assuming that the military and naval expenditure might be reduced three million dollars, which would still leave a deficiency of two millions and a half, and would require an increase of customs-duties. If three millions and a half could be saved, members wanted to know why the whole military and naval expenditure, which had required only six millions in 1809, might not be cut off.

Macon, who supported Randolph with the ardor of 1798, urged nothing less than this sweeping reform.

"If the army were disbanded and the navy sold," he argued,[1] "we should not perhaps want half a million, — not a million and a half, on the outside. That might be obtained by loans payable at short date. . . . You must get clear of the navy-yards; if you do not put them down, unquestionably they will put you down. How is it with the army? Has it been employed to more advantage? Its situation is too melancholy to be spoken of; and if anything could disgust the people of the territory we acquired some years since, it must be the management of that army, for however much they hear of our good government, after such a specimen they must have a despicable opinion of it indeed. . . . I will not raise a tax of a cent to support the present plan. I have no hesitation in saying that I shall feel bound to vote down the additional force of six thousand men whenever the subject shall come before us. I voted for it; but found that then, as now, we talk a great deal about war, and do nothing."

Not a member supported Eppes's motion for increased taxes. Democrats and Federalists, one after another, rose to oppose an increase, and to favor disbanding the additional army.

[1] Annals of Congress, 1809–1810, p. 1828.

" I shall certainly vote to reduce the army of the United States," said Burwell of Virginia ;[1] " and if the House should decide that it will not employ the navy of the United States in the protection of commerce, I shall certainly vote also to reduce the naval establishment. I am perfectly convinced that the circumstances under which I voted for the increase of the army and navy have passed away ; and as our revenue has diminished, I shall vote for a reduction of our expenses. . . . So far from considering the country in a deplorable situation, as my colleague (Mr. Randolph) has represented it, I think that in many points of view we have every reason to congratulate ourselves. It is a singular phenomenon to see any nation enjoying peace at this time. This exemption from the general lot claims the gratitude of every man in the country. So far as I am concerned in the affairs of the nation, I have but a single object in view, — namely, to preserve peace ; and my votes are predicated on that ground."

The war men voted with the peace men for reasons given by Troup of Georgia :[2] —

" I am as well convinced of the fact as that I am now addressing you, that the people will not consent to pay an additional tax for the support of armies and navies raised to oppose the injurious acts of the belligerents against our rights, after we have abandoned those rights and dishonorably withdrawn from the contest."

After much contradictory talk of this kind, Nelson of Maryland told the House that they were behaving like schoolboys.

[1] Annals of Congress, 1809–1810, pp. 1855–1857.
[2] Annals of Congress, 1809–1810, p. 1862.

" It is a perfect child's game," said he.[1] " At one session we pass a law for raising an army, and go to expense ; in another year, instead of raising money to pay the expense by the means in our power, we are to disband the army we have been at so much pains to raise. We shall well deserve the name of children instead of men if we pursue a policy of this kind."

The warning had no perceptible weight with the House, where the peace party were in a majority and the war party were in a passion, not with the foreign enemy, but with their neighbors and friends. Richard M. Johnson almost avowed that he should vote for reducing army and navy in order to punish the men who had made them useless : —

" To our humiliation and everlasting degradation we have refused to use the means in our power to induce foreign nations to do us justice. . . . The annals of human nature have not given to the world the sad example of a nation so powerful, so free, so intelligent, so jealous of their rights and at the same time so grossly insulted, so materially injured, under such extraordinary forbearance. . . . We are afraid to trust ourselves, and we pretend that we are afraid to trust the people. My hopes have rested and always will rest upon the people ; they constitute my last hope. We may disgrace ourselves, but the people will rise in the majesty of their strength, and the world will be interested in the spectacle."

With the advocates of war in a temper so unmanageable, and the advocates of peace in a majority so

[1] Annals of Congress, 1809–1810, p. 1864.

decisive, the House showed unanimity by passing in
committee, without a dissenting voice, a Resolution
that the military and naval establishments ought to
be reduced.   April 16 this vote was reached in committee; and the next day, by a vote of sixty to
thirty-one, the Resolution was formally adopted by
the House.   Of the minority, two thirds were Northern men and all were Republicans.

In obedience to the order, Randolph promptly reported a bill for reducing the navy.[1]   All the gunboats, all but three of the frigates, and all other
armed vessels — three only excepted — were to be sold,
their officers and crews discharged; the navy-yards,
except at Boston, New York, and Norfolk, to be dis-
used, and the marine corps reduced to two companies.
A few days later, April 24, Smilie of Pennsylvania
reported a bill for a similar reduction of the military
establishment to three regiments.   These measures
seemed to carry out the express will and orders of
the House; but no sooner did the House go into
committee than the members astonished themselves
by striking out each section in succession.   Gunboats,
frigates, navy-yards, and marines, each managed in
turn to obtain a majority against reduction.

Then Randolph rose, — not in wrath, for he spoke
with unusual calm, but with a force which warranted
the sway he so often exercised over men whose minds
were habitually in doubt.   He had ever believed, he
said, that the people of the United States were des-

[1] Annals of Congress, 1809–1810, p. 1933.

tined to become a great naval power, but if anything
could prevent this result it would be the premature
attempts of the last two Administrations to force it.
A naval power necessarily grew out of tonnage and
seamen, but both tonnage and seamen had been syste-
matically discouraged : —

" It has always been understood, according to my view
of the subject, that one of the principal uses of a navy
was to protect commerce ; but our political rule for some
time past has been that of inverse proportion, and we
have discovered that commerce is the natural protector
of a navy."

The inconsistency of Jefferson's principles and
practice was a target which could be hit by the most
inexperienced marksman, but Randolph struck it with
something more solid than an epigram when he discussed its expense.

" Against the administration of Mr. Adams," he said,
" I, in common with many others, did and do yet entertain a sentiment of hostility, and have repeatedly cried out
against it for extravagance and for profusion and for
waste — wanton waste — of the public resources. I find,
however, upon consideration, — whether from the nature
of men, or from the nature of things, or from whatever
other cause, — that that Administration, grossly extravagant as I did then and still do believe it to have been,
if tried by the criterion of the succeeding one, was a
pattern of retrenchment and economy."

In order to prove this charge he attacked Robert
Smith's administration of the navy, asserting that

while in 1800 each seaman cost about four hundred
and seventy-two dollars a year, in 1808 each seaman
cost nearly nine hundred dollars a year; and that
the same excess existed in regard to officers, marines,
clothing, and provisions : —

"Yes, sir! we have economized until we absolutely
have reduced the annual cost of a seaman from $472 —
as it was under the very wasteful expenditure of Mr.
Adams's administration — down to the moderate sum of
$887. We have economized until a paltry fleet consisting
of vessels built to our hand, to say nothing of those that
have been sold, and the warlike stores of which have
been retained and preserved, — which fleet was built,
equipped, and every cannon and implement of war purchased under the old Administration, — has cost us twelve
million dollars, when it cost the preceding Administration
but nine millions."

Only one member replied on behalf of the Government to these criticisms. Burwell Bassett of the
naval committee ventured somewhat timidly to defend, not so much Robert Smith as Secretary Hamilton, who, he said, had reduced expenses at the
navy-yard about one third. Most of the frigates had
been so thoroughly repaired as to be more valuable
than when first built. In the navy-yard itself everything was in good condition and well conducted.
Bassett's testimony hardly met Randolph's charges,
but the House sustained him on every point; and
Boyd of New Jersey so far forgot the respect due to
a former vote, in which the House had resolved by a

majority of two to one that the army and navy ought
to be reduced, as to say that never since the government was formed had so preposterous a proposition
been offered. The end of the session arrived before
the discussion ceased.

The same inability to act, even where no apparent
obstacle existed, was shown in regard to the United
States Bank, whose charter, granted for twenty years
by the First Congress in February, 1791, was to expire March 4, 1811. In the days of Federalist sway
the Republicans had bitterly opposed the Bank and
denied the constitutional power of Congress to grant
the charter; but during the eight years of Jefferson's
rule the Bank had continued without a question to
do the financial work of government, and no other
agency existed or could be readily created capable of
taking the place of this machine, which, unlike any
other in the government, worked excellently well.

If its existence was to be continued, public interest
required that the Act should be passed at this session,
since the actual charter was to expire in ten months.
If a new charter was to be refused, public interest
required even more urgently that ample warning of
so radical a change should be given, that the Treasury
might not be suddenly crippled or general bankruptcy
be risked without notice.

No complaint of any kind was at that time made
against the Bank; no charge was brought against it
of interference in politics, of corrupt influence, or of
mismanagement. Gallatin was known to favor it;

the President was not hostile, nor was any influence in the government opposed; the Federalists who had created were bound to support it; and except for the principles of some Southern Republicans who regarded functions of government as germs of despotism, every political faction in the country seemed consenting to the charter. January 29 the subject was referred to a special committee. The committee reported a Resolution, and in due course John Taylor of South Carolina brought in a bill, the result of negotiations between the Treasury and the Bank, granting a new charter on condition that the Bank should increase its capital two-and-a-half million dollars, half of which should be paid outright to the government; that, further, the Bank should bind itself to lend the government at three months' notice any amount not exceeding in the whole five million dollars at a rate not exceeding six per cent; that on all government deposits above the sum of three millions, which should remain for one year, the Bank should pay interest at the rate of three per cent; and that the government should have the right at any time to increase the capital stock, and subscribe and own the new stock to a fixed amount. These terms were especially valuable at the moment, because they assisted the Treasury to meet an actual deficit, and provided, as far as human foresight went, for financial dangers that might rise from further foreign troubles. No serious opposition showed itself. April 21 the House, by a majority of seventy-five to thirty-five, voted to accept the

price fixed for the charter ; but the session closed
without further action.

When Congress adjourned, May 2, 1810, the result
attained during five months passed in continuous
labor amounted to little more than the constitutional
necessities of government, — the appropriation bills ;
a loan for five million dollars ; an Act for taking a
census of persons ; an Act appropriating sixty thousand dollars toward making the Cumberland Road ;
an appropriation of five thousand dollars for experiments on Fulton's torpedoes ; in regard to foreign
affairs, Giles's Resolution blaming the conduct of the
British minister, and Macon's or Taylor's Act, which
condoned that conduct.   The old Non-intercourse
Act of March 1, 1809, expired by limitation with the
expiring Congress May 1, 1810.

"We adjourned last night," wrote Randolph to Nicholson the next day,[1] "a little after twelve, having terminated a session of more than five months by authorizing
a loan of as many millions, and — all is told.   The incapacity of Government has long ceased to be a laughing
matter.   The Cabinet is all to pieces, and the two Houses
have tumbled about their own ears."

With all Randolph's faults, he had more of the
qualities, training, and insight of a statesman than
were to be found elsewhere among the representatives in the Eleventh Congress ; and although himself
largely the cause of the chaos he described, he felt its
disgraces and dangers.   Society in general troubled

[1] Nicholson MSS.

itself little about them. The commercial class, pleased
to be freed from restraints, and the agricultural class,
consoled by the fair prices of their produce, thought
as little as possible about their failure in government;
what was called good society for the most part drew
a bitter pleasure from it. Yet beneath the general
physical contentment almost equally general moral
disgust existed and made itself felt. President Madison, who was in the best position to gauge popular
opinion, began to suspect the hardly perceptible movement of a coming tide. After the adjournment he
wrote to William Pinkney at London :[1] —

   " Among the inducements to the experiment of an
unrestricted commerce now made were two which contributed essentially to the majority of votes in its favor,
— first, a general hope, favored by daily accounts from
England, that an adjustment of differences there, and
thence in France, would render the measure safe and
proper ; second, a willingness in not a few to teach the
advocates for an open trade the folly as well as degradation of their policy. . . . It will not be wonderful, therefore, if the passive spirit which marked the late session
of Congress should at the next meeting be roused to the
opposite point, more especially as the tone of the nation
has never been so low as that of its representatives."

Madison still held to his favorite doctrine, and
meant no more by his warning than that the Eleventh
Congress might be expected to reimpose measures of
commercial restriction : —

   [1] Madison to Pinkney, May 23, 1810; Works, ii. 474.

" The experiment [of free commerce] about to be made will probably open too late the eyes of the people to the expediency and efficacy of the means [the embargo] which they have suffered to be taken out of the hands of the Government and to be incapacitated for future use." [1]

This condolence with Jefferson over the fate of their experiment showed the direction toward which Madison's eyes were still turned; but, though a firm believer in his own theory of peaceable coercion, he was ready and had always been ready to accept and carry out any stronger scheme that Congress might prefer. He had no definite plan of his own; he clung to the idea that England and France could be brought by patience to respect neutral claims of right; but he felt that the actual submission made by Congress was apparent rather than real, and might be followed within a year by renewed resistance.

Meanwhile nothing could be more dangerous to the Americans than the loss of self-respect. The habit of denouncing themselves as cowards and of hearing themselves denounced as a race that cared only for money tended to produce the qualities imputed. Americans of 1810 were persuaded that they could not meet Englishmen or Frenchmen on equal terms, man against man, or stand in battle against the veterans of Napoleon or Nelson. The sense of national and personal inferiority sank astonishingly deep. Reasonable enough as regarded the immense

[1] Madison to Jefferson, April 23, 1810; Works, ii. 472.

superiority of Europe in organization, it passed bounds
when it condemned everything American as contemptible, or when the Federalist gentry refused to
admit the Democrats of Pennsylvania or the Republicans of Virginia or the Government at Washington
into the circle of civilized life.   Social self-abasement
never went so far as in its efforts to prove to Francis James Jackson, the British minister, that he was
right in treating the national government with contempt.   Englishman as Jackson was, and ready to
assume without question every claim of superiority
that might be made for his country or his class, he
was surprised at the force of American allegiance to
himself.   As he travelled northward, after his dismissal from Washington, his private letters gave a
strange idea of the chaos in American society.   He
wrote from Philadelphia, —

" The tide has turned completely in our favor.   At
Washington they are in a state of the most animated
confusion, the Cabinet divided, and the Democratic party
going various ways. . . .   Their foreign politics embarrass them even more than home ones.   One moment they
want another embargo ; the next, to take off the restrictions ; then, to arm their merchantmen ; and next, to
declare war.   In short, they do not know what to be
at. . . .   Notwithstanding all that has passed, — which
would fill volumes to relate in full, — and the Government being at open war with me, ' the respectability ' has
been both here and at Baltimore so anxious to show that
they did not share the sentiments of the Democrats that
we have had throngs of visitors and innumerable invita-

tions that we could not accept, though we have dined at
home but twice during the month we have been here. To
prevent this, the savages have threatened in one of their
papers to tar and feather every man who should ask me
to his house." [1]

Pleased with his social success at Baltimore and
Philadelphia, Jackson found New York and New
England fairly delightful. His vogue in Baltimore
and Philadelphia meant little more than curiosity to
see his wife and her toilettes; but as he approached
New England he became a personage in politics, and
received attentions such as he could hardly have expected even from those European courts whose civility
lingered in his mind. February 25 he wrote from
New York: [2] —

" As we get farther north and east, the said Yankees
improve very much. New York is a fine town, unlike
any other in America, and resembling more the best of
our country towns, with the additional advantage of the
finest water that can be imagined. There is as much life
and bustle as at Liverpool or any other of our great
commercial towns; and like them New York has inhabitants who have made and are making rapid and brilliant
fortunes by their enterprise and industry. . . . We have
met with unbounded civility and good-will, and may be
said to live here in triumph. We are now engaged to
dinner every day but two, till the end of the first week
in March. . . . The governor of Massachusetts has written to me to invite me to Boston, where, he says, he and

[1] Bath Archives, Second Series, i. 78.
[2] Bath Archives, Second Series, i. 82.

many others will be happy to receive me. That State, which is one of the most populous and enlightened of the States of the Union, and, as you know, is the birthplace of American independence, has done more toward justifying me to the world than it was possible from the nature of things that I or any other person could do in the present stage of the business. The legislature, which is not a mob like many that have passed resolutions, has agreed to a report of a joint committee, and passed resolutions in conformity with it, exculpating me altogether, and in the most direct manner censuring the conduct of the President and of the general government."

Boston newspapers of Feb. 9, 1810, contained the report and resolutions in which the Massachusetts legislature, by a vote of two hundred and fifty-four to one hundred and forty-five, declared that "they can perceive no just or adequate cause" for breaking relations with the British minister, F. J. Jackson; and this challenge to their own Government, backed by Governor Gore's invitation of Jackson to Boston, was intended to carry political weight, even to the extent of forcing Madison to renew political relations, as he had been forced to resume commercial relations, with England. Had public opinion taken the intended course, Jackson's visit to Boston would have marked a demonstration of popular feeling against the national government; nor were the Federalists in any way parties consenting to the defeat of the scheme. The measures adopted by the Massachusetts legislature in February came before the people at the State election early in April, only six weeks after the

General Court and Governor Gore had condemned
Madison.   More than ninety thousand votes were cast,
and the Republican party, by a majority of about two
thousand, not only turned Governor Gore out of office,
but also chose a General Court with a Republican majority of twenty.   At the same time similar changes
of public opinion restored New Hampshire to Republican control, and strengthened the Republicans in
New York and the Middle States.   Not a doubt could
exist that the country sustained Madison, and that
Jackson was not only an object of decided unpopu-
larity in America, but was far from being favored in
England.   The advantage to be derived from his visit
to Boston was no longer evident, and after Governor
Gore ceased to hold office, the good taste of acting
on an invitation thus practically withdrawn seemed
doubtful ; but Jackson was not daunted by doubts.

Holding the promise of his Government that his
mission should last at least a year, Jackson beguiled
the interval by such amusements as offered themselves.   In May he retired to a country-house on the
North River, about eight miles above New York, where
he caught a glimpse of an American invention which,
as he had the good sense to suspect, was more important than all the diplomatic quarrels in which he
had ever engaged : —

" One of the curiosities that we daily see pass under
our windows is the steamboat, — a passage-vessel with
accommodation for near a hundred persons.   It is moved
by a steam-engine turning a wheel on either side of it,

which acts like the main wheel of a mill, and propels the vessel against wind and tide at the rate of four miles an hour. As soon as it comes in sight there is a general rush of our household to watch and wonder till it disappears. They don't at all know what to make of the unnatural monster that goes steadily careering on, with the wind directly in its teeth as often as not. I doubt that I should be obeyed were I to desire any one of them to take a passage in her." [1]

After thus entertaining himself on the Hudson, the British minister made his triumphal trip to Boston early in June, where he found a gratifying welcome from society if not from the governor and legislature : —

" At Boston, ' the headquarters of good principles,' we were feasted most famously, and I made there many interesting acquaintances. After living nine days in clover at about eighteen of the principal houses, — having never less than two engagements per day, — they gave me on the 10th a public dinner, at which near three hundred persons were present, and where we had toasts and cheering and singing in the best style of Bishopsgate Street or Merchant Taylor's Hall. A party of gentlemen met me at the last stage on entering Boston, and accompanied me to the first on my departure. At another public dinner I was invited to on the 4th of June (the Ancient and Honorable Artillery election dinner), and at which the governor, who is a Democrat, was present, the clergy, the magistrates, the heads of the University of Cambridge, and the military came to the top of the room in their respective bodies to be introduced to and to

[1] Bath Archives, Second Series, i. 118.

compliment me.   There is at Washington in consequence
much ' wailing and gnashing of teeth.' "

At the public dinner given to Jackson June 11,
after the guest of the evening had retired, Senator
Pickering gave a toast which became a party cry:
" The world's last hope, — Britain's fast-anchored
isle ! " [1]

From the moment the State officials withdrew from
the reception, little importance attached to the private acts of a society which might easily look with
interest at the rare appearance of a British minister in Boston ; but the political and social feeling
was the same as though Governor Gore were still
in power, and created natural disgust among Republicans, who believed that their Federalist opponents
aimed at a dissolution of the Union and at a retreat
within the protection of Great Britain.   If such ideas
existed, they showed themselves to Jackson in no
recorded form.   His visit to Boston was a social
amusement ; and he regarded it. like the conduct of
Congress, as a triumph to himself only because it
increased the mortifications of President Madison,
which counterbalanced in some degree his own want
of energetic support from Canning's successor at the
Foreign Office.

The history of Jackson and his mission did not
quite end with his departure from Boston in June,
1810, under escort of a mounted procession of Boston
Federalists.   He thence went to Niagara, — a difficult

[1] Upham's Life of Pickering, iv. 172.

journey; and descending to Montreal and Quebec, returned to Albany, where he had the unusual experience of seeing himself burned in effigy.

During all these wanderings he was a victim to the constant annoyance of being able to quarrel neither with President Madison nor with his new official chief, who showed a wish to quarrel as little as possible. Jackson was as willing to find fault with one Government as with the other.

" I look forward with full confidence," he wrote to his brother,[1] " for a full approbation of what I have done. Ministers cannot disapprove of though they may be sorry for it; and if they are sorry, it must be for the trouble it occasions them, for as I have told them there is no loss of any adjustment of difficulties, that being impracticable with this country upon the principles of my instructions. I hope they are adopting the line that I recommended to them, — that of procrastinating any decision whatever; but they might as well have told me so for my own guidance and information, instead of leaving me a prey to all the lies and misrepresentations which the Democrats have found it necessary to propagate on the subject for election purposes. It would be an absolute disgrace to the country, and would produce an impression never to be got over here, — the ill effects of which in all future transactions we should not fail to be made sensible of, — if another minister were to be sent out without some sort of satisfaction being taken or received for the treatment I have experienced. They ought to insist on my being reinstated."

[1] Bath Archives, Second Series, i. 109.

The British government held a different opinion ; and accordingly, at the expiration of his stipulated twelve months, Sept. 16, 1810, Jackson set sail for Europe, leaving J. P. Morier in charge of the British legation at Washington.

CHAPTER XI.

If the Non-intercourse Act of March 1, 1809, irritated Napoleon, Macon's Act of May 1, 1810, might be expected to work in a manner still more active.

The story has shown that Napoleon, toward the end of the year 1809, felt many difficulties in giving new shape to his American policy after it had been ruined by the Non-intercourse Act. His fixed idea required the seizure of every American ship in Europe beyond the borders of France, as he had for years seized American ships in his own ports. In part this wish sprang from the Continental system, and was excused to some extent by the plea that American commerce could be carried on only under British protection; in part the seizure of American ships was a punishment for defying the Emperor's orders; and in part it was due to his necessities of finance.

December 19, 1809, Napoleon wrote a brief order to Berthier, ordering the seizure of all American vessels in the Spanish ports within his control;[1] vessels and cargoes, he said, were to be considered good prize. Having taken this measure, he called a council of

[1] Napoleon to the Prince of Neuchatel, Dec. 19, 1809; Correspondance, xx. 78.

ministers for the next day, and ordered Maret to
bring there " everything relating to the judgments of
the prize-court; to the merchandise sequestered in
the ports, which is spoiling. If you have not all the
information, ask the Minister of Finance." [1]

The meaning of this preparation was to be sought
in the Cabinet itself, and in the Emperor's surround-
ings.   Peace with Austria left many vexations in
Napoleon's path.   Perhaps the unhappy situation of
his brother Joseph at Madrid troubled him less than
the difficulty of reconciling the Empress Josephine
to a divorce, or the mortifications of negotiating for
a wife among Russian, German, and Austrian prin-
cesses ; but annoyances like these, though serious for
ordinary men, could not be compared with the constant trouble created by the Continental system of
commercial restrictions and the want of money it
caused.   Threatened with financial difficulties, and
obliged to study economies as well as to press contributions of war, the Emperor found himself met by
something resembling opposition among his own ministers.   As was his habit, he yielded at first to the
advice he disliked, and promised to do something
for French industry.   In November he appointed a
new Minister of the Interior, Montalivet, and lectured
him on the slowness of his bureaus in acting for the
good of commerce.[2]   From such a mouth such a

[1] Napoleon to Maret, Dec. 19, 1809; Correspondance, **xx.** 77.
[2] Note pour le Comte de Montalivet, 16 Nov. 1809; Correspondance, **xx.** 35.

lesson startled the hearer, and Montalivet threw himself with zeal into the prescribed work. To Fouché the Emperor read another lecture compared with which the discourse to Montalivet was commonplace. Fouché, a pronounced opponent of Napoleon's commercial restrictions, during the Emperor's absence in Austria distributed too freely his licenses for foreign trade : " I recognize always the same course in your acts," Napoleon wrote him. " You have not enough legality in your head." [1]

While thus teaching one minister to cherish commerce, and another to respect legality, the Emperor listened to Champagny, who lost no chance of advising the encouragement of neutral trade ; and these three ministers — Champagny, Fouché, and Montalivet — found a strong ally in the Minister of the Treasury, Mollien, who has left the recorded opinion that the Imperial system of commercial restriction was " the most disastrous and the most false of fiscal inventions." [2] The bias of Decrès, the Minister of Marine, may be inferred from a story told by Marshal Marmont,[3] who, coming to Paris at the close of 1809, called on his old friend and talked with the enthusiasm of a successful soldier about the Emperor. " Well, Marmont," replied Decrès, " you are pleased at being made a marshal ; you see everything in

[1] Napoleon to Fouché, Sept. 29, 1809; Correspondance, xix. 535.

[2] Mémoires, iii. 134.

[3] Mémoires de Marmont, iii. 336.

bright colors. Do you want me to tell you the truth and to unveil the future ? The Emperor is mad — absolutely mad ! He will upset us all, and everything will end in a terrible disaster." Taken in connection with King Louis' attitude in Holland, the Cabinet opposition of December, 1809, amounted to rebellion against Napoleon's authority.

At the Cabinet council of December 20 Montalivet made a written report on the subject of American cotton, which threw so much blame on the Imperial policy as to call a written contradiction from Napoleon. "An American vessel," the Emperor replied the next day,[1] " coming from Louisiana to France will be well received here, no act of the government forbidding the admission of American ships into French ports." The Americans, he explained, had prohibited commerce with France while permitting it with Holland, Spain, and Naples ; and in consequence " his Majesty has used his right of influence over his neighbors because he was unwilling that they should be treated differently from France, and he has sequestered the ships destined for their ports ; " but no such provision had been made against American ships entering French ports.

Naturally piqued at an Imperial assertion that he had shown ignorance of facts that deeply concerned his department, Montalivet sent to the Treasury for information, with which, a few days afterward, he

[1] Note pour le Ministre de l'Intérieur, 21 Dec. 1809; Correspondance, xx. 81.

routed the Emperor from the field. Unable to answer him, Napoleon referred his report to Gaudin, Minister of Finance, with a curious marginal note, which showed — what his ministers evidently believed — that the Emperor understood neither the workings of his own system nor the laws of the United States : —

" Referred to the Minister of Finance to make me a report on this question : (1) How is it conceivable that American ships come from America in spite of the embargo? (2) How distinguish between ships coming from America and those coming from London?"

Armstrong obtained immediate and accurate knowledge of this struggle in council. Only a week after the Emperor wrote his note on the margin of Montalivet's report, Armstrong sent home a despatch on the subject : [1] —

" The veil which for some weeks past has covered the proceedings of the Cabinet with regard to neutral commerce is now so far withdrawn as to enable us to see with sufficient distinctness both the actors and the acting. The Ministers of Police and of the Interior (Fouché and Montalivet) have come out openly and vigorously against the present anti-commercial system, and have denounced it as ' one originating in error and productive only of evil, and particularly calculated to impoverish France and enrich her enemy.' While they have held this language in the Cabinet they have held one of nearly the same tenor out of it, and have added (we may sup-

[1] Armstrong to R. Smith, Jan. 6, 1810; MSS. State Department Archives.

pose on sufficient authority) the most solemn assurances that the Emperor ' never meant to do more than to prevent the commerce of the United States from becoming *tributary* to Great Britain ; that a new decision would soon be taken by him on this subject, and that from this the happiest results were to be expected.' "

As though to prevent President Madison from showing undue elation at this announcement for the fiftieth time that the happiest results were to be expected from the future, Armstrong wrote another letter, four days afterward,[1] on the new confiscations and their cause. Frenchmen he said would reason thus : " There is a deficit of fifty millions in the receipts of last year. This must be supplied. Why not then put our hands into the pockets of your citizens once more, since, as you continue to be embroiled with Great Britain, we may do it with impunity." Armstrong was angry, and could not analyze to the bottom the Emperor's methods or motives. Thiers, in later years having the advantage of studying Napoleon's papers, understood better the nature of his genius. " To admit false neutrals in order to confiscate them afterward, greatly pleased his astute (*rusé*) mind," wrote the French historian and statesman,[2] " little scrupulous in the choice of means, especially in regard to shameless smugglers who violated at once the laws of their own country and those of the

[1] Armstrong to R. Smith, Jan. 10, 1810; MSS. State Department Archives. Cf. Thiers' Empire, xii. 45.

[2] Thiers, xii. 48, 49.

country that consented to admit them." This description could not properly be applied to Americans,
since they violated neither their own law nor that of
France by coming to Amsterdam, San Sebastian, and
Naples ; but Thiers explained that the Emperor considered all Americans as smugglers, and that he wrote
to the Prussian government : " Let the American
ships enter your ports ! Seize them afterward. You
shall deliver the cargoes to me, and I will take them
in part payment of the Prussian war-debt." [1]

Meanwhile the confiscation of American ships
helped in no way the objects promised by Napoleon
to Montalivet and Fouché. At a loss to invent a
theory on which neutrals could be at the same time
plundered and encouraged, the Emperor referred the
subject to Champagny, January 10, in an interesting
letter.[2] He called for a complete history of his relations with the United States since the treaty of Mor-
fontaine. He ordered the recall of Turreau, in whom
he said he had little confidence, and who should be
replaced by a more adroit agent : —

" Have several conferences, if necessary, with the
American minister as well as with the Secretary of Legation who has just come from London ; in short, let me
know your opinion on the measures proper to be taken to
get out of the position we are in (*pour sortir de la position où nous nous trouvons*)."

[1] Thiers, xii. 50.
[2] Napoleon to Champagny, Jan. 10, 1810; Correspondance,
xx. 109.

" All the measures I have taken, as I have said several times, are only measures of reprisal. . . . It was only to the new extension given to the right of blockade that I opposed the Decree of Berlin; and even the Decree of Berlin ought to be considered as a Continental, not as a maritime blockade, for it has been carried out in that form. I regard it, in some sort, only as a protest, and a violence opposed to a violence. . . . Down to this point there was little harm. Neutrals still entered our ports; but the British Orders in Council necessitated my Milan Decree, and from that time there were no neutrals. . . . I am now assured that the English have given way; that they no longer levy taxes on ships. Let me know if there is an authentic act which announces it, and if there is none, let me know if the fact is true; for once I shall be assured that a tax on navigation will not be established by England, I shall be able to give way on many points."

All Napoleon's ministers must have known that these assertions of his commercial policy were invented for a momentary purpose. He had himself often declared, and caused them to declare, that his Continental system, established by the Berlin Decree and enforced before the Orders in Council were issued, had a broad military purpose quite independent of retaliation, — that it was aimed at the destruction of England's commerce and resources. As for his profession of ignorance that England had abandoned her transit duties on neutral merchandise, every minister was equally well aware that only six months before, the Emperor had discussed with them the measures to be taken in consequence of that abandonment; had sent them the draft of a new decree founded upon it, and had finally decided to do nothing only because England had again quarrelled with America over Erskine's arrangement. The pretexts alleged by Napoleon were such as his ministers could not have believed; but they were satisfied to obtain on any grounds the concessions they desired, and Champagny — or as he was thenceforward called, the Duc de Cadore — sent to Armstrong for the information the Emperor professed to want.

January 18, M. Petry, at the order of Cadore, called on the American minister, and requested from him a written memorandum expressing the demands of his Government. Armstrong drew up a short minute of the provisions to be made the material of a treaty.[1] The first Article required the restoration of sequestered property; the next stipulated that any ship which had paid tribute to a foreign Power should be liable to confiscation, but that with this exception commerce should be free. Cadore sent this paper to the Emperor, and within a few hours received a characteristic reply.

" You must see the American minister," wrote Napoleon.[2] " It is quite too ridiculous (*par trop ridicule*) that he should write things that no one can comprehend.

[1] Armstrong to R. Smith, Jan. 28, 1810 ; Document G. MSS. State Department Archives.

[2] Napoleon to Champagny, Jan. 19, 1810 ; Correspondance, xx. 132.

I prefer him to write in English, but fully and in a manner that we can understand. [It is absurd] that in affairs so important he should content himself with writing letters of four lines. . . . Send by special courier a cipher despatch to America to let it be understood that that government is not represented here; that its minister does not know French; is a morose man with whom one cannot treat; that all obstacles would be raised if they had here an envoy to be talked with. Write in detail on this point."

Petry returned to Armstrong with the condemned paper, and received another, somewhat more elaborate, but hardly more agreeable to the Emperor. January 25, Cadore himself sent for the American minister, and discussed the subject. The Emperor, he said, would not commit himself to the admission of colonial produce; he wished to restrict American commerce to articles the growth or manufacture of the two countries; he would not permit his neighbors to carry on a commerce with America which he denied to himself; but the " only condition required for the revocation by his Majesty of the Decree of Berlin will be a previous revocation by the British government of her blockade of France, or part of France (such as the coast from the Elbe to Brest, etc.), of a date anterior to that of the aforesaid decree; and if the British government would then recall the Orders in Council which had occasioned the Decree of Milan, that decree should also be annulled." This pledge purported to come directly from the

Emperor, and at Armstrong's request was repeated in the Emperor's exact words.[1]

Neither the Minister of the Interior, the Minister of the Treasury, nor the Emperor in these discussions alluded to the proposed Decree of Vienna, the draft of which was sent to Paris in August, confiscating all American ships in reprisal for the seizures of French ships threatened by the Non-intercourse Act. Although that decree was the point which the Emperor meant to reach, not until January 25 — when Champagny, after dismissing Armstrong, reported the interview to Napoleon, bringing with him at the Emperor's request the text of the Non-intercourse Act — did the Emperor at last revert to the ideas of the Vienna Decree. The long hesitation proved how little satisfactory the plea of retaliation was ; but no other excuse could be devised for a measure which Napoleon insisted upon carrying out, and which Champagny had no choice but to execute. The Emperor dictated the draft of a note,[2] in which the principles of confiscation were to be laid down : —

" If American ships have been sequestered in France, France only imitates the example given her by the American government ; and the undersigned recalls to Mr. Armstrong the Act of Congress of March 1, 1809, which orders in certain cases the sequestration and confiscation of French ships, excludes them from American

[1] Note pour le Général Armstrong, 25 Jan., 1810.   Correspondance, xx. 141.

[2] Projet de Note, Jan. 25, 1810 ; Correspondance, xx. 141.

ports, and interdicts France to the Americans. It is in
reprisal of this last provision that the American ships
have been seized in Spain and Naples.   The league
against England, which has the cause of neutrals for its
object, embraces now all the Continental peoples, and
permits none of them to enjoy commercial advantages of
which France is deprived. France will permit it in no
place where her influence extends ; but she is ready to
grant every favor to the ships of a neutral Power which
shall not have subjected themselves to a tribute, and
shall recognize only the laws of their own country, not
those of a foreign government. . . . If the Minister of
the United States has the power to conclude a convention
proper to attain the object indicated, the undersigned is
ordered to give all his care to it, and to occupy himself
upon it without interruption."

Perhaps this was the only occasion in Napoleon's
life when he stood between a nation willing to be
robbed and a consciousness that to rob it was a
blunder. The draft of his note showed his embarrassment. Remarkable in many ways, it required special notice in two points. The proposed Vienna Decree confiscated American ships because French ships
were forbidden under threat of confiscation to enter
American ports. The note of January 25 suggested
a variation from this idea. American ships were to
be confiscated everywhere except in France, because
they were forbidden to enter France. As they were
also confiscated in France because they were forbidden to leave America, the Emperor had nothing more
to demand. His reasoning was as convincing as a

million bayonets could make it; but perhaps it was
less Napoleonic than the avowal that for six months
the Emperor had been engaged in inveigling American property into neutral ports in order that he might
seize it.

Apparently Cadore still raised obstacles to the
Emperor's will. For some three weeks he held this
note back, and when at last, February 14, he sent it
to Armstrong, he made changes which were not all
improvements in the Emperor's text. Indeed, Napoleon might reasonably have found as much fault with
Champagny as he found with some of his generals,
for failing to carry out the orders he dictated : —

" His Majesty could place no reliance on the proceedings of the United States, who, having no ground of
complaint against France, comprised her in their acts
of exclusion, and since the month of May have forbidden
the entrance of their ports to French vessels, under the
penalty of confiscation. As soon as his Majesty was
informed of this measure, he considered himself bound
to order reprisals on American vessels, not only in his
territory, but likewise in the countries which are under
his influence. In the ports of Holland, of Spain, of
Italy, and of Naples, American vessels have been seized
because the Americans have seized French vessels."

After such long discussions and so many experiments, Napoleon had become reckless of appearances
when he allowed his foreign secretary to send this
note of Feb. 14, 1810, in which every line was a
misstatement, and every misstatement, as far as con-

cerned America, was evident in its purpose; while
apart from these faults, the note erred in trying to
cover too much ground of complaint against the
United States. Napoleon had, in the projected Decree of Vienna, ordered retaliation everywhere for the
confiscation threatened by the Non-intercourse Act.
Made to feel the impossibility of this course, he
changed his ground, continuing to confiscate American ships in France under the old Bayonne Decree,
and ordering the sequestration of American ships
throughout the rest of Europe on the plea that other
countries must not enjoy a commerce interdicted to
France. Cadore's note abandoned this ground again,
in order to return to the doctrine of the projected
Vienna Decree; and in the effort to give it a color
of reason, he asserted that the Americans had seized
French vessels.

Such a letter was a declaration of war six months
after beginning hostilities; and it made no offer of
peace except on condition that the United States
should pledge themselves to resist every British blockade which was not real in the sense defined by
Napoleon. Armstrong wrote to his Government, in
language as strong as he could use, that nothing was
to be expected from a policy that had no other
foundation than force or fraud. His angry remonstrances had embroiled him with the Emperor, and
he was on the point of quitting France. Under such
circumstances he did not insist on breaking off further conversations with Petry, but February 25 he

positively assured Petry that neither would the President and Senate ratify, nor would he himself as negotiator accept, a treaty in any form which did not provide reparation for the past as well as security for the future ;[1] and March 10 he replied to the Duc de Cadore in what the Emperor would have called a morose tone, denying every assertion made in Cadore's note, — reminding Cadore that the Emperor had received knowledge of the Non-intercourse Act at the time of its passage without a sign of protest or complaint; and, finally, renewing his old, long-standing grievances against " the daily and practical outrages on the part of France."[2]

When the Emperor received Armstrong's letter, which was excessively strong, and ended in a suggestion that Napoleon was trying to cover theft by falsehood, he showed no sign of anger, but became almost apologetic, and wrote to Cadore,[3] —

" Make a sketch of a reply to the American minister. It will be easy for you to make him understand that I am master to do here what America does there ; that when America embargoes French ships entering her ports, I have the right to reciprocate. You will explain to him how that law came to our knowledge only a short time ago, and only when I had knowledge of it did I

[1] Armstrong to R. Smith, Feb. 25, 1810 ; MSS. State Department Archives.

[2] Armstrong to Cadore, March 10, 1810 ; State Papers, iii. 381.

[3] Napoleon to Cadore, March 20, 1810; Correspondance, xx. 273.

immediately prescribe the same measure; that a few days before, I was busying myself with provisions for raising the actual prohibitions on American merchandise, when the course of commerce (*la voie du commerce*) made known to me that our honor was involved, and that no compromise was possible; that I conceive America as entitled to prevent her ships from coming to England and France; that I approved this last measure, though there was much to be said about it; but that I cannot recognize that she should arrogate the right of seizing French ships in her ports without putting herself in the case of incurring reciprocity."

One must answer as one can the question why Cadore, who had in his hands Armstrong's letter of April 29, 1809,[1] officially communicating the Non-intercourse Act, should not have suggested to Napoleon that some limit to his failings of memory ought to be observed. Napoleon's memory was sometimes overtasked by the mass of details he undertook to carry in his mind, but a striking incident always impressed itself there. Mme. de Rémusat[2] told how Grétry, who as member of the Institute regularly attended the Imperial audiences, was almost as regularly asked by Napoleon, "Who are you?" Tired at last of this rough question, Grétry replied by an answer equally blunt: "Sire, toujours Grétry;" and thenceforward the Emperor never failed to remember him. The United States in a similar tone recalled their affairs to the Emperor's memory by the Non-

[1] State Papers, iii. 324.   See *supra*, p. 135.
[2] Mémoires, ii. 77.

intercourse Act; but had this " toujours Grétry " not
been enough, Napoleon's financial needs also made
him peculiarly alive to every event that could relieve
them, and his correspondence proved that the Non-
intercourse Act as early as May, 1809, impressed him
deeply.   Yet in March, 1810, he not only convinced
himself that this Act had just come to his knowledge,
producing in him an outburst of national dignity, but
he also convinced his Minister of Foreign Relations,
who knew the contrary, that these impressions were
true, and made him witness them by his signature.

Acting without delay on the theory of sudden
passion, the Emperor signed, three days afterward,
March 23, a decree known as the Decree of Rambouillet, in which the result of these long hesitations
was at last condensed.[1]   This document was a para-
phrase of the projected Decree of Vienna of Aug. 4,
1809; and it showed the tenacity with which Napoleon, while seeming to yield to opposition, never
failed to return to a purpose and effect its object.
In order to carry out the Decree of Vienna in that
of Rambouillet he was forced into a *coup d'état*.   He
had not only to expel his brother Louis from Holland,
and annex Holland to France, but also to drive his
ablest minister, Fouché, from the Cabinet.

Of the steps by which he accomplished his objects,
something can be seen in his letters ; of his motives,
no doubt ever existed.   Armstrong described them
in strong language ; but his language was that of a

[1] State Papers, iii. 384.

party interested. Thiers recounted them as a pane-
gyric, and his language was even clearer than Armstrong's. He made nothing of the Emperor's pretence
that his seizures were in reprisal for the Non-intercourse Act. "This was an official reason (*une raison
d'apparat*)," said Thiers.[1] "He was in search of a
specious pretext for seizing in Holland, in France, in
Italy, the mass of American ships which smuggled
for the English, and which were within his reach.
He had actually sequestered a considerable number;
and in their rich cargoes were to be found the means
of furnishing his Treasury with resources nearly
equal to those procured for him by the contributions
of war imposed on the vanquished."

The system of treating the United States as an
enemy conquered in war rested on a foundation of
truth; and as usual with conquered countries it met
with most resistance, not from them but from by-
standers. The Emperor of Russia, the kings of
Prussia, Sweden, and Denmark, the Hanse Towns,
and King Louis of Holland were the chief obstacles
to the success of the scheme to which they were
required to be parties. King Louis of Holland
refused to seize the American ships at Amsterdam,
and forced his brother to the conclusion that if
nothing else could be done, Holland must be annexed
to France.

For many reasons the annexation of Holland met
with little favor in the Emperor's family and among

[1] Empire, xii. 45.

his Council. Chief among its opponents was Fouché, who sacrificed himself in his efforts to prevent it. Driven to the conviction that nothing but peace with England could put an end to the Emperor's experiments on the welfare of France, Fouché resolved that peace should be made, and invented a scheme for bringing it about. As Minister of Police he controlled secret means of intrigue, and probably he acted without concert with his colleagues; but the motives which guided him were common to almost all Napoleon's Cabinet. The only difference between ministers was, that while Cadore, Montalivet, Mollien, and Decrès stopped their opposition when it became dangerous, Fouché undertook to act.

Something of this came to Armstrong's ears. As early as January 10 [1] he reported a remark which he could not understand. " ' Do not believe,' said a minister to me the other day, ' that peace between us and England is impossible. If we offer to her the commerce of the world, can she resist it?' " Unknown to Armstrong, Napoleon had already made an advance to England. For this purpose he employed Labouchere, the chief banker of Holland, whose association with the Barings of London fitted him to act as an intermediary. The message sent by the Emperor through Labouchere could hardly be called an offer of terms; it amounted only to a threat that unless England made peace Holland should be annexed to

[1] Armstrong to R. Smith, Jan. 10, 1810 ; MSS. State Department Archives.

France, and every avenue of illicit commerce in
northern Europe should be stopped. In itself this
message could hardly serve as ground for a treaty;
but Fouché, without the Emperor's knowledge, sent
to London at the same time, about January 18, a
secret agent named Fagan, to suggest that if Great
Britain would abandon Spain, France would join in
creating from the Spanish-American colonies a monarchy for Ferdinand VII., and from Louisiana, at the
expense of the United States, a kingdom for the
French Bourbons.[1]

This last idea bore on its face the marks of its
origin. Fouché had listened to Aaron Burr, who after
years of effort reached Paris, and presented to the
government a memoir showing that with ten thousand regular troops, and a combined attack from
Canada and Louisiana, the destruction of the United
States was certain.[2] The scheme for placing the
Spanish Bourbons on a Spanish-American throne
probably came from the same Ouvrard whom Napoleon imprisoned at Vincennes, and whom Fouché
took into favor.

Labouchere and Fagan went to England, and early
in February had interviews with the British ministers,
who quickly dismissed them. The only impression
made on the British government by the double mis-

[1] Thiers, xii. 126.
[2] Armstrong to R. Smith, July 18, 1810 ; MSS. State Department Archives.   Cf. Correspondance de Napoleon, xx. 450,
451, *note.*

sion was one of perplexity at the object of an errand which appeared too absurd for discussion. The two agents returned to the Continent, and reported the result of their journey. Meanwhile Napoleon ordered Marshal Oudinot to march his army-corps into Holland, a step which brought King Louis to immediate submission. " I promise you," wrote Louis, " to follow faithfully all the engagements you shall impose upon me. I give you my word of honor to follow them faithfully and loyally from the moment I shall have undertaken them." [1] While Cadore was still negotiating with Armstrong for an arrangement with America, he was also employed in framing a treaty with Louis, which exacted the seizure of all American ships and merchandise in Dutch ports.[2] Louis came to Paris, and March 16 signed the treaty which by a secret stipulation provided for the seizure of American property.[3]

Matters stood thus April 1, 1810, when the ceremonies of the Imperial marriage interrupted for the moment further action. Napoleon had carried his point in regard to the punishment of America ; but the difficulties he had already met were trifling compared with the difficulties to come.

[1] Thiers, xii. 117.

[2] Napoleon to Champagny, Feb. 22, 1810 ; Correspondance, xx. 235.

[3] Thiers, xii. 117.

CHAPTER XII.

Napoleon set out, April 27, with his new Empress on a wedding journey to Holland. In the course of his journey an accident revealed to him the secret correspondence which Fouché had conducted through Fagan with the British government. Nothing criminal was alleged, nor was it evident that the Minister of Police had acted contrary to the Emperor's admitted wishes; but since the fall of Talleyrand, Fouché alone had considered himself so necessary to the Imperial service as to affect independence, and the opportunity to discipline him could not be lost. June 3 he was disgraced, and exiled to Italy. General Savary, Duc de Rovigo, succeeded him as Minister of Police.

The fate of King Louis was almost equally swift. When he returned to Holland after promising entire submission and signing the treaty of March 16, he could not endure the disgrace of carrying his pledges into effect. He tried to evade the surrender of the American ships, and to resist the military occupation of his kingdom. He showed public sympathy with the Emperor's opponents, and with riotous popular proceedings at Amsterdam. Once more the Emperor

was obliged to treat him as an enemy. June 24
the French troops were ordered to occupy Amsterdam, and July 3 Louis, abdicating his throne, took
refuge in Germany. July 8 Napoleon signed a Decree annexing Holland to France.[1]

The United States at the same time received their
punishment for opposing the Imperial will. The
Decree of Rambouillet, though signed March 23, was
published only May 14, when the sequestrations previously made in Holland, Spain, Italy, and France
became in a manner legalized. The value of the
seizures in Holland and Spain was estimated by the
Emperor in arranging his budget for the current
year as follows: [2] American cargoes previously seized
at Antwerp, two million dollars; cargoes surrendered
by Holland, two million four hundred thousand dollars; seizures in Spain, one million six hundred
thousand dollars.

In this estimate of six million dollars the seizures
in France, Denmark, Hamburg, Italy, and Naples
were not included. The American consul at Paris
reported to Armstrong that between April 1809 and
April 1810 fifty-one American ships had been seized
in the ports of France, forty-four in the ports of
Spain, twenty-eight in those of Naples, and eleven
in those of Holland.[3] Assuming an average value

---

[1] Napoleon to Decrès, 8 July, 1810.   Correspondance, xx. 450.

[2] Note, July 5, 1810 ; Correspondance, xx. 444.

[3] Rapport à l'Empereur, 25 Août, 1810; Archives des Aff.
Étrs. MSS.

of thirty thousand dollars, these one hundred and
thirty-four American ships represented values exceeding four millions. Adding to Napoleon's estimate of six millions the Consul's reported seizure
of seventy-nine ships in France and Naples, a sum
of nearly $8,400,000 was attained. In this estimate
the seizures at Hamburg, in Denmark, and in the
Baltic were not included. On the whole the loss
occasioned to Americans could not be estimated at
less than ten millions, even after allowing for English property disguised as American. The exports
from the United States during the six months after
the embargo amounted to fifty-two million dollars,[1]
exclusive of the ships; and as England offered a less
profitable market than the Continent, one fifth of
this commerce might easily have fallen into Napoleon's hands. Twenty years afterward the government
of France paid five million dollars as indemnity for a
portion of the seizures, from which Napoleon by his
own account received not less than seven millions.

Profitable as this sweeping confiscation was, and
thoroughly as Napoleon overbore opposition in his
family and Cabinet, such measures in no way promised to retrieve the disaster his system suffered from
the defection of America. While England protected
American ships in their attempts to counteract his
system in Spain, Holland, and in the Baltic, the
Emperor regarded American trade as identical with

[1] Gallatin to the Speaker, Feb. 7, 1810 ; State Papers, Commerce and Navigation, i. 812.

British, and confiscated it accordingly; but by doing
so he exhausted his means of punishment, and since
he could not march armies to New York and Baltimore as he marched them to Amsterdam and Hamburg, he could only return on his steps and effect
by diplomacy what he could not effect by force. The
Act of March 1, 1809, was a thorn in his side; but
the news which arrived toward the end of June, 1810,
that Congress had repealed even that slight obstacle
to trade with England made some corrective action
inevitable. The Act of May 1, 1810, struck a blow at
the Emperor such as no Power in Europe dared aim,
for it threw open to British trade a market in the
United States which would alone compensate England
for the loss of her trade with France and Holland.
Macon's Act made the Milan Decree useless.

Napoleon no sooner learned that Congress had
renewed intercourse with England and France, than
he wrote an interesting note[1] to Montalivet dated
June 25, the day after he ordered his army to seize
Amsterdam.

"The Americans," he said, "have raised the embargo on their ships so that all American ships can leave
America to come to France; but those which should
come here would be sequestered, because all would either
have been visited by English ships or would have touched
in England. It is therefore probable that no American
ship will come into our ports without being assured of
what France means to do in regard to them."

[1] Notes pour le Ministre de l'Intérieur, 25 Juin, 1810; Correspondance, xx. 431.

France could evidently do one of three things, — either avowedly maintain her decrees, or expressly revoke them, or seem to revoke them while in fact maintaining them. The process by which Napoleon made his choice was characteristic.

" We may do two things," he continued, — " either declare that the Decrees of Berlin and Milan are repealed, and replace commerce where it formerly was ; or announce that the Decrees will be repealed September 1, if on that date the English have repealed the Orders in Council. Or the English will withdraw their Orders in Council, and then we shall have to ascertain whether the situation that follows will be advantageous to us."

Assuming that the decrees and orders were withdrawn, and American ships admitted as neutrals, the Emperor explained how he should still enforce his system as before : —

" This situation will have no influence on the customs legislation, which will always regulate arbitrarily duties and prohibitions. The Americans will be able to bring sugar and coffee into our ports, — the privateers will not stop them because the flag covers the goods ; but when they come into a port of France or a country under the influence of France, they will find the customs legislation, by which we shall be able to say that we do not want the sugar and coffee brought by the Americans because they are English merchandise ; that we do not want tobacco, etc. ; that we do not want such or such goods, which we can as we please class among prohibited goods. Thus it is evident that we should commit ourselves to nothing."

Again and again, orally and in writing, in the presence of the whole Council and in private to each minister, the Emperor had asserted positively and even angrily that "all the measures I have taken, as I have said several times, are only measures of reprisal;" yet after assuming that his reprisals had succeeded, and that England had withdrawn her orders as France should have withdrawn her decrees, he told Montalivet, as though it were a matter of course, that he should carry out the same system by different means. This method of fighting for the rights of neutrals differed but little, and not to advantage, from the British method of fighting against them.

The Emperor put his new plan in shape. He proposed to recognize neutral rights by issuing licenses under the name of permits for a score of American vessels, and for the introduction of Georgia cotton, the article for which Montalivet made his long struggle. This measure was to be so organized that the shipments could take place only in a single designated port of America, only with certificates of origin delivered by a single French consul also to be designated; that the ship could enter only at one or two designated ports of France; that independently of the certificates of origin a cipher-letter should be written to the Minister of Foreign Relations by the consul who should have given them; finally, that the ships should be required to take in return wines, cognac, silks, and other French goods for the value of the cargo.

Deep was Armstrong's disgust when an Imperial Decree [1] appeared, dated July 15, authorizing licenses for thirty American ships to sail from Charleston or New York under the rigorous conditions detailed by this note; but the thirty licenses were merely a beginning. Once having grasped the idea that something must be done for French industry, the Emperor pressed it with his usual energy and with the usual results. During the months of June and July, while annexing Holland to his empire, he worked laboriously on his new commercial system. He created a special Council of Commerce, held meetings as often as twice a week, and issued decrees and orders by dozens. The difficulty of understanding his new method was great, owing to a duplication of orders not unusual with him; the meaning of a public decree was affected by some secret decree or order not made public, and as never failed to happen with his civil affairs, the whole mass became confused.

Apparently the new system [2] rested on a decree of July 25, 1810, which forbade any ship whatever to leave a French port for a foreign port without a license; and this license, in the Emperor's eyes, gave the character of a French ship to the licensed

[1] State Papers, iii. 400.

[2] Napoleon to Prince Lebrun, Aug. 20, 1810; Correspondance, xxi. 53.

vessel, — " that is to say, in two words, that I will
have no neutral vessel ; and in fact there is none
really neutral, — they are all vessels which violate
the blockade and pay ransom to the English." In
other words the Emperor's scheme was founded on
his Berlin and Milan Decrees, and left them intact
except within the operation of the licenses. " For
these [licensed] ships," he said,[1] " the Decrees of
Berlin and Milan are null and void ; . . . my licenses are a tacit privilege of exemption from my
decrees, on condition of conforming to the rules prescribed by the said licenses." The licenses themselves were classified in thirty different series,[2] —
for the ocean, the Mediterranean, England, etc.,
— and prescribed the cargoes to be carried both
on the inward and outward voyages.[3] They made
no distinction between neutrals and enemies ; the
license that authorized a voyage from London was
the same, except for its series, as that which covered
a cargo of cotton from Charleston; and such distinction as appeared, was limited to imposing on the
neutral additional trouble to prove that his goods
were not English. In theory the import of such
British merchandise as would relieve England's distress was forbidden, and the export of French mer-

[1] Napoleon to Eugene Napoleon, Sept. 19, 1810 ; Correspondance, xxi. 134.

[2] Napoleon to Montalivet, Aug. 10, 1810 ; Correspondance,
xxi. 29.

[3] Napoleon to Montalivet, Aug. 11, 1810 ; Correspondance,
xxi. 35.

chandise was encouraged, not only in order to assist French industry, but also in order to drain England of specie. Especially the sugar, coffee, and cotton of the colonies were prohibited; but when captured by privateers or confiscated on land, colonial produce was first admitted to the custom-house at a duty of fifty per cent, and then sold for the benefit of the Imperial treasury.

This system and tariff Napoleon imposed on all the countries subject to his power, including Switzerland, Naples, Hamburg, and the Hanse Towns; while he exerted all his influence to force the same policy on Prussia and Russia. As far as concerned the only neutral, the United States, the system classified American ships either as English when unlicensed, or as French when licensed; it imposed Imperial functions inconsistent with local law on the French consuls in America, and violated both international and municipal law only to produce another form of the Berlin and Milan Decrees, in some respects more offensive than the original.

The character and actions of Napoleon were so overpowering that history naturally follows their course rather than the acts of the undecided and unenergetic governments which he drove before him; and for this reason the replies made by Secretary Robert Smith to the flashes of Imperial temper or policy have not hitherto been noticed. In truth, Secretary Smith made no attempt to rival Napoleon in originality or in vigor of ideas or ex-

pression. Neither his genius nor that of Madison
shone bright in the lurid glare of the Emperor's
planet. When Champagny's letter of Aug. 22, 1809,
reached Washington with its novel views about floating colonies, rights of search, identity of blockade
with siege, and warning of confiscations in Holland,
Spain, and Italy, President Madison, replying through
Robert Smith, Dec. 1, 1809, contented himself with
silence in regard to the threats, and with a mild
dissent from the Emperor's exposition of the *jus
gentium.* " However founded the definition of M.
Champagny may be in reason and general utility,
and consequently however desirable to be made the
established law on the subject of blockades, a different practice has too long prevailed among all nations, France as well as others, and is too strongly
authenticated by the writers of admitted authority,
to be combated by the United States."

A touch of Madison's humor brightened the monotony of these commonplaces, but was not granted
the freedom which the subject might have allowed.
The President felt no wish to dwell on what was
unreasonable or violent in Napoleon's conduct.   He
passed lightly over the floating colony, ignored the
threatened seizure of American commerce, and fast-
ened on the closing paragraph of Champagny's note,
which promised that if England would revoke her
blockades, the decrees of France should fall of themselves. This proposition, defined by Champagny and
commented by Armstrong, required that England

should admit the whole doctrine of floating colonies and siege-blockades. Madison knew it to be impracticable and deceptive; but he was not bound to go beyond the letter of the pledge, and although he declined to admit Napoleon among those "writers of admitted authority" whose law prevailed among nations, he instructed Armstrong to act without delay in the sense of Champagny's suggestion.

"You will of course," wrote Secretary Smith to Armstrong, Dec. 1, 1809, "understand it to be wished that you should ascertain the meaning of the French government as to the condition on which it has been proposed to revoke the Berlin Decree. On the principle which seems to be assumed by M. Champagny, nothing more ought to be required than a recall by Great Britain of her proclamation or illegal blockades which are of a date prior to that of the Berlin Decree, or a formal declaration that they are not now in force." [1]

January 25, 1810, Armstrong asked Cadore the question thus dictated, and received for answer that the Emperor required only the revocation of the British blockades as a condition of recalling the Decree of Berlin, — a reply which Armstrong communicated the same day to Minister Pinkney at London. No further instructions from Washington seem to have reached the United States Legation at Paris until news arrived that on May 1 the Non-intercourse Act had been repealed. No official information of the repeal was received by Armstrong, but an American who

[1] Robert Smith to Armstrong, Dec. 1, 1810; State Papers, iii. 326.

brought despatches from Pinkney in London brought
also a printed copy of the Act of May 1, 1810. In
the want of official advices, probably July 9, Armstrong communicated the Act of May 1 to the Duc de
Cadore in the unofficial form of a newspaper. Cadore
replied that being so entirely unofficial, it could not
be made the ground-work of any government proceeding;[1] but he took it to the Emperor, and Armstrong
waited for some striking exhibition of displeasure.

From that moment Armstrong's relations with
Cadore became mysterious. Something unrecorded
passed between them, for, July 19 Napoleon ordered
Cadore to write to the French ambassador at St.
Petersburg a message for the American minister at
that Court:[2] —

" Charge the Duc de Vicence to tell Mr. Adams that
we have here an American minister who says nothing ;
that we need an active man whom one can comprehend,
and by whose means we could come to an understanding
with the Americans."[3]

For three weeks Napoleon made no decision on
the subject of the American Act; then, after settling
the annexation of Holland, he wrote to Cadore
July 31:[4] —

[1] Armstrong to Robert Smith, July 10, 1810 ; MSS State
Department Archives.

[2] Napoleon to Champagny, 19 July, 1810; Correspondance,
xx. 505.

[3] Napoleon to Champagny, 13 July, 1810 ; Correspondance,
xx. 554.

[4] Correspondance, xxi. 1.

" After having much reflected on the affairs of America, I have thought that to repeal my Decrees of Berlin and Milan would have no effect; that it would be better for you to make a note to Mr. Armstrong by which you should let him know that you have put under my eyes the details contained in the American newspaper; that I should have liked to have a more official communication, but that time passes, and that, — since he assures me we may regard this as official, — he can consider that my Decrees of Berlin and Milan will have no effect, dating from November 1; and that he is to consider them as withdrawn in consequence of such Act of the American Congress, on condition that (*à condition que*) if the British Council does not withdraw its Orders of 1807, the United States Congress shall fulfil the engagement it has taken to re-establish its prohibitions on British commerce. This appears to me more suitable than a decree which would cause a shock (*qui ferait secousse*) and would not fulfil my object.   This method appears to me more conformable to my dignity and to the seriousness of the affair."

The Emperor himself, August 2, dictated the letter, — the most important he ever sent to the United States government.   During the next three days he made numerous changes in the draft; but at last it was signed and sent to the American Legation.[1] Upon that paper, long famous as Cadore's letter of Aug. 5, 1810, turned the course of subsequent events; but apart from its practical consequences the student of history, whether interested in the

[1] Cadore to General Armstrong, Aug. 5, 1810 ; State Papers, iii. 386.

character of Napoleon or of Madison, or in the legal
aspects of war and peace, or in the practice of governments and the capacity of different peoples for
self-government, could find few examples or illus-
trations better suited to his purpose than the letter itself, the policy it revealed, and the manner in
which it was received by the United States and
Great Britain.

Cadore began by saying that he had communicated
to the Emperor the newspaper containing the Act of
Congress of May 1.   The Emperor could have wished
that all the acts of the United States government
which concerned France had always been officially
made known to him : —

" In general, he has only had indirect knowledge of
them after a long interval of time.   From this delay
serious inconveniences have resulted which would not
have existed had these acts been promptly and officially
communicated.

" The Emperor applauded the general embargo laid
by the United States on all their vessels, because that
measure, if it has been prejudicial to France, had in it
at least nothing offensive to her honor.   It has caused
her to lose her colonies of Martinique, Guadeloupe, and
Cayenne ; the Emperor has not complained of it.   He
has made this sacrifice to the principle which has determined the Americans to lay the embargo. . . . The Act
of March 1 [1809] raised the embargo and substituted
for it a measure the most injurious to the interests of
France.   This Act, of which the Emperor knew nothing
until very lately, interdicted to American vessels the com-

merce of France at the time it authorized that to Spain, Naples, and Holland, — that is to say, to the countries under French influence, — and denounced confiscation against all French vessels which should enter the ports of America.   Reprisal was a right, and commanded by the dignity of France, — a circumstance on which it was impossible to make a compromise (*de transiger*).   The sequestration of all the American vessels in France has been the necessary consequence of the measure taken by Congress."

This preamble, interesting for the novelty of its assertions both of fact and law, led to the conclusion that the Act of May 1, 1810, was a retreat from the Act of March 1, 1809, and warranted France in accepting the offer extended by both laws to the nation which should first " cease to violate the neutral commerce of the United States."

" In this new state of things," concluded Cadore, " I am authorized to declare to you, sir, that the Decrees of Berlin and Milan are revoked, and that after November 1 they will cease to have effect, — it being understood (*bien entendu*) that in consequence of this declaration the English are to revoke their Orders in Council, and renounce the new principles of blockade which they have wished to establish ; or that the United States, conformably to the Act you have just communicated, cause their rights to be respected by the English."

No phraseology could have more embarrassed President Madison, while, as Napoleon had remarked to Montalivet a few days before, " it is evident that we

commit ourselves to nothing." [1] So closely was the
Imperial promise imitated from that given by Erskine that the President could hardly reject it, although no American merchant would have risked so
much as a cargo of salt-fish on a pledge of such
a kind from such a man. As though to warn the
Americans, Napoleon added personal assurances that
gave to the whole proceeding an unpleasant air of
burlesque : —

"It is with the most particular satisfaction, sir, that
I make known to you this determination of the Emperor.
His Majesty loves the Americans. Their prosperity and
their commerce are within the scope of his policy. The
independence of America is one of the principal titles
of glory to France. Since that epoch the Emperor is
pleased in aggrandizing the United States ; and under all
circumstances that which can contribute to the independence, to the prosperity, and to the liberty of the Americans the Emperor will consider as conformable with the
interests of his Empire."

One might doubt whether Napoleon or Canning
were the more deficient in good taste ; but Americans whose nerves were irritated to fury by the irony
of Canning, found these expressions of Napoleon's
love rather absurd than insulting. So little had the
mere fact of violence to do with the temper of politics, compared with the sentiments which surrounded
it, that Napoleon could seize without notice ten
million dollars' worth of American property, impris-

[1] Notes, etc., June 25, 1810 ; Correspondance, xx. 431.

oning the American crews of two or three hundred
vessels in his dungeons, while at the same instant
he told the Americans that he loved them, that their
commerce was within the scope of his policy, and as
a climax avowed a scheme to mislead the United
States government, hardly troubling himself to use
forms likely to conceal his object; yet the vast majority of Americans never greatly resented acts which
seemed to them like the exploits of an Italian brigand
on the stage.   Beyond doubt, Napoleon regarded his
professions of love and interest not as irony or extravagance, but as adapted to deceive.   A few weeks
earlier he sent a message to the Czar of Russia, who
asked him to disavow the intention of restoring the
kingdom of Poland.   " If I should ever sign," replied
Napoleon,[1] " a declaration that the kingdom of Poland shall never be restored, it would be for the reason that I intended to restore it, — a trap I should
set for Russia ; " and in signing a declaration to the
President that his decrees were repealed, he set a
trap for the United States, which he baited with professions of love that to a more refined taste would
have seemed fatal to his object.

This mixture of feline qualities, — energy, astuteness, secrecy, and rapidity, — combined with ignorance
of other natures than his own, was shown in the
act with which he concluded his arrangements of
Aug. 5, 1810.   About a fortnight before, by a secret

[1] Napoleon to Caulaincourt, July 1, 1810 ; Correspondance,
xx. 158.

decree dated July 22, 1810,[1] he had ordered the proceeds of the American cargoes seized at Antwerp and in Dutch and Spanish ports, valued by him at six million dollars, to be turned into the Treasury as a part of his customs revenue devoted to the service of 1809–10. In French ports he held still some fifty ships in sequestration. Cadore's letter of August 5 mentioned these ships as sequestered, — a phrase implying that they would be held subject to future negotiation and decision, liable to be returned to their owners; yet on the same day Napoleon signed another secret decree[2] which condemned without hearing or judgment all the ships and cargoes declared to be still in sequestration by the letter that could hardly have yet been sent from Cadore's office. Every vessel which had arrived in French ports between May 20, 1809, and May 1, 1810, suffered confiscation by this decree, which further ordered that the American crews should be released from the dungeons where they were held as prisoners of war, and that from August 5 to November 1, 1810, American ships should be allowed to enter French ports, but should not discharge their cargoes without a license.

The Decree of August 5 was never made public. Armstrong indeed employed the last hours of his stay in Paris in asking whether the French government meant to admit further negotiation about these

[1] Gallatin's Writings, ii. 211.
[2] Gallatin's Writings, ii. 198.

seizures,[1] and Cadore replied that the law of reprisals
was final;[2] but when Albert Gallatin, as minister at
Paris some ten years afterward, happened to obtain
a copy of the document, he expressed his anger at its
secrecy in language such as he used in regard to no
other transaction of his public life. "No one can
suppose," he wrote,[3] "that if it had been communicated or published at the same time, the United
States would with respect to the promised revocation
of the Berlin and Milan Decrees have taken that
ground which ultimately led to the war with Great
Britain. It is indeed unnecessary to comment on
such a glaring act of combined injustice, bad faith,
and meanness as the enacting and concealment of
that decree exhibits." These epithets would not
have disturbed Napoleon. Politics were to him a
campaign, and if his opponents had not the sense
to divine his movements and motives, the disgrace
and disaster were none of his.

More mysterious than the conduct of Napoleon
was that of Armstrong. Contenting himself with
whatever the Emperor ordered, he refrained in his
despatches from saying more than was necessary for
the record. He protected himself from Napoleon's
personal attack by sending to the Duc de Cadore an
undated letter,[4] referring to the archives of Cadore's

[1] Armstrong to Cadore, Sept. 7, 1810 ; State Papers, iii. 388.

[2] Cadore to Armstrong, Sept. 12, 1810 ; State Papers, iii. 388.

[3] Gallatin to J. Q. Adams, Sept. 15, 1821 ; Gallatin's Writings, ii. 196.

[4] State Papers, iii. 387.

department for proof that every public measure of the
United States had been promptly and officially communicated to the French government; but he wrote
home no report of any conference with Cadore, he
expressed no opinion ʿ ; to the faith of the Emperor's
promise, made no further protest against the actual
reprisals, and required no indemnity for past spoliations. In fact, no action was asked from him; but
he lent himself readily to the silence that was needed.
Cadore reported[1] to the Emperor that Armstrong
" before his departure wishes to open (*engager*) none
of those difficult questions which he foresees must
rise between the two governments, in order to arrive
in America without having seen the fading of the
glory he attaches to having obtained the Note of
August 5." Too happy in the good fortune that
threw an apparent triumph into his hands at the
moment when he was ending his diplomatic career
in disgust, he felt anxious only to escape before
another turn of the wheel should destroy his success.
He remained in Paris more than a month after receiving Cadore's letter of August 5, but reserved for a
personal interview whatever information he had to
give the President; and his letters, like his despatches, expressed no inconvenient opinions. Sept.
12, 1810, his long and extremely interesting mission
ended, and he quitted Paris on his homeward journey,
leaving the Legation in charge of Jonathan Russell

[1] Rapport à l'Empereur, Août, 1810 ; Archives des Aff. Étr.
MSS. vol. lxiv. pièce 81.

of Rhode Island.   Armstrong's last official act was to
write from Bordeaux a letter to Pinkney at London,
declaring that the conditions imposed by Napoleon on
the repeal of his decrees were " not *precedent*, as has
been supposed, but *subsequent*." [1]

[1] Armstrong to Pinkney, Sept. 29, 1810; State Papers, iii. 386.

CHAPTER XIII.

WHILE Napoleon labored to reconstruct his system mutilated by American legislation, the Government of Great Britain sank lower and lower toward disappearance, while the star of Spencer Perceval shone alone with dull lustre on the British horizon. When the Portland ministry went to pieces in September, 1809, Perceval became of necessity master of the empire. Canning had quarrelled with him, and refused office except as prime minister. Castlereagh had been so lately disgraced that he could bring only weakness to the Government if he rejoined it. Both Castlereagh and Sidmouth refused to serve with Canning on any terms. The Whigs, represented by Lord Grenville and Lord Grey, were excluded by the King's prejudices, by their own pledges to the Irish Catholics, and by the great preponderance of Tory opinion in the country. The Duke of Portland was dying; King George himself was on the verge of insanity, and every one supposed that the Prince of Wales, if he became regent, would at once appoint a ministry from among his Whig friends. This stalemate, where every piece on the chessboard stood in the way of its neighbor, and none could move while the King and Spencer Perceval remained, seemed likely to end in the destruction of the British empire. An economist wiser and better educated than Napoleon might easily have inferred, as he did, that with time England must succumb.

Perceval and his remaining friends — Liverpool, Bathurst, Eldon — looked about them for allies. They would not, indeed they could not, surrender the government to others, for no one offered to take it. In the House of Lords they were strong, but in the Commons they had no speaker except Perceval, while the opposition was strengthened by Canning, and Castlereagh could not be safely reckoned as more than neutral. They sought for allies both old and young in the Commons, but their search was almost fruitless. They could find only young Viscount Palmerston, about five-and-twenty years of age, who took the subordinate place of Secretary at War.

Nothing remained but to carry on the government by the Peers, with Perceval as its only important representative in the Commons. The Lord Hawkesbury of 1802, who had become Lord Liverpool at his father's death, and was actually head of the Home Office, succeeded Castlereagh as head of the War Department. Spencer Perceval took the Duke of Portland's place as first Lord of the Treasury, retaining his old functions as Chancellor of the Exchequer. These changes brought no new strength

into the Cabinet; but Canning's place at the Foreign Office remained to be filled, and common consent fixed upon one person as alone competent to
bring with him to the position a weight of character that could overbalance the losses the Cabinet had
suffered.

This person, hitherto unmentioned, was Richard
Colley Wesley, or Wellesley, born in Ireland in 1760,
eldest son of the first Earl of Mornington, whose
younger son Arthur was born in 1769. Another
brother, Henry, born in 1773, rose to high rank in
diplomacy under the later title of Lord Cowley. In
1809 these three brothers were all actively employed
in the public service; but the foremost of the three
was the eldest, the Marquess Wellesley, whose reputation still overshadowed that of Arthur, then just
called to the peerage Sept. 4, 1809, as Viscount Wellington of Talavera, in reward of his recent battle
with Marshal Victor.

An Irish family neither wealthy nor very distinguished, the Wellesleys owed their success to their
abilities. The second Lord Mornington, Marquess
Wellesley, sprang into fame as a favorite of William
Pitt, who showed his power by pushing young men
like Richard Wesley and George Canning into positions of immense responsibility. Perhaps the favor
shown to the former may in part have had its source
in some resemblance of character which caused Pitt
to feel a reflection of himself, for Mornington was a
scholar and an orator. His Latin verses were an or-

nament of Eton scholarship; his oratory was classic
like his verses; and his manners suited the scholarship of his poetry and the Latinity of his orations.
Lord Mountmorris, one of his antagonists in the
Irish Parliament of 1783, ridiculed his rhetoric:
"If formidable spectres portending the downfall of
the Constitution were to appear in this House, I
admit that the noble Lord is frightened with becoming dignity. The ancient Roscius or the modern
Garrick could not stand with a better grace at the
appearance of a spectre." The orator whose air of
dignity Lord Mountmorris thought so studied was
then twenty-three years old, and apparently never
changed his manner. In the British Parliament,
thirteen years afterward, Sheridan described him as
presenting the same figure that Mountmorris laughed
at. "Exactly two years ago," said Sheridan in 1796,
"I remember to have seen the noble Lord with the
same sonorous voice, the same placid countenance,
in the same attitude, leaning gracefully upon the
table, and giving an account from shreds and patches
of Brissot that the French republic would last but
a few months longer." The aristocratic affectations,
if they were affectations, of Lord Mornington were
conspicuous; but no man could safely laugh at one
of the Wellesleys. In 1797 Mr. Pitt suddenly sent
this ornament of the peerage to India as governor-
general, and the world learned that since the time
of Clive no surer or bolder hand had guided the
empire of England in the East.

When he took charge of the Indian government, French influence contested his own at more than one court of the powerful native princes, while his resources were neither great nor easily concentrated. During the eight years of his sway he extirpated French influence; crushed the power of Tippoo Sultaun; conquered the empire of Mysore, which had again and again won victories over English armies within sight of Madras; broke up the Mahratta confederacy; and doubled the British territory in India, besides introducing or planning many important civil reforms. He shocked the Court of Directors by arbitrary rule, extravagance in finance, and favoritism toward his younger brothers; but success was the decisive answer to hostile criticism, and even fanatics could hardly affirm that a governor-general, though he might have every virtue, was fit for his place if he refused the services of Arthur Wellesley when they might be had for the asking.

When Lord Wellesley, created an Irish marquess and English baron, returned to England in 1806, he came home with the greatest name in the empire next to that of Pitt.[1] He was asked to join the Portland Administration, but declined. Canning was said to have taken offence at his refusal;[2] but at last in disgust with Perceval, Canning connected himself more closely than ever with the Marquess, doubtless in the hope of forcing Castlereagh

[1] Memoirs of R. Plumer Ward, i. 424.

[2] Buckingham Memoirs, iv. 390.

out in order to bring Wellesley in.[1] At Canning's
request in April, 1809, the Marquess was appointed
to the important and difficult post of Ambassador
Extraordinary to the Supreme Junta of Spain, then
at Seville ; while at the same time his brother Arthur
was made general-in-chief in the Peninsula. Lord
Wellesley went to Spain with the understanding that
he was soon to return and enter the Cabinet.[2] In
October he learned that Canning had broken up the
Cabinet, and that while Canning himself on one
side expected the Wellesleys' support, Perceval on
the other was begging for it, and the Whigs were
waiting with open arms to welcome their alliance.
Canning's duel took place Sept. 21, 1809. October 5 Spencer Perceval wrote to Wellesley at Seville,
asking him to accept the Foreign Office; while at the
same time Canning informed the King that Lord
Wellesley would retire from office with himself.

In such a situation the most astute politician
could not trust his own judgment. No one could
say whether Wellesley's strength would invigorate
the Government, or whether Perceval's weakness
would exhaust Wellesley as it had exhausted Canning. Canning and Wellesley held the same estimate
of Perceval. Canning had succeeded only in ruin-
ing himself by struggling to rid the Government of
that incubus, as he regarded it, and Wellesley had

[1] Wellington to Wellesley, Oct. 5, 1809 ; Supplementary
Despatches, vi. 386.
[2] Buckingham Memoirs, iv. 392.

no better right to expect success. On the other
hand, if the Marquess should join the Government
he might assist his brother Arthur, who needed support at home. Probably this idea turned the scale;
at all events Wellesley accepted Perceval's offer,
and gave his Administration a chance of life.

Wellesley could have had no hope of effecting any
considerable object except by carrying out Canning's scheme, which required that Spencer Perceval
should be forced from power before the Government could be placed on a strong foundation. His
first experiences showed him the difficulties in his
way.

December 6, 1809, the Marquess was sworn as
Secretary of State. A few days afterward he appointed his brother Henry to the post he had himself
vacated, of Envoy to the Spanish Junta at Seville.
The favoritism was unfortunate, but Wellesley
troubled himself little about odium; his single
thought was to support his " brother Arthur,"
while England was far from showing equal zeal
in Arthur's support. In spite of the success at
Talavera, Lord Wellington had been obliged to retreat into Portugal; the Spanish army led by infe-
rior generals ventured to march on Madrid, and
November 19 was annihilated by the French at
Ocaña, some fifty miles south of that city, leaving
the whole south and east of Spain unprotected.
The French were certain to reoccupy Seville if not
to attack Cadiz. Affairs in the Peninsula were at

least as unpromising as they had ever been, and
Englishmen might be excused for doubting the
policy of wasting British resources in fretting one
extremity of Napoleon's enormous bulk.

While the Wellesley interest concentrated on the
Peninsula, the Foreign Office was interested in wider
fields. The new secretary was expected to devise
some system of trade with the Spanish-American
colonies which should meet approval from the Junta,
jealous with good reason of any foreign interference
with Mexico and Peru; but above all he was required
to take in hand the quarrel with the United States,
and if possible to retrieve the mistakes of Canning.
He had been only a few weeks in office when news
arrived that President Madison refused to hold further relations with F. J. Jackson, the British minister, and that Madison and Jackson were only agreed
in each requiring the punishment of the other. Pinkney soon appeared at the Foreign office with a request
for Jackson's recall.

Lord Wellesley was in character to the full as
arbitrary as George Canning. Seven years of imperial power in India had trained him in habits of
autocratic authority; but he was a man of breeding,
courteous, dignified, and considerate of others' dignity. In India he had shown what Canning thought
himself to possess, — the hand of iron in the velvet
glove. Without a tinge of Canning's besetting vice,
the passion to be clever, Wellesley never fell into the
fault of putting sarcasms or epigrams into his state

papers. So little offensive was he in manner, that although he brought about a war between England and the United States no American held him as an enemy, or retained so much ill-feeling toward him as to make even his name familiar to American ears. In truth his subordinate position in the Government prevented the exercise of his powers, and left him no opportunity to develop the force of that character which had crushed Tippoo Sultaun and tamed the Mahrattas. His colleagues allowed him to show only the weaknesses of a strong nature, which may have been increased to vices by the exhaustion of eight years' severe labor in an Indian climate. What he might have done had he taken Perceval's place no one can say; what he did or failed to do is more easily told.

When Pinkney came to explain the President's action and wishes in regard to Jackson, Wellesley, in a manner that seemed to the American minister both frank and friendly, showed only the wish to conciliate. In a short time Pinkney became so intimate with the new Foreign Secretary as to excite comment. Nothing could be more encouraging than his reports to the President of the change in disposition which had come over the Foreign Office. Jan. 2, 1810, Pinkney, in a long note, explained to Wellesley the President's reasons for breaking off relations with Jackson.[1] His tone was conciliatory, professing only the wish for friendly accommodation; and Wel-

[1] Pinkney to Wellesley, Jan. 2, 1810; State Papers, iii. 352.

lesley on his side not only received the note without objection, but encouraged the hope that the President's wishes would be gratified. Pinkney reported that in conversation Lord Wellesley had promised at once to send out a new envoy of diplomatic rank; to lose no time in settling the "Chesapeake" affair; and afterward to take up the commercial questions which had made the substance of Monroe's treaty three years before. The cordiality of these promises satisfied Pinkney that they were not meant to deceive. If any one was deceived, the victim was not Pinkney but Wellesley himself, who overrated his own power and underrated the inert resistance of Spencer Perceval and the army of selfish interests at his back. Even Jackson's affair was not easily managed. Jackson could not be disavowed, for he had done nothing more than his orders required him to do; nor could a new minister be appointed until the year elapsed which Canning promised for the term of Jackson's mission. Between Canning on one side and Perceval on the other, Wellesley found himself unable to act, and resorted to delays.

Not until March 14 did Pinkney receive the promised reply[1] to his note of January 2; and this reply was not all that Wellesley had given him to expect. Compared with Canning's notes, Wellesley's letter might be called affectionate; but it was less definite than Pinkney would have liked. His Majesty, said Wellesley, regretted that the President should have

[1] State Papers, iii. 355.

interrupted communications before his Majesty could manifest his invariable disposition to maintain the relations of amity with the United States. Mr. Jackson had most positively assured his Government that it was not his purpose to give offence by anything he said or did; in such cases the usual course would have been to convey a formal complaint, which would have prevented the inconvenience of a suspension of relations. Yet his Majesty, always disposed to pay the utmost attention to the wishes and sentiments of States in amity with him, had directed the return of Mr. Jackson, though without marking his conduct with any expression of displeasure, inasmuch as Mr. Jackson's "integrity, zeal, and ability have long been distinguished in his Majesty's service," and he seemed to have committed no intentional offence on the present occasion. Jackson was ordered to deliver his charge into the hands of a properly qualified person, while his Majesty "would receive, with sentiments of undiminished amity and good-will, any communication which the Government of the United States may deem beneficial to the mutual interests of both countries."

This was but Canning once more, without the sarcasm. With his grand air of sultan and viceroy, Wellesley ignored the existence of complaints, and professed himself "ready to receive, with sentiments of undiminished amity and good-will, any communication which the Government of the United States may deem beneficial;" but when his course led, two years afterward, to the only communication which could logically result, — a declaration of war, — Wellesley declared in Parliament[1] "that a more unjust attack was never made upon the peace of any nation than that of the American government upon England;" and that "the American government had been long infected with a deadly hatred toward this country, and (if he might be allowed an unusual application of a word) with a deadly affection toward France." He blamed only his own colleagues, who "ought in fact to have expected and been fully prepared for war with America."

That the American government and people were infected with a deadly hatred toward England, if not already true, was becoming true with a rapidity which warranted Wellesley in taking it for fact, if he could do nothing to prevent it; but he should at least have explained the reasons why his colleagues, who in his opinion showed culpable neglect, failed to expect war or to prepare for it. In truth his colleagues had as little reason to expect war with America as he had to charge the American government with "deadly affection" toward France. They would do nothing to conciliate the United States because they had what seemed the best ground for thinking that the United States were already conciliated, and that the difficulties between America and France were such as to prevent America from quarrelling with England. Wellesley's note was written March 14; Louis

[1] Cobbett's Debates, Nov. 30, 1812; xxiv. 33, 34.

of Holland, March 16, signed the treaty obliging him
to seize the American ships in his ports ; Napoleon
signed, March 23, the Rambouillet Decree.   In every
country within French control Napoleon was waging
avowed war against the United States in retaliation for the Non-intercourse Act ; while in America,
March 31, Congress abandoned the idea of even a
Navigation Act against England, and May 1 restored
relations with her, without asking an equivalent or
expressing unfriendly feeling.   Under such circumstances, ministers more intelligent than Spencer Perceval were warranted in thinking that the part of
wisdom was to leave American affairs alone.

The point was all-important in the story of the
war.   Governments rarely succeed in forethought,
and their favorite rule is to do nothing where nothing
need be done.   Had the British government expected
war, even Spencer Perceval would have bestirred himself to prevent it ; but ministers neither expected nor
had reason to expect hostilities.   On the contrary,
the only bright spot in Perceval's horizon was the
United States, where his influence seemed paramount.
The triumph of Perceval's policy there gave him
strength at home to disregard Wellesley's attempts
at domination.   An intelligent by-stander, through
whom Lord Wellesley kept up relations with the
Whigs, wrote, May 1, to the Marquess of Buckingham a letter,[1] which threw light on the ideas then
influencing Wellesley : —

[1] Buckingham Memoirs, iv. 438.

" The only hope Perceval can naturally have is in the turn which peace, or rather accommodation, with America may give the public mind ; as also the successes in Spain against France which may be looked for. The former, in my opinion, as well from the devotion of Pinkney to Lord Wellesley as the late rapacious act of Bonaparte, may be looked on as certain."

This letter, showing the certainty felt by all parties in American friendship, happened to be written on the day when the President signed the Act restoring commercial relations. After all that had occurred, — seizures, blockades, impressments, and Orders in Council ; the " Chesapeake " affair, Rose's mission, Canning's letters, Erskine's arrangement, and Jackson's dismissal, — the British government counted its American policy as its chief success, and had the strongest reasons for doing so. American legislation was controlled by British influence, and Napoleon reasonably thought that neither robbery nor magnanimity would affect the result.

The Marquess of Buckingham's friend gave him exact information, as the news a few weeks later, of the Act of May 1, proved ; but evidence much more convincing of the confidence felt by ministers in the attitude of America was given by George Canning, who claimed the credit for having brought about that settlement which gave a new lease of life to the Perceval Administration.   June 15, a week before Parliament rose, Canning spoke.[1]

[1] Cobbett's Debates, xvii. 742.

" The recent proceedings of Congress," he said, " have effected so much of what it was the anxious wish of the Government of which I was a member to attain, that I trust all our difficulties with America may be speedily adjusted.   In truth I had never much doubt upon my mind that America, if left to her own policy and to the effect of those discussions which would take place in her own legislatures, general and provincial, would at no distant period arrive at that point at which, by the late Act of Congress, she appears to have arrived.   No man is more anxious than I am for an amicable accommodation with that Power ; but I trust at the same time that the change in the policy of the United States has not been effected by any improper concessions on our part, — a circumstance which I can fully disclaim during the period that I remained in office.   I should rather hope that it has been the consequence of a determined adherence to that system which has been so often declaimed against in this House, but which has proved as clearly beneficial to the commercial interests as it has been consistent with the political dignity of this nation."

While it was possibly true, or soon became true, that the United States were, as Wellesley afterward alleged, infected by a deadly hostility to England, neither Wellesley nor Canning, nor any other English statesman in the year 1810, suspected the strength of that passion, or dreamed of shaping a policy to meet the hatred which ought to have been constantly in their minds.   Wellesley's personal wishes were not easy to fathom, but they probably leaned, under Pinkney's influence, toward conciliation.   His actual measures showed a want of decision, or a degree of feebleness, unsuspected in his character.

Quite early in Wellesley's career as Foreign Secretary, an opportunity occurred to test his energies. January 25, 1810,[1] Armstrong sent to Pinkney a copy of Napoleon's offer to withdraw the Decree of Berlin, if England would withdraw her previous blockade of the coast from Elbe to Brest. Nothing could be easier for England. The blockade of May 16, 1806, had been invented by Charles James Fox at the beginning of his short Administration as an act of friendship toward the United States, in order to evade the application of Sir William Scott's legal principles; it was strictly enforced only between Ostend and the Seine, a short strip of coast within the narrow seas completely under British control, and in part visible from British shores, while the subsequent Orders in Council had substituted a series of other measures in place of this temporary device, until at last the blockade of Holland and the Empire, from the river Ems to Trieste, — in which, April 26, 1809, the restrictive system of England was merged, — seemed to sweep away all trace of the narrower restraint. No one but Sir William Scott could say with certainty, as matter of law, whether Fox's blockade was or was not in force; but for years past England had established a depot at Helgoland in the mouth of the Elbe, for no other purpose than to violate its own blockade by smuggling merchandise into Germany, Denmark,

[1] Armstrong to Pinkney, Jan. 25, 1810 ; State Papers, iii. 350.

and Holland.   From every point of view the continued existence of Fox's blockade seemed impossible
to suppose.

February 15 Pinkney wrote to Wellesley, asking
whether that or any other blockade of France previous
to January, 1807, was understood to be in force.[1]
March 2 Wellesley replied that the restrictions imposed in May, 1806, " were afterward comprehended
in the Order of Council of Jan. 7, 1807, which order
is still in force." [2]   This reply encouraged Pinkney
to infer that Fox's blockade had merged in Howick's
Order in Council.   March 7 he wrote again to the
Marquess,[3] —

" I infer . . . that the blockade . . . is not itself in
force, and that the restrictions which it established rest
altogether, so far as such restrictions exist at this time,
upon an Order or Orders in Council issued since the first
day of January, 1807."

To this easy question, which seemed hardly worth an-
swering in the negative, Wellesley replied, March 26,[4]

" The blockade notified by Great Britain in May, 1806,
has never been formally withdrawn.   It cannot, therefore, be accurately stated that the restrictions which it
established rest altogether on the Order of Council of
Jan. 7, 1807 ; they are comprehended under the more
extensive restrictions of that Order."

[1] Pinkney to Wellesley, Feb. 15, 1810 ; State Papers, iii. 350.
[2] Wellesley to Pinkney, March 2, 1810 ; State Papers, iii. 350.
[3] Pinkney to Wellesley, March 7, 1810 ; State Papers, iii. 350.
[4] Wellesley to Pinkney, March 26, 1810 ; State Papers, iii. 356.

This explanation, however satisfactory it might be to the admiralty lawyer who may have framed it, conveyed no clear idea to the diplomatic mind. The question whether the blockade of 1806 was or was not still in force remained obscure. Pinkney thought it not in force, and wrote to Armstrong,[1] —

" Certainly the inference is that the blockade of 1806 is virtually at an end, being merged and comprehended in an Order in Council issued after the date of the Edict of Berlin. I am, however, about to try to obtain a formal revocation of that blockade, and of that of Venice [July 27, 1806], or at least a precise declaration that they are not in force."

His hopes were not strong, but he returned patiently to his task, and April 30 wrote a third letter to Lord Wellesley,[2] in which he recited Napoleon's promise in full, and begged Wellesley to say " whether there exists any objection on the part of his Majesty's government to a revocation, or to a declaration that they are no longer in force, of the blockades in question, especially that of May, 1806."

Already Pinkney had waited nearly three months for a plain answer to a question which ought certainly to have received a satisfactory reply within a week. He was destined to wait longer ; indeed, the United States waited two years for their answer before they declared war. The reason for this incomprehensible behavior, at a moment when America was thought to

[1] Pinkney to Armstrong, April 6, 1810 ; State Papers, iii. 355.
[2] Pinkney to Wellesley, April 30, 1810 ; State Papers, iii. 357.

be friendly, cannot be fully explained; but evidence published in his brother's papers seems to show that Marquess Wellesley favored giving up not only Fox's blockade, but also the principle of commercial restrictions represented both in the Orders of November, 1807, and in the blockade of April, 1809. "He only agreed with his colleagues in the legality and propriety of the orders when first enacted. He contended that they had ceased to be applicable to the state of affairs ; that they had become inexpedient with regard to England, and would certainly produce a war with America."[1] That he insisted on this opinion in the Cabinet, or forced an issue with his colleagues on the point, is not to be supposed; but without doubt the treatment his opinions and authority received in the Cabinet was the cause of his strange conduct toward the American minister.

Pinkney's last letter about Fox's blockade was dated April 30. As early as April 25 every well-informed man in London knew that Wellesley was on bad terms with his colleagues. The Marquess of Buckingham's correspondent had the news from Wellesley's own mouth :[2] —

"Lord Wellesley complains that he has no weight whatever in Council; that there is nothing doing there which marks energy or activity; that the affairs of the country are quite at a standstill, and are likely to remain so ; and that so little is his private interest in any of the

[1] Memorandum ; Supplementary Despatches, vii. 264.

[2] Cf. Lewis's Administrations, 323, *note*.

departments, that since his accession to office he has not been able to make an exciseman. . . . Add to all this that he hates, despises, and is out of friendship or even intimacy with every one of his colleagues at this moment." [1]

Two years afterward the Marquess repeated the same story in public : [2] —

" Lord Wellesley," he declared, speaking in the third person, " had repeatedly, with great reluctance, yielded his opinions to the Cabinet on many other important points [besides the war in the Peninsula]. He was sincerely convinced by experience that in every such instance he had submitted to opinions more incorrect than his own, and had sacrificed to the object of accommodation and temporary harmony more than he could justify in point of strict public duty. In fact he was convinced by experience that the Cabinet neither possessed ability nor knowledge to devise a good plan, nor temper and discernment to adopt what he now thought necessary, unless Mr. Perceval should concur with Lord Wellesley. To Mr. Perceval's judgment or attainments Lord Wellesley, under the same experience, could not pay any deference without injury to the public service."

Probably Wellesley did not conceal in Council the opinion of his colleagues which he freely expressed in society. In every way they annoyed him. A scholar, who prided himself on his classical studies and refined tastes, he found these colleagues altering his state papers and criticising his style. " He had

[1] Buckingham Memoirs, iv. 435.
[2] Statement, etc.; Cobbett's Debates, xxiii. 367, *note.*

thought he was among a Cabinet of statesmen," he said; " he found them a set of critics." His own criticisms occasionally touched matters more delicate than style. Once at a Cabinet meeting Lord Westmoreland, the Privy Seal, put his feet on the table while Wellesley was talking. The Foreign Secretary stopped short. " I will go on with my remarks," he said, " when the noble Lord resumes a more seemly attitude."

Americans could hardly be blamed for holding a low opinion of this Administration, when most intelligent Englishmen held the same. If Whigs or Liberals like Grenville, Brougham, and Sydney Smith were prejudiced critics, this charge could hardly be brought against Canning; but if Canning's opinion were set aside, the Wellesleys at least being identified with his administration had every reason to wish Perceval success. How the Marquess hated and despised Perceval ; how he struggled to get rid of him, and strained every nerve to bring Canning, Castlereagh, Sidmouth, Grey, or Grenville into the Government as a counter-balancing influence, can be read in the biographies of all these men, and of many less famous. London echoed with the Marquess's deep disgust; every man of fair parts in England sympathized with it, unless his personal interests or feelings bound him to blind devotion. The yoke hung heavy on Whigs and Tories alike. Even Lord Sidmouth rebelled against the commercial system to which Perceval clung more desper-

ately than to his offices or power. " Of that de-
structive system," wrote Sidmouth in the summer
of 1810,[1] " all are weary, ' praeter atrocem animum
Catonis.' "

Even Henry Wellesley, at Seville and Cadiz, felt
the same heavy hand deadening the effect of every
effort, and longed to do at Cadiz what Erskine had
done at Washington. March 4, 1810,[2] Perceval wrote
to Lord Wellesley begging him to instruct his brother
Henry to obtain from the Spanish Junta exclusive or
at least special privileges in the trade of the Spanish
colonies, such as would admit British consuls to the
chief places of South America, and " give us a decided benefit and preference in the trade." Of course
this preference was to be granted at the expense of
the United States, the solitary rival of England in
those waters, but " as nearly hostile to Spain as she
can be without actually declaring war against her."
Soon afterward the " Espagnol," a Spanish periodical
published in England, applauded revolutionary movements in Caracas and Buenos Ayres, while it asserted the impossibility of preventing the spread of
the spirit of independence in the Spanish-American
colonies.

" You can have no idea," wrote Henry Wellesley from
Cadiz, August 31, to his brother Arthur,[3] " of the ferment occasioned here by this article, which is attributed

[1] Pellew's Sidmouth, ii. 507.
[2] Walpole's Perceval, ii. 114.
[3] Wellington's Supplementary Despatches, vi. 583.

to the Government, — as it is supposed, and I believe
justly, that the ' Espagnol ' is patronized by the Government, and contains its sentiments with regard to the
occurrences in Spain and the measures necessary in the
present crisis of her affairs. . . . It is wonderful that
they cannot be satisfied in England with a commercial
arrangement which would be attended with immense
advantages to ourselves, and would likewise be greatly
beneficial to Spain.   I apprehend this to be the true
spirit of all commercial treaties ; and why are we to take
advantage of the weakness of Spain to endeavor to impose terms upon her which would be ruinous and disgraceful?   I have it in my power to conclude to-morrow
a commercial treaty which, without breaking in upon
the Spanish colonial laws, would pour millions into the
pockets of our merchants, and be equally advantageous
to the resources ; but this will not do, and we must either
have the trade direct with the colonies, or nothing.   However, I have received my answer, and the Government
will not hear of opening the trade."

The coincidence of opinion about Spencer Perceval
extended everywhere, except among the Church of
England clergy, the country squires, the shipping
interests, the Royal household at Windsor, and the
Federalists of Boston and Connecticut.   As though to
make him an object of execration, the long-threatened
storm burst on the trade and private credit of Great
Britain.   For some eighteen months gold stood at a
premium of about fifteen per cent ; the exchanges
remained steadily unfavorable, while credit was
strained to the utmost, until in July, 1810, half the

traders in England, and private banks by the score, were forced to suspend payment. Never before, and probably never since, has England known such a fall in prices and destruction of credit.[1]

This was the impending situation when Parliament adjourned, June 21, with no bright spot on its horizon but the supposed friendship of America. Meanwhile Pinkney wearied Wellesley for an answer to the question whether Fox's blockade was in force. June 10, June 23, and finally August 6, he renewed his formal request. " No importunity had before been spared which it became me to use." [2] He was met by the same torpor at every other point. Wellesley promised to name a new minister to Washington, but decided upon none. He invited overtures in regard to the " Chesapeake " affair, but failed to act on them. Rumor said that he neglected business, came rarely to Cabinet meetings, shut himself in his own house, saw only a few friends, and abandoned the attempt to enforce his views. He resolved to retire from the Cabinet, in despair of doing good, and waited only for the month before the next meeting of Parliament, which he conceived to be the most proper time for declaring his intention.[3]

In the midst of this chaos, such as England had

[1] Tooke's History of Prices.

[2] Pinkney to Robert Smith, Aug. 14, 1810; State Papers, iii. 363.

[3] Memorandum ; Supplementary Despatches of Lord Wellington, vii. 266.

rarely seen, fell Cadore's announcement of August 5 that the Imperial Decrees were withdrawn, *bien entendu* that before November 1 England should have abandoned her blockades, or America should have enforced her rights. Pinkney hastened to lay this information before Lord Wellesley, August 25, and received the usual friendly promises, which had ceased to gratify him. "I am truly disgusted with this," he wrote home, August 29,[1] "and would, if I followed my own inclination, speedily put an end to it." Two days afterward he received from Wellesley a civil note,[2] saying that whenever the repeal of the French Decrees should actually have taken effect, and the commerce of neutral nations should háve been restored to the condition in which it previously stood, the system of counteraction adopted by England should be abandoned. This reply, being merely another form of silence, irritated Pinkney still more, while his instructions pressed him to act. He waited until September 21, when he addressed to Wellesley a keen remonstrance. "If I had been so fortunate," he began,[3] "as to obtain for my hitherto unanswered inquiry the notice which I had flattered myself it might receive, and to which I certainly thought it was recommended by the plainest considerations of

[1] State Papers, iii. 366.

[2] Wellesley to Pinkney, Aug. 31, 1810 ; State Papers, iii. 366.

[3] Pinkney to Wellesley, Sept. 21, 1810; State Papers, iii. 368.

policy and justice, it would not perhaps have been necessary for me to trouble your Lordship with this letter;" and in this tone he went on to protest against the "unwarrantable prohibitions of intercourse rather than regular blockades," which had helped in nearly obliterating "every trace of the public law of the world":—

"Your Lordship has informed me in a recent note that it is 'his Majesty's earnest desire to see the commerce of the world restored to that freedom which is necessary for its prosperity;' and I cannot suppose that this freedom is understood to be consistent with vast constructive blockades which may be so expanded at pleasure as, without the aid of any new device, to oppress and annihilate every trade but that which England thinks fit to license. It is not, I am sure, to *such* freedom that your Lordship can be thought to allude."

The Marquess of Buckingham's well-advised correspondent some weeks afterward [1] remarked that "Pinkney, who was at first all sweetness and complaisance, has recently exhibited in his communications with Lord Wellesley an ample measure of republican insolence." Sweetness and insolence were equally thrown away. Pinkney's letter of September 21, like most of his other letters, remained unanswered; and before November 1, when Napoleon's term for England's action expired, a new turn of affairs made answer impossible. The old King was allowed to visit the death-bed of his favorite daughter

[1] Buckingham Memoirs, iv. 482.

the Princess Amelia; he excited himself over her wishes and farewells, and October 25 his mind, long failing, gave way for the last time. His insanity could not be disguised, and the Government fell at once into confusion.

CHAPTER XIV.

THE summer of 1810 was quiet and hopeful in
America. For the first time since December, 1807,
trade was free. Although little immigration occurred, the census showed an increase in population
of nearly thirty-seven per cent in ten years, — from
5,300,000 to 7,240,000, of which less than one hundred thousand was due to the purchase of Louisiana.
Virginia and Massachusetts still fairly held their own,
and New York strode in advance of Pennsylvania,
while the West gained little relative weight. Ohio
had not yet a quarter of a million people, Indiana
only twenty-four thousand, and Illinois but twelve
thousand, while Michigan contained less than five
thousand. The third census showed no decided
change in the balance of power from any point of
view bounded by the usual horizon of human life.
Perhaps the growth of New York city and Philadelphia pointed to a movement among the American
people which might prove more revolutionary than
any mere agricultural movement westward. Each
of these cities contained a population of ninety-six
thousand, while Baltimore rose to forty-six thousand,
and Boston to thirty-two thousand. The tendency

toward city life, if not yet unduly great, was worth noticing, especially because it was confined to the seaboard States of the North.

The reason of this tendency could in part be seen in the Treasury reports on American shipping, which reached in 1810 a registered tonnage of 1,424,000, — a point not again passed until 1826. The registered foreign tonnage sprang to 984,000, — a point not again reached in nearly forty years. New vessels were built to the amount of one hundred and twenty-seven thousand tons in the year 1810.[1] The value of all the merchandise exported in the year ending Sept. 30, 1810, amounted to nearly sixty-seven million dollars, and of this sum about forty-two millions represented articles of domestic production.[2] Except in the year before the embargo this export of domestic produce had never been much exceeded.[3] The imports, as measured by the revenue, were on the same scale. The net customs-revenue which reached $16,500,000 in 1807, after falling in 1808 and 1809 to about $7,000,000, rose again to $12,750,000 in 1810.[4] The profits of the export and import business fell chiefly to Boston, New York, Philadelphia,

[1] Statement, etc., Dec. 16, 1811; State Papers, Commerce and Navigation, i. 876.

[2] Gallatin to the Speaker, Feb. 6, 1811 ; State Papers, Commerce and Navigation, i. 866.

[3] Statement, etc., Dec. 16, 1811; State Papers, Commerce and Navigation, i. 929.

[4] Statement, etc., Feb. 28, 1812; State Papers, Finance, ii. 542–552.

and Baltimore, where the shipping belonged ; and
these cities could not fail to attract labor as well
as capital beyond the degree that a conservative
republican of the Revolutionary time would have
thought safe.

More than half of these commercial exchanges
were with England or her dependencies. Great
Britain and her American colonies, Portugal and
Spain in her military protection, and British India
consumed at least one half of the exports ; while
of the net revenue collected on imports, Gallatin
estimated six and a half millions as derived from
articles imported from Great Britain and the British
dependencies, all other sources supplying hardly six
millions.[1] The nature of these imports could be
only roughly given. In general, sugar, molasses,
coffee, wines, silk, and tea were not British ; but
manufactures of cotton, linen, leather, paper, glass,
earthen-ware, iron, and other metals came chiefly
from Great Britain. To the United States this
British trade brought most of the articles necessary to daily comfort in every part of the domestic
economy. The relief of recovering a full and cheap
supply exceeded the satisfaction of handsome profits
on the renewed trade. Experience of the hourly
annoyance, expense, and physical exposure caused
by deprivation of what society considered necessities rendered any return to the restrictive system

[1] Report on the Finances, Nov. 25, 1811 ; State Papers,
Finance, ii. 495

in the highest degree unwise, especially after the
eastern people acquired conviction that the system
had proved a failure.

Thus the summer passed with much of the old
contentment that marked the first Administration
of Jefferson. Having lost sight of national dignity,
the commercial class was contented under the protection of England; and American ships in the Baltic,
in Portugal, and in the West Indies never hesitated
to ask and were rarely refused the assistance of the
British navy.   From time to time a few impressments were reported ; but impressment had never
been the chief subject of complaint, and after the
withdrawal of the frigates blockading New York,
little was heard of British violence. On the other
hand, Napoleon's outrages roused great clamor in
commercial society, and his needless harshness to
every victim, from the Pope to the American sailors
whom he shut up as prisoners of war, went far to
palliate British offences in the eyes of American
merchants.

News of Napoleon's seizures at San Sebastian arrived before the adjournment of Congress May 1 ;
and as fresh outrages were reported from every quarter by every new arrival, and as Cadore's letters became public, even Madison broke into reproaches.
May 25 he wrote to Jefferson : [1] " The late confiscations by Bonaparte comprise robbery, theft, and
breach of trust, and exceed in turpitude any of

[1] Madison's Works, ii. 477.

his enormities not wasting human blood." These
words seemed to show intense feeling, but Madison's temper indulged in outbursts of irritability
without effect on his action; in reality, his mind
was bent beyond chance of change on the old idea
of his Revolutionary education, — that the United
States must not regard France, but must resist
Great Britain by commercial restrictions. " This
scene on the Continent," he continued to Jefferson,
" and the effect of English monopoly on the value
of our produce are breaking the charm attached
to what is called free-trade, foolishly by some and
wickedly by others." He reverted to his life-long
theory of commercial regulations.

A few days afterward Madison wrote to Armstrong
fresh instructions founded on the Act of May 1,
which was to be the new diplomatic guide. These
instructions,[1] dated June 5, were of course signed
by the Secretary of State, Robert Smith, who afterward claimed credit for them; but their style, both
of thought and expression, belonged to Madison.
Even the unfailing note of his mind — irritability
without passion — was not wanting. He would wait,
he said, for further advices before making the proper
comments on Cadore's letter of February 14 and on
its doctrine of reprisals. " I cannot, however, forbear
informing you that a high indignation is felt by the
President, as well as by the public, at this act of
violence on our property, and at the outrage both in

[1] State Papers, iii. 384.

the language and in the matter of the letter of the
Duc de Cadore." Turning from this subject, the despatch requested that Napoleon would make use of
the suggestion contained in the Act of May 1, 1810.
" If there be sincerity in the language held at different times by the French government, and especially
in the late overture, to proceed to amicable and just
arrangements in case of our refusal to submit to the
British Orders in Council, no pretext can be found
for longer declining to put an end to the decrees of
which the United States have so justly complained."
One condition alone was imposed on Armstrong preliminary to the acceptance of French action under
the law of May 1, but this condition was essential :

" If, however, the arrangement contemplated by the
law should be acceptable to the French government,
you will understand it to be the purpose of the President not to proceed in giving it effect in case the late
seizure of the property of the citizens of the United
States has been followed by an absolute confiscation,
and restoration be finally refused. The only ground
short of a preliminary restoration of the property on
which the contemplated arrangement can be made will
be an understanding that the confiscation is reversible,
and that it will become immediately the subject of discussion with a reasonable prospect of justice to our
injured citizens."

The condition thus prescribed seemed both reasonable and mild in view of the recent and continuous
nature of the offence ; but Madison could not, even

if he would, allow his own or public attention to
be permanently diverted from England. As early
as June 22 he had begun to reconstruct in his own
mind the machinery of his restrictive system. "On
the first publication of the despatches by the 'John
Adams,'" he wrote to Jefferson,[1] "so strong a feeling
was produced by Armstrong's picture of the French
robbery that the attitude in which England was
placed by the correspondence between Pinkney and
Wellesley was overlooked. The public attention is
beginning to fix itself on the proof it affords that
the original sin against neutrals lies with Great
Britain; and that while she acknowledges it, she
persists in it."

The theory of original sin led to many conclusions
hard to reconcile; but, as regarded Napoleon, Madison's idea seemed both sensible and dignified, — that
England's original fault in no way justified the recent
acts of France, which were equivalent to war on the
United States, not as one among neutrals, but as a
particular enemy. Fresh instructions to Armstrong,
dated July 5,[2] reiterated the complaints, offers, and
conditions of the despatch sent one month before.
Especially the condition precedent to action under
the law of May 1 was repeated with emphasis : —

" As has been heretofore stated to you, a satisfactory
provision for restoring the property lately surprised and
seized, by the order or at the instance of the French

[1] Madison's Works, ii. 480.
[2] State Papers, iii. 385.

government, must be combined with a repeal of the
French edicts with a view to a non-intercourse with
Great Britain, such a provision being an indispensable
evidence of the just purpose of France toward the United
States.   And you will moreover be careful, in arranging
such a provision for that particular case of spoliations,
not to weaken the ground on which a redress of others
may be justly pursued."

The instructions of June 5 and July 5 went their
way ; but although Armstrong duly received them,
and wrote to Cadore a letter evidently founded on
the despatch of June 5, he made no express allusion
to his instructions in writing either to the French
government or to his own.   Although he remained
in Paris till September 12, and on that day received
from Cadore an explicit avowal that the sequestered
property would not be restored, but that "the principles of reprisal must be the law," he made no
protest.

Equally obscure was the conduct of Madison.   Cadore's letter of August 5 announcing that the French
Decrees were withdrawn, on the understanding that
the United States should by November 1 enforce
their rights against England, reached Washington
September 25, but not in official form.   Nothing is
known of the impression it produced on the Cabinet ; nothing remains of any discussions that ensued.
If Gallatin was consulted, he left no trace of his
opinion.   Hamilton and Eustis had little weight in
deciding foreign questions.   Robert Smith within a

year afterward publicly attacked the President for
the course pursued, and gave the impression that it
was taken on Madison's sole judgment. The President's only authority to act at all without consulting Congress depended on the words of the law of
May 1: " In case either Great Britain or France
shall, before the third day of March next, so revoke
or modify her edicts as that they shall cease to
violate the neutral commerce of the United States,
which fact the President of the United States shall
proclaim by proclamation," the non-intercourse of
March 1, 1809, should at the end of three months
revive against the nation which had not revoked its
edicts. Under this authority, President Madison
was required by Cadore's letter to proclaim that
France had revoked or modified her edicts so that
they ceased to violate the neutral commerce of the
United States.

Madison was doubtless a man of veracity ; but
how was it possible that any man of veracity could
proclaim that France had revoked or modified her
edicts so that they ceased to violate the neutral
commerce of the United States when he had every
reason to think that at least the Bayonne Decree,
barely six months old, would not be revoked,
and when within a few weeks he had officially declared that the revocation of the Bayonne Decree
was " an indispensable evidence of the just purpose of France " preliminary to a non-intercourse
with England ? If the President in June and July

thought that provision indispensable to the true
intent of the law which he aided in framing, he
would assume something more than royal dispensing
power by setting the indispensable provision aside
in November.

This objection was light in comparison with others.
The law required the President to proclaim a fact, —
that France had revoked or modified her decrees so
that they ceased to violate the commerce of America.
Of this fact Cadore's letter was the only proof; but
evidently Cadore's letter pledged the Emperor to
nothing. " I am authorized to declare to you,"
wrote Cadore, " that the Decrees of Berlin and
Milan are revoked, and that after November 1 they
will cease to have effect, on the understanding that
in consequence of this declaration . . . the United
States, conformably to the Act you have just communicated, shall cause their rights to be respected
by the English." Napoleon not only reserved to himself the right of judging whether the measures to
be taken by the United States should " cause their
rights to be respected," but in doing so he reversed
the process prescribed by the Act, and required the
President to enforce his rights before the Emperor
should withdraw his decrees.

From the standpoint of morality, perhaps the most
serious objection of all was the danger of sacrificing
national and personal self-respect by affecting to regard as honest a promise evidently framed to deceive,
and made by a man whom Madison habitually charac-

terized in terms that implied, to speak mildly, entire want of confidence. If America would consent to assert her rights against England in no way more straightforward than this, she might perhaps recover her neutral profits, but hardly her national self-respect.

A few months afterward, when Robert Smith gave to the world the amusing but not wholly new spectacle of a Secretary of State attacking his own President for measures signed by his own name, Joel Barlow wrote for the " National Intelligencer " a defence of the President's course, in which he gave reasons supplied by Madison himself for holding that Cadore's letter satisfied the conditions of Macon's Act.

To the first objection, founded on the Rambouillet and Bayonne Decrees, Barlow replied that the American government had habitually distinguished between maritime edicts violating neutral rights and municipal edicts attacking private property. " We could not in strictness arraign such municipal spoliations under the head of violations of our *neutral* rights, nor of consequence regard them as contemplated by the Acts of Congress defining the acts whose revocation would satisfy the conditions of that Act." This reasoning, though not quite convincing, might have had weight but for two objections.   First, the President himself, in June and July, had declared these municipal spoliations to be contemplated by Macon's Act as " an indispensable evidence of the just pur-

pose of France;"[1] and, second, the President in
November notified Armstrong, that,[2] "in issuing the
proclamation, it has been presumed that the requi-
sition contained in that letter [of July 5] on the
subject of the sequestered property will have been
satisfied." Barlow's idea of a municipal spoliation,
independent of the *jus gentium*, was an afterthought
intended to hide a miscalculation.

One other argument was advanced by Barlow.
Erskine's arrangement having been accepted without
question of previous British spoliations, not only did
impartiality require the same treatment for France,
but a different rule " would have led to the embarrassment of obliging the Executive, in case the
British government should be desirous of opening
a free trade with the United States by repealing
its orders, to make it a prerequisite that Great
Britain also should indemnify for her respective
spoliations."

Such a prerequisite would have been proper, and
ought to have been imposed; but Barlow's argument
was again answered by the President himself, who
actually insisted on the demand against France, and
assumed the demand to be satisfied. If this was
partiality to England, the President was guilty of it.
Probably at the time he saw reasons for thinking

[1] Cf. Speech of Mr. Eppes, Feb. 2, 1811 ; Annals of Congress, 1810–1811, 866.

[2] Robert Smith to Armstrong, Nov. 2, 1810; State Papers,
iii. 389.

otherwise. The secrecy, the continuance, the pretext of the French seizures, their municipal and vindictive character and direct Imperial agency seemed to set them apart from those of England, which, although equally illegal, were always in the form of lawful trial and condemnation.

The same argument of impartiality served to justify immediate action on Cadore's offer as on Erskine's, without waiting for its execution. That one admitted mistake excused its own repetition in a worse form was a plea not usually advanced by servants, either public or private ; but in truth Erskine's pledge was distinct and unconditional, while Cadore's depended on the Emperor's satisfaction with a preliminary act. Had Erskine made his arrangement conditional on Canning's approval of the President's measures, Madison would certainly have waited for that approval before acting under the law ; and after the disastrous results of precipitancy in 1809, when no one questioned Erskine's good faith, wisdom called for more caution rather than less in acting, in 1810, on an offer or a pledge from a man in whom no one felt any confidence at all.

In truth, Madison's course in both cases was due not to logic, but to impatience. As Barlow admitted : " We know it had been the aim of our government for two or three years to divide the belligerents by inducing one or the other of them to revoke its edicts, so that the example would lead to a revocation by the other, or our contest be limited to a single one." Madison gave the same reason in a letter of October 19 to Jefferson: [1] " We hope from the step the advantage at least of having but one contest on our hands at a time." He was mistaken, and no one expressed himself afterward in language more bitter than he used against Napoleon for conduct that deceived only those who lent themselves to deception.

October 31, Robert Smith sent for Turreau and gave him notice of the decision reached by the President and Cabinet: [2] —

" The Executive," said Robert Smith, " is determined not to suffer England longer to trammel the commerce of the United States, and he hopes to be sustained by Congress. If, then, England does not renounce her system of paper-blockades and the other vexations resulting from it, no arrangement with that Power is to be expected; and consequently you will see, in two days, the President's proclamation appear, founded on the provisions of the law requiring the non-intercourse to be enforced against either nation which should fail to revoke its edicts after the other belligerent had done so. . . . Although we have received nothing directly from Mr. Armstrong on this subject, which is doubtless very extraordinary, we consider as sufficient for the Government's purposes the communication he made to Mr. Pinkney, which the latter has transmitted to us."

[1] Works, ii. 484.
[2] Turreau to Champagny, 1 November, 1810 (No. 1) ; Archives des Aff. Étr. MSS.

The next day Robert Smith made some further interesting remarks.[1] "The Executive thinks," he said, "that the measures he shall take in case England continues to restrict our communications with Europe will lead necessarily to war," because of the terms of the non-intercourse. "We have with us a majority of Congress, which has much to retrieve, and has been accused of weakness by all parties."

On leaving Smith, Turreau went to see Gallatin, "whose opinion in the Cabinet is rarely favorable to us."

"Mr. Gallatin (by the way long since on bad terms with Mr. Smith) told me that he believed in war; that England could not suffer the execution of measures so prejudicial to her, and especially in the actual circumstances could not renounce the prerogatives of her maritime supremacy and of her commercial ascendency."

Both Smith and Gallatin evidently expected that war was to result, not from the further action of the United States, but from the resentment and retaliation of England. They regarded the non-intercourse as a measure of compulsion which would require England either to resent it or to yield.

Having decided to accept Cadore's letter as proof that an actual repeal of the French Decrees, within the meaning of the Act of Congress, had taken place November 1, the President issued, November 2, his proclamation declaring that "it has been officially

[1] Turreau to Champagny, 2 November, 1810 (No. 6) ; Archives des Aff. Étr. MSS.

made known to this Government that the said edicts of France have been so revoked as that they ceased, on the said first day of the present month, to violate the neutral commerce of the United States;" and simultaneously Gallatin issued a circular to the collectors of customs, announcing that commercial intercourse with Great Britain would cease Feb. 2, 1811.

By this means Madison succeeded in reverting to his methods of peaceful coercion. As concerned England, he could be blamed only on the ground that his methods were admittedly inadequate, as Gallatin, only a year before, had officially complained. Toward England the United States had stood for five years in a position which warranted them in adopting any measure of reprisal. The people of America alone had a right to object that when Madison began his attack on England by proclaiming the French Decrees to be revoked, he made himself a party to Napoleon's fraud, and could scarcely blame the Federalists for replying that neither in honor nor in patriotism were they bound to abet him in such a scheme.

The Proclamation of Nov. 2, 1810, was not the only measure of the autumn which exposed the President to something more severe than criticism. At the moment when he challenged a contest with England on the assertion that Napoleon had withdrawn his decrees, Madison resumed his encroachments on Spain in a form equally open to objection.

The chaos that reigned at Madrid and Cadiz could not fail to make itself felt throughout the Span'sh empire. Under British influence, Buenos Ayres in 1810 separated from the Supreme Junta, and drove out the viceroy whom the Junta had appointed. In April of the same year Caracas followed the example, and entered into a treaty with England, granting commercial preferences equally annoying to the Spaniards and to the United States. Miranda reappeared at the head of a revolution which quickly spread through Venezuela and New Grenada. A civil war broke out in Mexico. Even Cuba became uneasy. The bulky fabric of Spanish authority was shaken, and no one doubted that it must soon fall in pieces forever.

England and the United States, like two vultures, hovered over the expiring empire, snatching at the morsels they most coveted, while the unfortunate Spaniards, to whom the rich prey belonged, flung themselves, without leadership or resources, on the ranks of Napoleon's armies. England pursued her game over the whole of Spanish America, if not by government authority, more effectively by private intrigue; while the United States for the moment confined their activity to a single object, not wholly without excuse.

As long as Baton Rouge and Mobile remained Spanish, New Orleans was insecure. This evident danger prompted Madison, when Secretary of State, to make a series of efforts, all more or less unfortunate, to gain possession of West Florida; and perhaps nothing but Napoleon's positive threat of war prevented the seizure of Baton Rouge during Jefferson's time. After that crisis, the subject dropped from diplomatic discussion; but as years passed, and Spanish power waned, American influence steadily spread in the province. Numerous Americans settled in or near the district of West Feliciana, within sight of Fort Adams, across the American border. As their number increased, the Spanish flag at Baton Rouge became less and less agreeable to them; but they waited until Buenos Ayres and Caracas gave notice that Spain could be safely defied.

In the middle of July, 1810, the citizens of West Feliciana appointed four delegates to a general convention, and sent invitations to the neighboring districts inviting them to co-operate in re-establishing a settled government. The convention was held July 25, and consisted of sixteen delegates from four districts, who organized themselves as a legislature, and with the aid or consent of the Spanish governor began to remodel the government. After some weeks of activity they quarrelled with the governor, charged him with perfidy, and suddenly assembling all the armed men they could raise, assaulted Baton Rouge. The Spanish fort, at best incapable of defence, was in charge of young Louis Grandpré, with a few invalid or worthless soldiers. The young man thought himself bound in honor to maintain a trust committed to him; he rejected the summons to surrender, and when the Americans swarmed over the ruinous bastions they found Louis Grandpré almost alone defending his flag. He was killed.

After capturing Baton Rouge, the Americans held a convention, which declared itself representative of the people of West Florida, and September 26 issued a proclamation, which claimed place among the curious products of that extraordinary time. " It is known to the world," began this new declaration of independence,[1] " with how much fidelity the good people of this territory have professed and maintained allegiance to their legitimate sovereign while any hope remained of receiving from him protection for their property and lives." The convention had acted in concert with the Spanish governor " for the express purpose of preserving this territory, and showing our attachment to the government which had heretofore protected us ; " but the governor had endeavored to pervert those concerted measures into an engine of destruction ; and therefore, " appealing to the Supreme Ruler of the world for the rectitude of our intentions, we do solemnly publish and declare the several districts composing the territory of West Florida to be a free and independent State."

A few days afterward the convention, through its president, wrote to the Secretary of State, Robert Smith, urging the annexation of the new territory to the United States, but claiming all the public lands

[1] State Papers, iii. 396.

in the province for "the people of this Commonwealth, who have wrested the government and country
from Spain at the risk of their lives and fortunes." [1]
These words accorded ill with their appeal to the
Supreme Ruler of the world for the rectitude of their
intentions, and their protest of " our inviolable fidelity
to our king and parent country while so much as a
shadow of legitimate authority remained to be exercised over us." Yet neither with nor without their
elaborate machinery of legitimate revolution could
Madison have anything to do with them.   Innumerable obstacles stood in his way. They declared the
independence of territory which he had long since appropriated to the United States. This course alone
withheld Madison from recognizing the new State ;
but other difficulties forbade any action at all. The
Constitution gave the President no power to use the
army or navy of the United States beyond the national limits, without the authority of Congress ; and
although extreme emergency might have excused the
President in taking such action, no emergency existed
in October, 1810, since Congress would meet within
six weeks, and neither Spain, France, nor England
could interfere in the interval. The President's only
legal course was to wait for Congress to take what
measures seemed good.

Madison saw all this, but though aware of his want
of authority, felt the strongest impulse to act without
it. He described his dilemma to Jefferson in a letter

[1] State Papers, iii. 395.

written before he received the request for annexation, then on its way from Baton Rouge : [1] —

" The crisis in West Florida, as you will see, has come home to our feelings and interests. It presents at the same time serious questions as to the authority of the Executive, and the adequacy of the existing laws of the United States for territorial administration. And the near approach of Congress might subject any intermediate interposition of the Executive to the charge of being premature and disrespectful, if not of being illegal. Still, there is great weight in the considerations that the country to the Perdido, being our own, may be fairly taken possession of, if it can be done without violence ; above all, if there be danger of its passing into the hands of a third and dangerous party."

Casuistry might carry the United States government far. The military occupation of West Florida was an act of war against Spain. " From present appearances," continued Madison, " our occupancy of West Florida would be resented by Spain, by England, and by France, and bring on, not a triangular, but quadrangular contest." Napoleon himself never committed a more arbitrary act than that of marching an army, without notice, into a neighbor's territory, on the plea that he claimed it as his own. None of Madison's predecessors ventured on such liberties with the law ; none of his successors dared imitate them, except under the pretext that war already existed by the act of the adverse government.

[1] Madison to Jefferson, Oct. 19, 1810 ; Works, ii. 484.

Madison was regarded by his contemporaries as a
precise, well-balanced, even a timid man, argumenta-
tive to satiety, never carried away by bursts of passion, fretful rather than vehement, pertinacious rather
than resolute, — a character that seemed incapable
of surprising the world by reckless ambition or law-
less acts ; yet this circumspect citizen, always treated
by his associates with a shade of contempt as a closet
politician, paid surprisingly little regard to rules of
consistency or caution. His Virginia Resolutions of
1798, his instructions in the Louisiana purchase, his
assumption of Livingston's claim to West Florida,
his treatment of Yrujo, his embargo policy, his acceptance of Erskine's arrangement, his acceptance of
Cadore's arrangement, and his occupation of West
Florida were all examples of the same trait ; and an
abundance of others were to come. He ignored caution in pursuit of an object which seemed to him
proper in itself ; nor could he understand why this
quiet and patriotic conduct should rouse tempests of
passion in his opponents, whose violence, by contrast, increased the apparent placidity of his own
persistence.

Forestalling the action of Congress which was to
meet within five weeks, President Madison issued,
Oct. 27, 1810, a proclamation announcing that Governor Claiborne would take possession of West
Florida to the river Perdido, in the name and behalf
of the United States. This proclamation, one of the
most remarkable documents in the archives of the

United States government, began by reasserting
the familiar claim to West Florida as included in the
Louisiana purchase : —

" And whereas the acquiescence of the United States
in the temporary continuance of the said territory under
the Spanish authority was not the result of any distrust
of their title, as has been particularly evinced by the
general tenor of their laws and by the distinction made
in the application of those laws between that territory
and foreign countries, but was occasioned by their conciliatory views, and by a confidence in the justice of
their cause, and in the success of candid discussion and
amicable negotiation with a just and friendly Power ;
. . . considering, moreover, that under these peculiar
and imperative circumstances a forbearance on the part
of the United States to occupy the territory in question,
and thereby guard against the confusions and contingen-
cies which threaten it, might be construed into a dereliction of their title or an insensibility to the importance
of the stake ; considering that in the hands of the United
States it will not cease to be a subject of fair and
friendly negotiation and adjustment ; considering finally
that the Acts of Congress, though contemplating a present possession by a foreign authority, have contemplated
also an eventual possession of the said territory by the
United States, and are accordingly so framed as in that
case to extend in their operation to the same," —

Considering all these reasons, substantially the
same self-interest by which France justified her decrees, and England her impressments, the President
ordered Governor Claiborne, with the aid of the

United States army, to occupy the country and to govern it as a part of his own Orleans territory.[1] By a letter of the same date the Secretary of State informed Claiborne, that, " if contrary to expectation, the occupation of this [revolutionized] territory should be opposed by force, the commanding officer of the regular troops on the Mississippi will have orders from the Secretary of War to afford you, upon your application, the requisite aid. . . . Should however any particular place, however small, remain in possession of a Spanish force, you will not proceed to employ force against it, but you will make immediate report thereof to this Department." [2] Having by these few strokes of his pen authorized the seizure of territory belonging to " a just and friendly Power," and having legislated for a foreign people without consulting their wishes, the President sent to the revolutionary convention at Baton Rouge a sharp message through Governor Holmes of the Mississippi territory, to the effect that their independence was an impertinence, and their designs on the public lands were something worse.[3]

A few days after taking these measures, Robert Smith explained their causes to Turreau in the same conversation in which he announced the decision to

[1] Proclamation, etc., Oct. 27, 1810 ; State Papers, iii. 397.

[2] Secretary of State to Governor Claiborne, Oct. 27, 1810 ; State Papers, iii. 396.

[3] Secretary of State to Governor Holmes, Nov. 15, 1810; State Papers, iii. 398.

accept Cadore's letter as the foundation of non-intercourse with England.   The wish to preclude British
occupation of Florida was the motive alleged by
Smith for the intended occupation by the United
States.[1]

" As for the Floridas, I swear, General, on my honor
as a gentleman," said Robert Smith to Turreau, October
31, " not only that we are strangers to everything that
has happened, but even that the Americans who have
appeared there either as agents or leaders are enemies
of the Executive, and act in this sense against the Federal government as well as against Spain. . . . Moreover these men and some others have been led into these
measures by the hope of obtaining from a new government considerable concessions of lands.   In any case you
will soon learn the measures we have taken to prevent
the English from being received at Baton Rouge as they
have been at Pensacola, which would render them absolute masters of our outlets by the Mobile and Mississippi.
We hope that your Government will not take it ill that
we should defend the part of Florida in dispute between
Spain and us ; and whether our pretensions are well-
founded or not, your interest, like ours, requires us
to oppose the enterprises of England in that country."

Claiborne took possession of the revolutionized districts   December 7, and the Spanish governor at
Mobile was not sorry to see the insurgents so
promptly repressed and deprived of their expected
profits.   Yet Claiborne did not advance to the Per-

[1] Turreau to Champagny, 1 Nov. 1810 (No. 2) ; Archives
des Aff. Étr. MSS.

dido; he went no farther than the Pearl River, and
began friendly negotiations with Governor Folch at
Mobile for delivery of the country still held by the
Spaniards between the Pearl and the Perdido.   Governor Folch had none but diplomatic weapons to use
in his defence, but he used these to save that portion
of the province for some years to Spain.

The four districts west of the Pearl River were
organized by Claiborne as a part of the territory of
Orleans, in which shape, the President's proclamation
had said, " it will not cease to be a subject of fair and
friendly negotiation and adjustment " with Spain.
Within a few weeks the President announced to
Congress in his Annual Message that " the legality
and necessity of the course pursued " required from
the Legislature " whatever provisions may be due to
the essential rights and equitable interests of the
people thus brought into the bosom of the American
family."   The difficulty of reconciling two such assertions perplexed many persons who in the interests
of law and of society wished to understand how a
people already brought into the bosom of the American family could remain a subject of fair negotiation
with a foreign Power.   The point became further
complicated by the admission of Louisiana as a State
into the Union, with the four districts which were
" to be a subject of fair and friendly negotiation."

The first result of these tortuous proceedings was
to call a protest from Morier, the British chargé at
Washington, who wrote to the Secretary of State,

December 15, a letter [1] containing one paragraph worth noting : —

" Would it not have been worthy of the generosity of a free nation like this, bearing, as it doubtless does, a respect for the rights of a gallant people at this moment engaged in a noble struggle for its liberty, — would it not have been an act on the part of this country dictated by the sacred ties of good neighborhood and friendship which exist between it and Spain, to have simply offered its assistance to crush the common enemy of both, rather than to have made such interference the pretext for wresting a province from a friendly Power, and that at the time of her adversity ? "

Spain had little reason to draw distinctions between friends, allies, and enemies.   She could hardly stop to remember that the United States were filching a petty sand-heap in a remote corner of the world, at a time when England was " wresting " not one but all the splendid American provinces from their parent country, and when France was kneeling on the victim's breast and aiming stab after stab at her heart.

[1] Morier to Robert Smith, Dec. 15, 1810; State Papers, iii. 399.

CHAPTER XV.

THE elections for the Twelfth Congress, as far as they took place in 1810, showed a change in public opinion, and not only reduced the Federalists to their old rank of a faction rather than a party, but also weakened the conservative Republicans of Jefferson's school; while the losses of both strengthened a new party, which called itself Republican, but favored energy in government. Henry Clay and William Lowndes, John C. Calhoun and Felix Grundy, Langdon Cheves and Peter B. Porter, whatever they might at times say, cared little for Jeffersonian or Madisonian dogmas. The election which decided the character of the Twelfth Congress, by choosing men of this character to lead it, decided also the popular judgment on the Eleventh Congress, which had as yet run only half its course. Rarely in American history has any particular Congress been held in high popular esteem, but seldom if ever was a Congress overwhelmed by contempt so deep and general as that which withered the Eleventh in the midst of its career. Not only did Republicans and Federalists think alike for once, but even among the members

themselves no one of weight had a good word to say
of the body to which he belonged.

Quick to feel a popular rebuke, Congressmen submitted to punishment, and obeyed the orders they
would rather have resisted ; but their work in such
a temper was sure to be done without good-will or
good faith, for a body which had lost its own respect
could hardly respect its successor. The American
system of prolonging the existence of one Legislature
after electing another, never worked worse in practice than when it allowed this rump Congress of
1809, the mere scourings of the embargo, to assume
the task of preparing for the War of 1812, to which
it was altogether opposed and in which it could not
believe. No Congress had been confronted by greater
perplexities. President Madison submitted to it a
number of Executive acts more than doubtful in
legality, which must all be approved ; and these
measures, when approved, led to a policy of war with
England and Spain, which required great increase
of Executive strength, careful reorganization of the
Executive machinery, especially great care of the
national credit and of its chief financial agents, —
political duties of extreme difficulty and delicacy.

President Madison's Annual Message, December 5,
called attention to such business as he wished to
present. Naturally, the revocation of the French
Decrees took the first place. The President assumed
that the revocation was complete, and that his proclamation was issued in regular course, " as pre-

scribed by law," the President having no discretion ;
but he admitted disappointment that the sequestered
property had not been restored.   " It was particularly
anticipated that, as a further evidence of just disposition toward them, restoration would have been immediately made of the property of our citizens, seized
under a misapplication of the principle of reprisals,
combined with a misconstruction of a law of the
United States.   This expectation has not been fulfilled."   England had not yet relinquished her illegitimate blockades, and she avowed that the blockade
of May, 1806, was comprehended in the subsequent
Orders in Council ; the withdrawal of that blockade
had therefore been required by the President as one
of the conditions of renewing intercourse with Great
Britain.   The state of the Spanish monarchy had
produced a change in West Florida, a district " which
though of right appertaining to the United States had
remained in the possession of Spain, awaiting the result of negotiations for its actual delivery to them."
The Spanish authority being subverted, the President did not delay taking possession ; " the legality
and necessity of the course pursued assure me of
the favorable light in which it will present itself to
the Legislature."

If this sketch of foreign affairs lacked perfect candor, the view of domestic concerns gave matter for
other doubts.   " With the Indian tribes," said the
Message, " the peace and friendship of the United
States are found to be so eligible that the general dis-

position to preserve both continues to gain strength."
The story of Tippecanoe and Tecumthe soon threw
new light on this assertion. To Indian friendship
domestic prosperity succeeded, and the Message
praised the economy and policy of manufactures.
" How far it may be expedient to guard the infancy
of this improvement in the distribution of labor by
regulations of the commercial tariff, is a subject
which cannot fail to suggest itself to your patriotic
reflections." A navigation law was also required to
place American shipping on a level of competition
with foreign vessels. A national university " would
contribute not less to strengthen the foundations
than to adorn the structure of our free and happy
system of government." Further means for repress-
ing the slave-trade were required. Fortifications,
arms, and organization of the militia were to be provided. The Military School at West Point needed
enlargement.

Congress found more satisfaction in Gallatin's Annual Report, sent to Congress a week afterward, than
they could draw from Madison's Message, for Gallatin told them that he had succeeded in bringing the
current expenses within the annual income; and
only in case they should decide to prohibit the importation of British goods after Feb. 2, 1811, should he
need further legislation both to make good the revenue and to enforce the prohibition.

Congress lost no time. West Florida called first
for attention; and Senator Giles, December 18, re-

ported a bill extending the territory of Orleans to the
river Perdido, in accordance with the President's
measures. In the debate which followed, Federalist
senators attacked the President for exceeding the
law and violating the Constitution. Their argument
was founded on the facts already told, and required
nothing more to support it; but the defence had
greater interest, for no one could foretell with certainty by what expedient senators would cover an
Executive act which, like the purchase of Louisiana
itself, had best be accepted in silence as plainly beyond the Constitution. Henry Clay acted as the
President's champion, and explained on his behalf
that the Act of Oct. 31, 1803, authorizing the President to occupy the ceded territory of Louisiana, was
still in force, although regular possession to the
Iberville had been taken, Dec. 20, 1803, in pursuance
of that Act, without further demand on the part of
the United States, and although the Act of March 20,
1804, providing for the temporary government of the
territory, declared that " the Act passed the 31st day
of October . . . shall continue in force until the 1st
day of October, 1804." In face of this double difficulty, — the exhaustion of the power and its express
limitation, — Clay asserted that the power had not
been exhausted, and that the limitation, though apparently general, was intended only for the provisional government established by another portion of
the Act of 1803. He produced in his support the
Act of Feb. 24, 1804, empowering the President to

erect West Florida into a collection district whenever he deemed it expedient. " These laws," continued Clay, " furnish a legislative construction of the treaty correspondent with that given by the Executive, and they vest in this branch of the government indisputably a power to take possession of the country whenever it might be proper in his discretion."

Congress approved this opinion, which was in truth neither weaker nor stronger than the arguments by which the Louisiana purchase itself had been sustained. Fate willed that every measure connected with that territory should be imbued with the same spirit of force or fraud which tainted its title. The Southern States needed the Floridas, and cared little what law might be cited to warrant seizing them ; yet a Virginia Republican should have been startled at learning that after October, 1803, every President, past or to come, had the right to march the army or send the navy of the United States at any time to occupy not only West Florida, but also Texas and Oregon, as far as the North Pole itself, since they claimed it all, except the Russian possessions, as a part of the Louisiana purchase, with more reason than they claimed West Florida.

As usual, the most pungent critic of Republican doctrines was Senator Pickering, who if he could not convince, could always annoy the majority. He replied to Clay, and in the course of his speech read Talleyrand's letter of Dec. 21, 1804, which put an end to Monroe's attempt to include West Florida in

the Louisiana purchase. Nothing could be more apt ;
but nothing could be more annoying to the Administration, for Talleyrand's letter was still secret.
Confidentially communicated with other papers to
Congress by Jefferson, Dec. 6, 1805, the injunction
of secrecy had never been removed, and the publication tended to throw contempt on Madison not only
for his past but particularly for his present dalliance
with Napoleon.   Pickering could charge, with more
than usual appearance of probability, that West
Florida was to be Madison's reward for accepting the
plainly deceptive pledge of Cadore's letter of August
5. The Senate, with some doubts, resented Pickering's conduct to a moderate extent. Samuel Smith
moved it to be " a palpable violation of the rules ; "
and with the omission of " palpable," the resolution
was adopted. The deference to Executive authority
which allowed so important a paper to be suppressed
for five years showed more political sagacity than was
proved in censuring Pickering by a party vote, which
he would regard as a compliment, because he read
a document that the Administration should have been
ashamed not to publish and resent.

The interlude helped only to embarrass the true
question, — what should be done with West Florida.
President Madison's doctrine, embodied in Giles's bill,
carried out the Livingston-Monroe theory that West
Florida belonged to Louisiana.   In theory, this arrangement might answer the purpose for which it
was invented ; but in fact West Florida did not be-

long to Louisiana, either as a Spanish or as an American province, and could not be treated as though it did. If Mobile Bay and the Gulf coast as far as the Perdido belonged to Louisiana, the territory afterward divided into the States of Alabama and Mississippi had no outlet to the gulf. Georgia would never consent to such treatment, merely to support President Madison in alleging that West Florida was occupied by him as a part of the Orleans territory. Senator Giles's bill was silently dropped.

The Senate reached this point December 31, but meanwhile the House reached the same stand-still from another side. December 17 the Speaker appointed a committee, with Macon at its head, to report on the admission of Orleans territory as a State. The admission of the State of Louisiana into the Union was for many reasons a serious moment in American history; but one of its lesser incidents was the doubt which so much perplexed the Senate, whether Louisiana included West Florida. If this was the case, then by the third article of the treaty of purchase the inhabitants of Mobile and the district between Mobile and Baton Rouge, without division, should be " incorporated in the Union of the United States, and admitted as soon as possible " to the Union as part of the territory of Orleans. This was the opinion of Macon and his committee, as it had been that of Giles and his committee, and of the President and his Cabinet. December 27 Macon reported a bill admitting Louisiana, with West Florida to the Perdido, as a State; but no sooner did the debates begin, than the Georgians for the first time showed delicacy in regard to the rights of Spain. Troup could not consent to include in any State this territory " yet in dispute and subject to negotiation." Bibb held the same misgivings : " The President by his proclamation, although he had required its occupation, had declared that the right should be subject to negotiation; now, if it became a State, would not all right of negotiation be taken from the President?" To prevent this danger, Bibb moved that West Florida, from the Iberville to the Perdido, should be annexed to the Mississippi Territory or made a separate government.

On the other hand, Rhea of Tennessee held that no other course was open to Congress than to admit the Orleans territory in its full extent as ceded by France, according to the President's assertion. The treaty was peremptory, and Congress was bound by it to annex no part of the Orleans purchase to a pre-existing territory. West Florida belonged to Louisiana, and could not lawfully be given to Mississippi.

The House tried as usual to defer or compromise its difficulty. January 9, Macon's bill was so amended as to withdraw West Florida from its operation; but when on the following day two members in succession asked the House to provide a government for West Florida, the House referred the motions back to the committee, and there the matter

rested.   No man knew whether West Florida belonged to Louisiana or not.   If the President was
right, Mobile and all the Gulf shore to a point within
ten miles of Pensacola, although still held by the
Spaniards, made part of the State of Louisiana, and
even an Act of Congress could not affect it; while
if this was not the case, the President in ordering the
seizure of West Florida had violated the Constitution
and made war on Spain.

Hardly had the House admitted its helplessness
in the face of this difficulty, when it was obliged
to meet the larger issue involved in the Louisiana
affair; for Jan. 14, 1811, Josiah Quincy, with extreme deliberation, uttered and committed to writing
a sentence which remained long famous : —

" If this bill passes, it is my deliberate opinion that
it is virtually a dissolution of this Union ; that it will
free the States from their moral obligation ; and, as it
will be the right of all, so it will be the duty of some,
definitely to prepare for a separation, — amicably if
they can, violently if they must."

The Speaker decided this language to be disor-
derly ; but the House, by a vote of fifty-six to fifty-
three, reversed the ruling, and Quincy went on argu-
ing, as Jefferson had argued eight years before, that
the introduction of new States, outside the original
Union, was no part of the compact, and must end in
overwhelming the original partners.

Quincy's protest wanted only one quality to give
it force.   He spoke in the name of no party to the

original compact. His own State of Massachusetts assented to the admission of Louisiana, and neither the governor nor the legislature countenanced the doctrine of Quincy and Pickering. If the partners themselves made no protest, the act had all the legality it needed, in the absence of appeal to higher authority ; but it consummated a change in the nature of the United States government, and its results, however slow, could not fail to create what was in effect a new Constitution.

The House, without further delay, passed the bill by a vote of seventy-seven to thirty-six. After some amendment by the Senate, and dispute between the Houses, the bill was sent to the President, and Feb. 20, 1811, received his signature. The Act fixed the Iberville and the Sabine for the eastern and western boundaries of the new State. Meanwhile West Florida remained, till further legislation, a part of Orleans Territory for all purposes except those of admission into the Union ; and, according to the view implied by the action of Executive and Legislature, the President retained power to order the military occupation of Texas under the Act of Oct. 31, 1803, subject to government afterward, like West Florida, by the proconsular authority of the Executive.

As though the Florida affair needed still further complication, the President, January 3, sent to Congress a secret message asking authority to seize East Florida : —

" I recommend . . . the expediency of authorizing the Executive to take temporary possession of any part or parts of the said territory, in pursuance of arrangements which may be desired by the Spanish authorities. . . . The wisdom of Congress will at the same time determine how far it may be expedient to provide for the event of a subversion of the Spanish authorities within the territory in question, and an apprehended occupancy thereof by any other foreign Power."

In secret session Congress debated and passed an Act, approved Jan. 15, 1811, authorizing the President to take possession of East Florida, in case the local authority should consent or a foreign Power should attempt to occupy it. The President immediately appointed two commissioners to carry the law into effect. The orders he gave them, the meaning they put on these orders, the action they took, and the President's further measures were to form another remarkable episode in the complicated history of Florida.

Congress next turned to the charter of the United States Bank; but if it succumbed before West Florida, it was helpless in dealing with finance. Long hesitation had ended by creating difficulties. Local interests hostile to the Bank sprang into existence. In many States private banks were applying for charters, and preparing to issue notes in the hope of seizing their share of the profits of the United States Bank. The influence of these new corporations was great. They induced one State legislature after another to

instruct their senators on the subject. That Massachusetts, Pennsylvania, and Maryland should wish to
appropriate the profits of the National Bank was not
surprising, but that Virginia and Kentucky should
make themselves instruments of the capitalist States
showed little knowledge of their true interests. As
the crisis came near, the struggle became hotter,
until it rivalled the embargo excitement, and every
hour of delay increased the vehemence of opposition
to the charter.

The Bank was vulnerable on more than one side.
Largely owned in England, it roused jealousy as a
foreign influence. Congress could hardly blame this
ownership, since Congress itself, in 1802, aided President Jefferson in selling to the Barings, at a premium
of forty-five per cent, the two thousand two hundred
and twenty Bank shares still belonging to the government. The operation brought to the Treasury
not only a profit of four hundred thousand dollars
in premiums, but also about thirteen hundred thousand dollars of British capital to be used for American purposes. Fully two thirds of the Bank stock,
amounting to ten million dollars, were owned in
England; all the five thousand shares originally
subscribed by the United States government had been
sold to England; and as the Bank was a mere creature of the United States government, these seven
millions of British capital were equivalent to a score
of British frigates or regiments lent to the United
States to use against England in war. By returning

them, the United States seriously weakened themselves and strengthened their enemy.

Unfortunately this interest was national. Local interests felt that Englishmen received profits which should belong to Americans; and capitalists in general were not inclined to lower their profits by inviting foreign capital into the country unless they shared its returns. The second misfortune of the Bank was that of being a Federalist creation, chiefly used for the benefit of Federalists, who owned most of the active capital in the country. The third objection went deeper. The Bank was the last vestige of strong government created by the Federalists, — a possible engine of despotism; and no one could deny that if decentralization was wise, the Bank should be suppressed. Finally, the Bank was a bulwark to Gallatin; its destruction would weaken Madison and drive Gallatin from office.

Doubtless the objections to the Bank were so strong as some day to become fatal. In a society and government so little developed as those of America, a National Bank was out of keeping with other institutions. Even in England and France these banks exercised more influence over the Treasury than was proper; and in America, if once the Bank should unite in political sympathy with the Government, it might do no little harm. The necessity for such an institution was merely one of the moment, but in the period of national history between 1790 and 1860, the year 1811 was perhaps the only moment when destruction of the Bank threatened national ruin. A financial cataclysm had prostrated credit from St. Petersburg to New Orleans. Prices were nominal. England owed America large sums of money, but instead of discharging the debt, she was trying to escape payment and withdraw specie. Already the supply of specie in the United States was insufficient to sustain the bank-note circulation. In New York city the State banks were supposed to hold not more than half a million dollars, and in Pennsylvania not much more than a million; while the Bank of the United States had lost three and a half millions in eleven months, and had but five and a half millions left.[1]

Meanwhile the State banks not only expanded their issues, but also rapidly increased in number. Suppression of the National Bank could not fail to stimulate this movement. " The banks established by the State legislatures will scramble for the privilege of filling the chasm to be made by the destruction of the Bank of the United States. Already are they preparing for the patriotic endeavor. Our State legislatures are to be importuned to become bank jobbers and joint undertakers and copartners in the enterprise." [2]   Nothing could prevent expansion of credit, drain of specie, bankruptcy and confusion of the currency ; and this was to be done at

[1] Speech of Mr. Tallmadge of Connecticut, Jan. 23, 1811 ; Annals of Congress, 1810–1811, p. 784.

[2] Speech of Jonathan Fisk of New York, Jan. 17, 1811 ; Annals of Congress, 1810–1811, p. 612.

the time the country entered into a war with the only Power whose influence could shake the Union to its foundation.

Madison stood aloof, and left on Gallatin the burden of the struggle ; but Gallatin's energies and influence could do little with the Eleventh Congress. He was strongest in the House ; but there the debate, after many speeches, ended, January 24, by a vote of sixty-five to sixty-four in favor of indefinite postponement, and by common consent all parties waited for the Senate to decide. The omen was not happy for the Treasury.

Gallatin had at last found a capable senator to support him. The political fortunes of William Henry Crawford, which ended only at the threshold of the White House, drew no small part of their growth from his courageous defence of the Treasury during these chaotic years. Crawford showed the faults of a strong nature, — he was overbearing, high-tempered, and his ambition did not spurn what his enemies called intrigue ; but he possessed the courage of Henry Clay, with more than Clay's intelligence, though far less than his charm. Crawford was never weak, rarely oratorical ; and if he was ever emotional he reserved his emotion for other places than the Senate. " One man at last appeared who filled my expectations," wrote Gallatin many years afterward to an old and intimate friend.[1] " This was Mr. Crawford, who united to a powerful mind a most correct

[1] Adams's Gallatin, p. 598.

judgment and an inflexible integrity, — which last quality, not sufficiently tempered by indulgence and civility, has prevented his acquiring general popularity." February 5 he introduced into the Senate a bill continuing the old Bank charter for twenty years on certain conditions; and February 11 he supported the bill in a speech remarkable for the severity of its truths. He began by challenging the Constitution itself : —

" Upon the most thorough examination [of the Constitution] I am induced to believe that many of the various constructions given to it are the result of a belief that it is absolutely perfect. It has become so extremely fashionable to eulogize this Constitution, whether the object of the eulogist is the extension or contraction of the powers of the government, that whenever its eulogium is pronounced I feel an involuntary apprehension of mischief."

Upon the party theory that Congress could exercise no implied power, and therefore could not charter a corporation, Crawford fell energetically, until he came in contact with the instructions of State legislatures, which he swept out of his path with actual contempt : —

" What is the inducement with these great States to put down the Bank of the United States? Their avarice combined with their love of domination ! . . . The great commercial States are to monopolize the benefits which are to arise from the deposits of your public money. The suppression of this Bank will benefit none of the interior or smaller States in which there is little or no revenue collected. As the whole benefit is to be engrossed by three or four of the great Atlantic States, so the whole of the power which the dissolution of this Bank will take from the national government will be exclusively monopolized by the same States."

Under Gallatin's teaching, Crawford bade fair to make himself, what the South so greatly needed, a statesman who understood its interests; but he was far in advance of his people. The society from which he sprang was more correctly represented by Giles, who answered him in the manner for which the Virginia senator had acquired unpleasant notoriety. February 14 John Randolph, who with all his faults was not so factious as to join in the scheme of the State banks, wrote to his friend Nicholson:[1] " Giles made this morning the most unintelligible speech on the Bank of the United States that I ever heard." Never had Giles taken more trouble to be judicial, candid, and temperate; no one could have admitted with more impartiality the force of his opponent's arguments; but his instincts, stronger than his logic, compelled him to vote against the Bank. The conclusion was as certain as the process was vague.

Henry Clay, who followed on the same side, ironically complimented the Virginia senator, who had " certainly demonstrated to the satisfaction of all who heard him both that it was constitutional and unconstitutional, highly proper and improper, to pro-

[1] Adams's Gallatin, p. 430.

long the charter of the Bank ; " but Clay's irony was
as unfortunate as Giles's logic.   The sarcasm thrown
at Giles recoiled on Clay himself, for he passed the
rest of his life in contradicting and repenting the
speech he made at this moment, in which he took
ground against the power of Congress to create corporations.   " The power to charter companies is not
specified in the grant, and, I contend, is of a nature
not transferable by mere implication.   It is one of
the most exalted attributes of sovereignty."   The
legislation of twenty years which enforced the opposite opinion he swept aside in his peculiar manner.
" This doctrine of precedents, applied to the legislature, appears to me to be fraught with the most
mischievous consequences."   With more than his
ordinary self-confidence, he affirmed that the Treasury
could be as well conducted without as with the Bank ;
and he closed with a burst of rhetoric hardly to be
paralleled in his oratory, by holding the Bank responsible for not preventing Great Britain from attacking
the " Chesapeake," impressing American seamen, and
issuing the Orders in Council.

Clay's excuse for extravagances like these was
neither his youth nor his ignorance of affairs nor his
obedience to instructions, nor yet a certain want of
tact which made him through life the victim of needless mistakes, but was rather the simple repentance
with which, within five years, he threw himself on
the mercy of the public, admitting that had he foreseen the effect of his course he would have acted in

a very different way.[1] Even for Giles some apology might be made, for no one could deny that consistency required him to vote as he did, and he could appeal to the record in his defence. The worst offender was not Giles or Clay, but Samuel Smith.

When Crawford flung so freely his charges of avarice and ambition about the Senate chamber, he had Samuel Smith directly in his eye; for Smith's action was avowedly controlled by his interests, and since his speech on Macon's bill his attitude toward public measures was better understood than before. No one could conceive Smith to be influenced by conscientious scruples about implied powers, but many persons besides Madison and Gallatin believed him to be selfish and grasping. Baltimore favored State banks, and Smith lent his reputation as a business man to the service of local politics and interests, except so far as in doing this he aimed at the overthrow of Gallatin. He gave what amounted to a pledge of his character as a merchant to the assertion that the State banks were better, safer, and more efficient agencies for the Treasury than the Bank of the United States could possibly be. In making the speech which advanced these doctrines, he threw out an express challenge to Gallatin. "The secretary is considered by his friends a very great man in fiscal operations; in commercial matters I may be permitted to have opinions of my own." As a commer-

[1] Address to Constituents; Annals of Congress, 1815–1816, p. 1193.

cial authority he asserted that government had much greater control over the State banks than over the United States Bank; that more confidence could be put in the security of the State banks than in that of the National Bank; that they could more easily effect the necessary exchanges; that they were as prudently conducted; that the National Bank did not act as a check upon them, but they acted as a check upon it; that the ordinary and extraordinary business of the Treasury could be as effectually and securely done by the State banks; and that the liquidation of the United States Bank would " be remembered nine days and not much longer." When five years afterward the fallacy of these opinions became too notorious for question, Smith did not, like Clay, throw himself on the justice of his country or admit his errors, but he voted to re-establish the Bank in a far more extensive form, and took the ground that it was the only means of repairing mistakes which he had been a principal agent in making.

The other speeches made in this debate, although quite equal in ability to these, carried less political weight, for they implied less factiousness. One remained, which excited no small curiosity and some amusement.

When the Senate, February 20, divided on the motion to strike out the enacting clause, seventeen senators voted for the Bank and seventeen voted against it. Nine Northern senators voted in its favor, including seven of the ten from New England,

and nine on the opposite side.   Eight Southern senators voted one way, and eight the other.   Of the
twenty-seven Republican senators, seventeen voted
against the Bank, and ten in its favor; while the
three senators who were supposed to be in personal
opposition to the President — Giles, Samuel Smith,
aud Michael Leib — all voted in opposition.   The
force of personal feeling was credited with still another vote; for when the result was announced, the
Vice-President, George Clinton, whose attitude was
notorious, made a short address to the effect that
" the power to create corporations is not expressly
granted ; it is a high attribute of sovereignty, and in
its nature not accessorial or derivative by implication,
but primary and independent."   On this ground he
threw his casting vote against the bill.

So perished the first Bank of the United States ;
and with its destruction the Federalist crisis, so long
threatened, began at last to throw its shadow over
the government.

CHAPTER XVI.

WHILE Congress recoiled from the problem of West Florida, and by a single voice decreed that the United States Bank should cease to exist, nothing had yet been decided in regard to England and France.

This delay was not due to negligence. From the first day of the session anxiety had been great; but decision, which even in indifferent matters was difficult for the Eleventh Congress, became impossible in so complicated a subject as that of foreign relations. The President's proclamation named Feb. 2, 1811, as the day when intercourse with England was to cease. Congress had been six weeks in session, and had barely a fortnight to spare, when at last the subject was brought before the House, January 15, by John W. Eppes of Virginia, chairman of the committees of Ways and Means and Foreign Relations, who reported a bill for regulating commercial intercourse with Great Britain. As a third or fourth commercial experiment, — a companion to the partial Non-intercourse Act of April, 1806; the embargo of December, 1807; and the total Non-intercourse Act of March, 1809, — the new bill promised more discontent in America than it was ever likely to create in England.

The measure was not a non-intercourse, but a non-importation, severe and searching, in some ways almost as violent as the embargo; and was to be passed by a Congress elected expressly for the purpose of repealing the embargo.

The proposed bill lay on the Speaker's table. February approached, and still Congress did nothing; yet this delay substituted in place of the Constitution a system of government by proclamation. In two instances involving not only foreign war, but also more than half the foreign trade and several principles of fundamental law, the country depended in February, 1810, on two Executive proclamations, which rested on two assertions of fact that no one believed to be true. In spite of Madison and his proclamations, West Florida was not a part of Louisiana; Napoleon had not withdrawn his decrees, — and Congress was unwilling to support either assertion.

Unless the Berlin and Milan Decrees were repealed Nov. 1, 1810, as Cadore's letter was held to promise, neither President nor Congress could reasonably take the ground that Cadore's letter, of itself, revived the non-intercourse against England. The United States had the right to make war on England with or without notice, either for her past spoliations, her actual blockades, her Orders in Council other than blockades, her Rule of 1756, her impressments, or her attack on the "Chesapeake," not yet redressed, — possibly also for other reasons less notorious; but the right to make war did not carry with it the right to require

that the world should declare to be true an assertion
which the world knew to be false.   Unless England
were a shrew to be tamed, President Madison could
hardly insist on her admitting the sun to be the
moon; and so well was Congress aware of this difficulty that it waited in silence for two months, until,
February 2, the President's proclamation went into
effect; while the longer Congress waited, the greater
became its doubts.

Only one proof could be admitted as sufficient evidence that the French Decrees were repealed.   The
Emperor had violated American rights by decree, and
until he restored them by decree no municipal order
of his subordinates could replace the United States
in the position they claimed.   For this reason the
President and Congress waited anxiously for news
from Paris to November 1, when the decree of appeal
should have issued.   The news came, but included no
decree.   The President then assumed that at least
the Decrees of Berlin and Milan would not be enforced in France after November 1; but letters from
Bordeaux, dated Dec. 14, 1810, brought news that two
American vessels which entered that port about December 1 had been sequestered.   No other American
vessels were known to have arrived in French ports
except with French licenses.

This intelligence was a disaster.   The President
communicated it to Congress in a brief message [1]
January 31; and so serious was its effect that on

[1] State Papers, iii. 390.

February 2, when the non-intercourse revived by proclamation, Eppes rose in the House and moved to recommit his bill on the ground that the behavior of France gave no excuse for action against England. " The non-intercourse went into operation to-day," he said. " It had been considered by the Committee of Foreign Relations that in the present state of our affairs it would be better to provide for the relief of our own citizens and suspend the passage of the law for enforcing the non-intercourse until the doubts hanging over our foreign relations were dissipated."

The opposition would have done well to let Eppes struggle with his difficulties as he best could without interference; but Randolph, who liked to press an advantage, professing a wish to relieve the President " from the dilemma in which he must now stand," moved the repeal of the Non-intercourse Act of March 1, 1809, — a step which if taken would have repealed also the President's proclamation. The motion brought on a premature debate. Out-reasoned, out-manœuvred, and driven to the wall, the Republicans could only become dogged and defiant. They took the ground that retreat was impossible. Eppes avowed that he considered the national faith pledged to France; and although he would not enforce the non-intercourse against England until he had certain knowledge that the French Decrees were withdrawn, he must have unequivocal evidence that France had " violated the faith pledged to this nation " before he would vote to repeal the law. Apologetic

throughout, he admitted that indemnity for the French
seizures had always been considered an essential part
of any arrangement with Napoleon, yet held that the
national faith was pledged to that arrangement, although an essential part of the Emperor's obligation
was omitted. Every speaker on the Republican side,
with the exception of Dr. Samuel L. Mitchill of New
York, asserted with increasing vehemence that the
Act of May 1, 1810, created a contract with France,
made perfect by Cadore's letter of August 5. This
legal view of Napoleonic statesmanship had much
force with the Republican lawyers of the Eleventh
Congress, although its necessary consequence followed
its announcement; for since law, whatever lawyers
might sometimes seem to assert, was not politics, —
differing especially in the point that law had a sanction of force, while international politics had none, —
and since Napoleon could in no way be controlled by
any sanction, and still less be trusted, the so-called
contract, while binding on America, in no way bound
France.

Even Langdon Cheves, the new member from South
Carolina, maintained that the United States could no
longer break their compact with the Emperor. " Was
it not better," he asked, " that the nation should preserve all it had left, — its good faith? Its property
and honor had been sacrificed, and all that was left
was its good faith." Cheves admitted that his doctrine of " good faith " had an ulterior motive, which
was to force a conflict with England. " He had

never been satisfied with the wisdom or propriety of the law of May last in any other view than one. He believed it would make the country act a part worthy of its character ; it would precipitate us on a particular enemy, — and this, he believed, the country required." He went so far as to assert " that the decrees were removed, and that if the violation of our rights continued to-morrow, yet the decrees were so revoked on the 1st of November last as that they did cease to violate our commerce. If our rights are now violated, it is a violation independent of the decrees, by the mere will of an arbitrary and powerful government." Rhea of Tennessee went further still. " If any compact," said he, " can be of greater dignity than a treaty, the law of May 1, made by the constituted authorities of the United States, and agreed to and acted on by the constituted authorities of France, forms that compact."

When one nation is agreed in the policy of fighting another any pretext will answer, and Government need not even be greatly concerned to give any reason at all ; but in the condition of America in 1810, grave dangers might result from setting aside the four or five just issues of war with England in order to insist on an issue that revolted common-sense. If ingenuity had been provoked to suggest the course which would rouse most repugnance in the minds of the largest possible number of Americans, no device better suited for its purpose than the theory of Eppes, Cheves, and Rhea could have been proposed ; and if they wished to exasperate the conscience of New England in especial to fanatical violence, they came nearest their end by insisting on an involuntary, one-sided compact, intended to force Massachusetts and Connecticut to do the will of the man whom a majority of the people in New England seriously regarded as anti-Christ. Even on the floor of the House no Republican could stand a moment before John Randolph without better protection than this compact with France, which France herself did not recognize.

"This is the 2d of February," said Randolph. "The time has arrived, the hour now is, when gentlemen by their own arguments, if their arguments be just, are bound to fulfil the contract, which I do not undertake to expound, but which they say has been made — certainly in a manner very novel to our Constitution — between the House of Representatives on the one hand and Bonaparte on the other, — a bargain which, like the bargains of old with the Devil, there is no shaking off. It is a bargain which credulity and imbecility enter into with cunning and power. . . . I call upon gentlemen to make good their promise to his Majesty the Emperor of the French and King of Italy ; to redeem their pledge ; to cut off in fact nearly the whole of our existing trade in return for the liberty of trading by license from the three favored ports which it has pleased his Imperial Majesty to privilege. No man believes — I beg pardon, sir ; I was going to say, but I will not, that no man believes one syllable of this breach of faith on our part. I have too much confidence in the honor of gentlemen not to be convinced that they have persuaded themselves to this effect, although it is incomprehensible to me.   Bound, sir, to whom? To Bonaparte? Bound to Shylock? Bound to render up not only the pound of flesh, but every jot of blood in the Constitution? Does he come forward with his pockets swelled with American treasure ; do his minions, fattened upon our soil, whether obtained by public rapine or private extortion, do they come forward, calling upon us to make sacrifices of our best interest on the shrine of their resentments, in the name, too, of good faith?"

The majority showed its usual weakness in debate, but rejected Randolph's motion by a vote of sixty-seven to forty-five; and after rejecting it, knew not what to do.   Eppes reported a new bill to suspend for a time the operation of the non-intercourse, and a new debate began.   February 9 Eppes rejoiced the House by opening a fresh hope of some decided policy. A new French minister was soon to arrive in place of Turreau, and further legislation must wait his arrival.

" He has left France," said Eppes, " at a time to bring us certain information on this question.   I have no wish to enter on this interesting question with a bandage round my eyes.   Whether France has complied with her engagements, whether France has failed in her engagements, cannot be a subject of ingenious speculation many days longer."

Further proceedings were suspended until Congress should learn what Napoleon's agent would say.[1]

[1] Robert Smith's Address to the People, June 7, 1811.

The new minister arrived almost immediately. Unlike Turreau, Serurier was a diplomate by profession. He had last served as French minister at the Hague, where, by no fault of his own, he drove King Louis of Holland from his throne. February 16 he was presented to the President, and the next day had a long interview with Robert Smith, who learned that he brought no instructions or information of any kind on the one subject that engrossed diplomatic attention. The scene with Francis James Jackson was repeated with the French minister. Again and again Smith pressed his inquiries, which Serurier politely declined to answer except by resenting any suggestion that the Emperor would fail to keep his word.[1]

After this interview, on the same day, the President apparently held a Cabinet meeting, and probably also consulted certain party leaders in Congress; but no record of such conferences has been preserved, nor is anything known of the arguments that ended in the most hazardous decision yet risked. If disagreement took place, — if Gallatin, Eppes, Robert Smith, or Crawford remonstrated against the course pursued, not a whisper of their arguments was heard beyond the Cabinet. Serurier himself is the only authority for inferring that some conference was probably held; but he knew so little, that in giving to his Government an account of his first day in Washington he closed the despatch by reporting in a few lines the decision, of which he could have hardly suspected the

[1] Serurier to Maret, Feb. 17, 1811; Archives des. Aff. Étr. MSS.

importance. His interview with Robert Smith took place on the morning of February 17 ; the afternoon was probably passed by the President and Cabinet in conference ; in the evening Mrs. Madison held a reception, where Serurier was received with general cordiality : —

" In coming away, Mr. Smith — probably intending to say something agreeable, and something that I might regard as the effect of our first conversations — assured me that he was authorized to give me the pledge that if (*pour peu que*) England should show the least new resistance to the withdrawal of her orders, the Government had decided to increase the stringency of the non-intercourse, and to give that measure all the effect it ought to have."

The decision to enforce and re-enforce the non-intercourse against England implied that the President considered Napoleon's Decrees to be withdrawn. February 17, at latest, the decision was made. February 19 the President sent to Congress a Message containing two French documents.[1] The first was a letter, dated December 25, from the Duc de Massa, Minister of Justice, to the President of the Council of Prizes, which recited the words of Cadore's letter and the measures taken by the American government in consequence, and ordered that all captured American vessels should thenceforward not be judged according to the principles of the Decrees of Berlin and Milan, which "shall remain suspended ;" but such captured vessels should be sequestrated, " the

[1] State Papers, iii. 393.

rights of the proprietors being reserved to them until the 2d of February next, the period at which the United States, having fulfilled the engagement to cause their rights to be respected, the said captures shall be declared null by the Council." The second letter, of the same date, was written by Gaudin, Duc de Gaete, Minister of Finance, to the Director-General of the Customs, directing him thenceforward not to enforce the Berlin and Milan Decrees against American vessels.

On these letters, not on any communications from Serurier, the President rested his decision that the Decrees of Berlin and Milan were so revoked as no longer to violate the neutral commerce of the United States. Obviously they failed to prove more than that the decrees were partially suspended. According to these orders the decrees were not under any circumstances to be revoked, but their operation upon American commerce in France was to cease in case the Emperor should be satisfied that America had previously enforced against England the principles of the decrees. This was the converse of the American demand, and was in effect the attitude of England. The same packet which brought Jonathan Russell's despatch containing the two letters of the French ministers brought also the " Moniteur " of December 15, which contained the Duc de Cadore's official Report on Foreign Relations, — a paper understood to express the Emperor's own language, and to be decisive as to the meaning of his foreign policy : —

" Sire, as long as England shall persist in her Orders in Council, your Majesty will persist in your decrees; will oppose the blockade of the Continent to the blockade of the coast, and the confiscation of British merchandise on the Continent to the pillage on the seas. My duty obliges me to say to your Majesty, You cannot henceforward hope to recall your enemies to more moderate ideas except by perseverance in this system."

These documents, combined with a knowledge of the license system, showed the true scope and meaning of Cadore's pledge so clearly as to leave no possibility of doubt. If America chose to accept these limitations of her neutral rights, she was at liberty to do so; but she could hardly require England to admit that the Berlin and Milan Decrees were in any sense revoked because American ships were thenceforward to be admitted to France subject to the system of those decrees. Napoleon concealed neither his policy nor his motives, and as these did not warrant the assertion that France had ceased to violate the neutral rights of America, President Madison was obliged to assume that the Emperor meant to do more. A month after his decision was made, he wrote to Jefferson a letter of speculation as to the reasons that prevented the Emperor from taking the action assumed to belong to his plans:[1] —

" It is, as you remark, difficult to understand the meaning of Bonaparte toward us. There is little doubt that his want of money and his ignorance of commerce have

[1] Madison to Jefferson, March 18, 1811; Works, ii. 490.

had a material influence. He has also distrusted the stability and efficacy of our pledge to renew the non-intercourse against Great Britain, and has wished to execute his in a manner that would keep pace only with the execution of ours, and at the same time leave no interval for the operation of the British Orders without a counter-operation in either his or our measures. In all this his folly is obvious."

Such language was not only inconsistent with the doctrine that the French Decrees stood repealed in such a manner as no longer to violate American commerce, but it also showed that Madison deceived himself as to Napoleon's character and his policy. Of all theories on which to found political action, the least reasonable was that of assuming Napoleon to be foolish ; yet his " obvious folly " was Madison's explanation of an ingenious and successful device to enforce the Continental system.

Having adopted a policy, Madison could not but carry it to its practical results. Robert Smith came to him February 20 with the draft of a note addressed to Serurier, asking for information as to the withdrawal of the decrees, — a course similar to that adopted with Jackson. " I was, to my astonishment, told by him that it would not be expedient to send to Mr. Serurier any such note. His deportment during this interview evinced a high degree of disquietude, which occasionally betrayed him into fretful expressions." [1]

[1] Address to the People of the United States, by Robert Smith, 1811.

Smith did not understand the uselessness of asking Serurier for information he could not give, after deciding to act on such information as though it had been given. Although every one knew privately that Serurier would say nothing on the subject, the President could not afford to give the silence official emphasis; and he probably regarded Smith's attempt to do so as a part of his general effort to discredit the whole system of commercial restrictions. The proposed letter to Serurier could be of no use except to embarrass Congress in legislating against England. Already the first steps for this purpose had been arranged, and the next day, February 21, Eppes moved in the House to amend his bill by substituting two new sections, which revived the non-intercourse of March, 1809, against England in respect to all vessels which left a British port after Feb. 2, 1811, and forbade the courts to entertain the question whether the French edicts were or were not revoked.

Nothing short of a revolution in the form of government could force such a bill through Congress at so late an hour; but the Republican party having decided on the measure, did not shrink from employing the means.

February 23 the House went into committee and took up Eppes's new bill. That it was unsatisfactory could not be denied. Robert Wright of Maryland — a new member, of the war party — moved to amend by requiring from England an arrangement about impressments as an additional condition of restoring intercourse, and had the Government intended to make war its ultimate object it would have adopted Wright's motion; but the House had no such object. Impressment was not one of the grievances which of late had been urged against England; indeed, the subject had somewhat fallen out of sight, and so little did the House care to insist upon it, that only twenty-one votes supported Wright's motion. On the other hand, the conduct of France was hotly discussed, but only by Federalists. The Republicans sat silent.

After one day's debate the bill was reported, and February 26 the true struggle began. The House sat eighteen hours, while the minority consumed time by long speeches and dilatory motions. During the last four hours no quorum was present, and the Speaker decided that in the absence of a quorum no compulsory process could be issued. When the House reassembled at half-past ten on the morning of February 27, long speeches were resumed. The evening session began at six o'clock, when on both sides patience was exhausted. Randolph made two successive motions to postpone. Eppes declared that Randolph's motive was to delay and defeat the bill; Randolph retorted by the lie direct, and for a time the House fell into confusion, while Eppes wrote a challenge on the spot, and sent it by Richard M. Johnson to Randolph, who left the House to instruct his second.

Until half-past two o'clock in the morning of February 28 time was consumed in these tactics, — about eighty members being present, and the majority keeping silence. At that hour Barent Gardenier was on the floor making another diffuse harangue, when Thomas Gholson of Virginia called for the previous question on the last motion before the House. According to the rules, Speaker Varnum stated the motion: " Shall the main question be now put ? " It was decided in the affirmative. Gardenier immediately attempted to speak on the main question, when Gholson called him to order. Then followed the *coup d'état.*

" The Speaker decided that according to the late practice of the House it was in order to debate the main question after the previous question had been taken. He said that this practice had been established by the House by a decision two years ago, in opposition to an opinion which he himself had always entertained and had then declared. His decision on that occasion was reversed, and he felt himself bound by that expression of the House."

Gholson appealed. The Speaker decided that the appeal was debatable, but his decision was reversed by a vote of sixty-six to thirteen. The House then, without a division, reversed his first ruling, and ordered that thenceforth, after the motion for the previous question should have been decided in the affirmative, the main question should not be debated.

By this means and by persistent silence the majority put an end to debate. When Randolph returned to the hall and heard what had been done, he burst

into reproaches that the House had disgraced itself;
but his outcry, which like his language to Eppes was
attributed to drink, received no answer except cries
to order.   Further resistance was not carried to extremes; perhaps the dilatory tactics of later times
were hardly applicable to so small a body as the
House of 1811, or needed time for development; at
all events the bill was forced to its passage, and at
about five o'clock on the morning of February 28 the
House passed it by a vote of sixty-four to twelve.
March 2 it passed the Senate, and was approved by
the President.   Of all the Republicans, Macon alone
in the House and Bradley of Vermont in the Senate
voted against it.   Matthew Lyon, who also opposed it,
left the House in disgust without voting.

The rule of the previous question thus adopted has
been the subject of much criticism, and doubtless
tended among other causes to affect the character of
the House until in some respects it became rather a
court of registration than a deliberative body.   With
few exceptions in history, this result has proved inevitable in large assemblies whose cumbrous ineffi-
ciency has obstructed public needs or interests; and
perhaps the House of Representatives in 1811 was not
to blame for seeking to correct vices inherent in its
character.   Such great and permanent changes implied a sufficient cause behind them, even though
they led to worse evils.   The previous question was
a rude expedient for removing wanton obstruction,
and might have been the source of benefit rather

than of injury to the public service had the House
succeeded in giving its new character systematic improvement; but in American history the previous
question became an interesting study, because it
marked deterioration. Of all the defences provided
by the Constitution for special or feeble interests, the
right of debate was supposed to be the most valuable; and nowhere was this right so necessary as in
Congress. Not even in the courts of justice was
deliberation more essential than in the House of
Representatives. The Republicans came into office
in 1801 to protect special and feeble interests, and
had no other reason for existence than as the enemies of centralized power; yet circumstances drove
them to impose silence on the voice of a minority
that wanted only to prevent an improper act, and
they did so by methods substantially the same as
those used by Cromwell or Napoleon. In neither case
was the minority consulted or its protest regarded.
The difference was rather in the character of the
actors. The great usurpers of history had in one
sense a sufficient motive, for they needed the power
they seized, and meant to use it. The Republican
majority in the Eleventh Congress neither needed
power nor meant to use it. Their object was not
to strengthen government, or to prepare for war,
or even to suppress popular liberties for their own
pleasure, but merely to carry out an Executive scheme
which required no haste, and was to be followed by
no strong measures. As far as human intelligence

could be called blind, the intelligence which guided
the House was the blind instinct of power.

The same instinct was shown in the behavior of
Congress toward other matters of legislation. Under
Executive pressure, the Acts authorizing or approving
the seizure of East and West Florida, the admission
of Louisiana as a State, and the revival of non-
intercourse against England were passed; and this
series of measures seemed to a large minority a domestic revolution preliminary to foreign war. Naturally the Federalists and independent Republicans
looked for the measures to be taken in order to meet
or to escape the dangers thus invited. The Federalists had no small share of English respect for whatever was fixed, and they needed only to be satisfied
that the Union was strong in order to yield whatever
obedience it required; but they wondered how Madison with his weak Cabinet and Eppes with his still
less intelligent majority meant to create and handle
the weapons that were to drive Old England from
the ocean and to hold New England on the land.
They could not believe that a government would
fling itself headlong out of the window in order
to oblige the people to save it from breaking its
neck.

So far from grasping at weapons, Congress and the
Executive seemed bent only on throwing away the
weapons they held. The Bank perished almost with
the same breath that revived the non-intercourse
against England. By abolishing the Bank, Congress

threw away a large sum of money which Gallatin hoped to employ for his current demand and for possible war. By forbidding the importation of English merchandise, Congress further struck off one half the annual revenue. Gallatin foresaw the danger to the Treasury long before it was realized, and January 28 wrote a letter to Eppes advising a general increase of duties on such importations as might be permitted by law. February 6 Eppes reported from the Ways and Means Committee a bill to this effect; but the House failed to act upon it. Congress would consent to no new taxation; and as the Treasury could not be allowed to fail in its engagements, the House authorized a loan of five million dollars.

Such financial expedients looked toward any result except a policy of vigor, and the rest of the winter's legislation bore out the belief that no vigor was in the mind of Government. The Tenth Congress had increased the military establishment, until in 1808 the appropriations exceeded $4,700,000. The Eleventh Congress reduced them in 1809–1810 to about $3,100,000 ; in 1811 Congress appropriated barely $3,000,000. The naval appropriations in 1809 reached nearly $3,000,000; in 1810 they were reduced to about $1,600,000 ; in 1811 Congress appropriated $1,870,000. Even in a time of profound peace, when no thought of war disturbed the world, such armaments would have been hardly sufficient for purposes of police on the coasts and in the territories.

A short debate took place at the last moment of

the session, on a bill authorizing the President to accept a corps of fifty thousand volunteers. The measure had been reported by Crawford of Georgia in the Senate, from a committee appointed to consider the occupation of West Florida. March 1 the Senate passed the bill without a division, for it implied neither a new principle nor any necessary expense; while the President, without such authority, would find himself helpless to deal with any trouble that might arise from the affairs of Florida. When the bill reached the House, John Dawson of Virginia urged its adoption; " it was incumbent on them," he said, " to do something to provide for defence." Matthew Lyon said he had frequently voted. for such bills when there was no prospect of war; " and now, when we were going to war [with Spain], and giving the provocation ourselves, he was of opinion it ought to be passed." The House, without a division, indefinitely postponed the bill; and thus refusing to do more business of any kind, toward midnight of Sunday, March 3, the Eleventh Congress expired, leaving behind it, in the minds of many serious citizens, the repute of having brought Government to the last stage of imbecility before dissolution.

CHAPTER XVII.

THE government of the United States reached, March 4, 1811, the lowest point of its long decline. President Madison had remained so passive before domestic faction, while so active in foreign affairs, that the functions of government promised to end in confusion. Besides the greater failures of the last session, more than one personal slight had been inflicted on the President. He obtained the confirmation of Joel Barlow as Armstrong's successor at Paris, by a vote of twenty-one to eleven in the Senate ; but when he nominated Alexander Wolcott of Connecticut to succeed Justice Cushing on the Supreme Bench, he met a sharp rebuff. The selection was far from brilliant, but New England offered no great choice among Republicans suited to the bench. Sullivan was dead; Levi Lincoln declined the office ; Barnabas Bidwell, detected in a petty defalcation, had absconded to Canada ; Joseph Story, still a young man, only thirty-one years of age, was obnoxious to many Republicans on account of his hostility to the embargo, and particularly to Jefferson, who took personal interest in this appointment.[1] The

[1] Jefferson to Madison, Sept. 27, 1810 ; Works, v. 548.

President could think of no one who brought stronger recommendations than Wolcott, and accordingly sent his name to the Senate. A few days afterward John Randolph wrote to his friend Nicholson,[1] —

"The Senate have rejected the nomination of Alexander Wolcott to the bench of the Supreme Court, twenty-four to nine. The President is said to have felt great mortification at this result. The truth seems to be that he is President *de jure* only. Who exercises the office *de facto* I know not, but it seems agreed on all hands that 'there is something behind the throne greater than the throne itself.'"

February 21 the President nominated J. Q. Adams, then absent as minister at St. Petersburg, to the same place, and the Senate unanimously confirmed the appointment. The rejection of Wolcott had no meaning further than showing the opinion held by the Republican party of their President's judgment.

"Our Cabinet presents a novel spectacle in the world;" continued Randolph. "Divided against itself, and the most deadly animosity raging between its principal members, — what can come of it but confusion, mischief, and ruin? Macon is quite out of heart."

Gallatin was also out of heart. The conduct of Duane and his "Aurora" put additional venom into the wounds made by the session. Commonly some foundation of truth or probability lay beneath political attacks; some show of evidence or some responsible voucher was alleged if not produced, and the charges

[1] Adams's Gallatin, p. 430.

against public men, to be accepted, were shaped to suit the known character and habits of the victims ; but this was not the case with Duane's assertions of Gallatin's wealth, speculations, embezzlements, and secret intrigues.   Duane assumed the truth of his own inventions, and although few persons might be so credulous as to believe him, many were so far influenced as to draw aside and leave Gallatin and the Smiths to fight out their battles as they liked. This withdrawal of active support chiefly weakened the Administration.   President Madison had no hold over his friends so long as he refused to declare whom he regarded as friends.   He lost not only the Smiths, but also Gallatin, by standing aloof.

" Things as they are cannot go on much longer," wrote Randolph, February 17. " The Adminstration are now in fact aground at the pitch of high tide, and a spring tide too.   Nothing then remains but to lighten the ship, which a dead calm has hitherto kept from going to pieces.   If the cabal succeed in their present projects, and I see nothing but promptitude and decision that can prevent it, the nation is undone."

This judgment was so far true that none but persons hostile to all central government could look toward the future without alarm ; for if the system continued in the future to lose energy as in the ten years past, the time was not far distant when the country must revert to the old Confederation, or to ties equally weak.   Such a result was the outcome of Randolph's principles, and he should have welcomed it; but Randolph was a creature of emotions; with feminine faults he had feminine instincts and insight, which made him often shrink from results of his own acts. At this crisis he showed more political judgment than could be expected from wiser men. Though a Republican of the narrowest Virginia creed, he would take part with none of the factions that racked the government. He opposed vehemently not only the legislative assertion that the French Decrees were withdrawn, but also the legislative violence that overthrew the constitution of the House by means of the previous question. If Randolph was wrong on either of these points, he was at least wrong in company with history itself. He favored his old policy of peace, economy, and a decentralized government, and lost his temper with his colleague Eppes, to the verge of a duel; but for this course he was little to be blamed, since the policy was that of his party, and the contest was not of his making. He gave to Gallatin all the support he had to give. Though more deeply committed than any regular party man to the Constitutional doctrines of narrow construction, he voted with the friends of the Bank. "Randolph's opinion on the bill to renew the charter of the United States Bank is, I believe, unknown to every person except himself," wrote Macon, February 20,[1] — although Macon, himself opposed to the Bank, was Randolph's intimate friend. Disgusted with the factiousness of others, Randolph became

[1] Macon to Nicholson, Feb. 20, 1811 ; Nicholson MSS.

almost statesmanlike, and for a brief moment showed
how valuable he might have been had his balance
equalled his intelligence.

Randolph had long since ceased to hold direct relations with Gallatin, but neither then nor ever afterward did he doubt that Gallatin was the only capable
character in the Government, and that he must be
supported. " The cabal," whose influence excited disgust in his mind as it did in that of Macon, ought
to be put down, and Randolph said plainly to Gallatin's friends that the President must be compelled to
do it.[1] This dreaded cabal drew life only from the
President himself ; in any other sense it was a creature of the imagination. So little did Randolph and
Macon know about it that they called its members
" the invisibles," and puzzled themselves to account
for the influence it appeared to exert. In truth, the
cabal had no strength that warranted the alarm it
roused. Samuel Smith's abilities have shown themselves in the story. Few men of the time stand more
definitely imaged than he in speeches, letters, intrigues, and ambitions, for the exactest measure-
ment ; but measured in whatever way he pleased, he
was rather mischievous than alarming. His brother
Robert, whom he had made Secretary of State, was
a mere instrument. Giles possessed more ability, but
could never become the leader of a party, or win the
confidence of the public. Vice-President Clinton and
his friends were an independent faction, ready to

[1] Adams's Gallatin, p. 431.

coalesce with the Smiths and Giles for any personal objects; but they had little more capacity than the Marylanders. Michael Leib and Duane of the "Aurora" were more useful as intriguers, because they had less to lose; but they were also more dangerous to their friends. Seven or eight Federalist senators also could be depended upon as allies for all ordinary purposes of faction. Yet in such a combination no solidarity existed; no common head, no plan, no object held its members together. The persons engaged in this petty and vexatious war on the Administration could not invent a scheme of common action, or provide a capable leader, or act in unison on any two measures. As Randolph justly said : [1]

"I am satisfied that Mr. Gallatin, by a timely resistance to their schemes, might have defeated them and rendered the whole cabal as impotent as Nature would seem to have intended them to be ; for in point of ability (capacity for intrigue excepted), they are utterly contemptible and insignificant."

Randolph had ruined himself by impetuosity ; his only idea of resistance implied violence. Gallatin never used the knife except when every other means had been tried ; but when he did so, his act was proof that no other outlet could be opened by the clearest head and the most patient temper of his time. For two years he had waited, while the problem he placed before Madison and Jefferson in 1809 became more perplexed and less soluble with every month; but

[1] Adams's Gallatin, p. 432.

when the Eleventh Congress expired, he reached the same conclusion with Randolph, that promptitude and decision could alone save Madison. Acting on this belief, he wrote a letter of resignation.[1]

" It appears to me," he told the President, " that not only capacity and talents in the Administration, but also a perfect heartfelt cordiality among its members, are essentially necessary to command the public confidence, and to produce the requisite union of views and action between the several branches of government. In at least one of these points your present Administration is defective ; and the effects, already sensibly felt, become every day more extensive and fatal. New subdivisions and personal factions, equally hostile to yourself and the general welfare, daily acquire additional strength. Measures of vital importance have been and are defeated ; every operation, even of the most simple and ordinary nature, is prevented or impeded ; the embarrassments of government, great as from foreign causes they already are, are unnecessarily increased ; public confidence in the public councils and in the Executive is impaired, — and every day seems to increase every one of these evils. Such a state of things cannot last ; a radical and speedy remedy has become absolutely necessary."

Gallatin's resignation obliged the President to act. How long he might still have waited had Gallatin taken no step, only those can say who best understand the peculiarities of his temper ; but in any case he could hardly have much longer postponed a crisis. Not only were his ablest supporters, like Crawford,

[1] Adams's Gallatin, p. 434.

as impatient as Randolph of the situation, but his own personal grievances were becoming intolerable. He could acquiesce with patience while Gallatin and the Treasury were sacrificed ; but he could not bear to be crossed in his foreign policy, or to be opposed on his sensitive point, — the system of commercial restrictions. Gallatin probably liked the non-intercourse as little as it was liked by the Smiths ; but he did not, as a Cabinet minister, intrigue against the President's policy, while Robert and Samuel Smith did little else.

When Gallatin, probably March 5, sent, or brought, his resignation to the White House, Madison declined to accept it, and at once authorized Gallatin to sound James Monroe on the offer of the State Department. Gallatin sent for Richard Brent, Giles's colleague in the Senate, who wrote to Monroe March 7. Brent's letter, followed by others, opened another act in the political drama, for it made Monroe Secretary of State and President of the United States, and prolonged the Virginia dynasty for eight years ; but in order to reach this result, Monroe himself had to thread more than one dark and dangerous passage, which would have wrecked the fortunes of any man not born to carry a charmed political life.

Monroe's return to the paths of promotion had been steady and even rapid. In 1808 he was the rival candidate for the Presidency, on the ground that he leaned toward reconciliation with England, while Madison leaned toward France. Without wholly abandoning this attitude, Monroe was invited to become the Republican governor of Virginia ; and when attacked for his want of sympathy with Madison, he made explanations, both public and private, which so much irritated his old friend John Randolph as to draw from him a letter, Jan. 14, 1811,[1] telling Monroe of reports industriously circulated, "that in order to promote your election to the chief magistracy of this Commonwealth, you have descended to unbecoming compliances with the members of the Assembly, not excepting your bitterest personal enemies ; that you have volunteered explanations to them of the differences heretofore subsisting between yourself and the Administration which amount to a dereliction of the ground which you took after your return from England, and even of your warmest personal friends." The charge was never answered to Randolph's satisfaction.[2]   Monroe could not publicly avow that he had made a succession of mistakes, partly under Randolph's influence, which he wished to correct and forget ; but on this tacit understanding he was elected governor of Virginia, and for the rest of his life became to John Randolph an object of little esteem considering the confidence and admiration he had so long inspired.

More than most men, Randolph could claim the merits of his own defects. If he was morbidly proud and sensitive, he was at least quick to understand

[1] Adams's Randolph, p. 243.
[2] Monroe to Randolph, Feb. 13, 1811; Monroe MSS.

when he had lost a friend. Of him Monroe rid himself without trouble ; but Monroe labored under the
misfortune that his other oldest and best friends were
of the same political stamp. Chief among these, the
Mentor of Virginia politics, was John Taylor of
Caroline, — a man whose high character, consistent
opinions, and considerable abilities made him a valuable ally. Another was Littleton Walker Tazewell.
To them, after the rupture with Randolph, Monroe
wrote, excusing his course in becoming the Republican candidate for governor, and reasserting in sufficiently strong terms his want of confidence in
President Madison : [1] —

" I fear, if the system of policy which has been so
long persevered in, after so many proofs of its dangerous
tendency, is still adhered to, that a crisis will arise the
dangers of which will require all the virtue, firmness, and
talents of our country to avert. And that it will be persevered in seems too probable while the present men
remain in power. . . . And if the blame of improvident
and injudicious measures is ever to attach to them among
the people, it must be by leaving to the authors of those
measures the entire responsibility belonging to them."

Within six weeks after this letter had been written,
Monroe was asked to join the men in power, and to
share the blame of those " improvident and injudicious measures," the responsibility for which ought,
as he conceived, to be left entirely to their authors.
He wrote at once to Colonel Taylor for advice ; and

[1] Monroe to Tazewell, Feb. 6, 1811 ; Monroe MSS.

the reply threw much light on the personal and public motives supposed to guide the new Secretary of State.   Colonel Taylor advised Monroe to accept the President's invitation, for several reasons.[1]   Assuming that Monroe was to succeed Madison as the next Republican candidate for the Presidency, he took for granted that Monroe was to follow the lines of his old opinions, and to correct Madison's leanings toward France.

"Our foreign relations," continued Taylor, "seem to be drawing to a crisis, and you ought to be in the public eye when it happens, for your own sake, independently of the services you can render your country.   It is probable that this crisis will occur on a full discovery that France will not do our commerce any substantial good without an equivalent which would amount to its destruction.   So soon as this discovery is made, the Government, in all its departments, will alter its policy, and your occupancy of a conspicuous station will shed upon you the glory of its having come round to your opinion."

Colonel Taylor gave no thought to the opposite possibility that Monroe might come round to the opinion of the Government; yet his argument seemed to place Monroe in a position where, if he could not convert Madison, he would have no choice but to let Madison convert him.

"This offer to you is an indication of a disposition in Mr. Madison to relieve himself of the burden [of certain

[1] Colonel Taylor to Monroe, March 24, 1811; Monroe MSS. State Department Archives.

persons and measures] ; and if you suffer yourself to lose
the benefit of this disposition, another will gain it to
your inestimable injury.   Suppose this other should be
a competitor for the Presidency, will it not be a decisive
advantage over you?   General Armstrong is probably
taking measures for this object. . . . One consideration
of great weight is that the public think you an honest
man.   If this opinion is true, the acceptance seems to
be a duty toward relieving it from the suspicion that
there are too many avaricious or ambitious intriguers
of apparent influence in the government.   I suppose the
President and Gallatin (whom I know) to be wholly
guided by what they think to be the public good ; and
should you happen to concur with them, it will abate
much of the jealousy (though I hope it will never be
smothered) with which Executive designs are viewed ;
and to moderate it, under the perilous situation of the
country, is in my view desirable."

The country reached a perilous pass when John
Taylor of Caroline made plans to strengthen the
Executive ; but he could not have calculated on
Monroe's readiness to follow this course so far as
it ended in leading him.   Taylor's advice threw
Monroe into the full current of Executive influence.
Alliance with Madison and Gallatin, rupture with
France, antagonism to the Smiths and Clintons,
jealousy of Armstrong, and defiance of Duane were
sound policy, and united honesty with self-interest ;
but their success depended on elements that Taylor
could not measure.

That Monroe shared these views, that they were

in fact the common stock of his personal party,
might be seen not only in his previous letters, but
even more in his reply to Senator Brent,[1] written
March 18.

"You intimate," said Monroe to Brent, "that the
situation of the country is such as to leave me no alternative. I am aware that our public affairs are far from
being in a tranquil and secure state. I may add that
there is much reason to fear that a crisis is approaching
of a very dangerous tendency, — one which menaces the
overthrow of the whole Republican party. Is the Administration impressed with this sentiment, and prepared
to act on it? Are things in such a state as to allow the
Administration to take the whole subject into consideration, and to provide for the safety of the country and
of free government by such measures as circumstances
may require, and a comprehensive view of them suggest?
Or are we pledged by what is already done to remain
spectators of the interior movement, in the expectation
of some change abroad as the ground on which we are
to act? I have no doubt, from my knowledge of the
President and Mr. Gallatin, — with the former of whom
I have been long and intimately connected in friendship,
and for both of whom, in great and leading points of
character, I have the highest consideration and respect,
— that if I came into the Government the utmost cordiality would subsist between us, and that any opinions
which I might entertain and express respecting our
public affairs would receive, so far as circumstances
would permit, all the attention to which they might be
entitled; but if our course is fixed, and the destiny of

[1] Adams's Gallatin, p. 435; Gallatin's Writings, i. 497.

our country dependent on arrangements already made, I do not perceive how it would be possible for me to render any service at this time in the general government."

If the President's proclamation of Nov. 2, 1810, and the Act of Congress passed March 2, 1811, three weeks before Monroe wrote this letter, had not fixed the course and destiny of the country, instructions to Pinkney and Jonathan Russell — on which those two agents had already acted, and which would be the first papers to be read by Monroe as Secretary of State — seemed certainly to fix beyond recall the course about which Monroe inquired. Even a man more liberal than Madison in professions might have hesitated to say that the future secretary was free to break with France, or to enter on other arrangements with England than those already imposed. Monroe's letter implied disapproval of the course hitherto taken, and a wish, if possible, to change it. Madison was well acquainted not only with Monroe's opinions on foreign affairs, but also with those of Monroe's friends, who held that the course taken by the President ought to be reversed ; and with this knowledge of all the circumstances Madison replied [1] to Monroe's inquiry : —

" With the mutual knowledge of our respective views of the foreign as well as domestic interests of our country, I see no serious obstacle on either side to an association

[1] Madison to Monroe, March 26, 1811 ; Monroe MSS. State Department Archives.

of our labors in promoting them.   In the general policy
of avoiding war by a strict and fair neutrality toward the
belligerents, and of settling amicably our differences with
both, — or with either, as leading to a settlement with
the other, — or, that failing, as putting us on better
ground against him, there is and has been an entire concurrence among the most enlightened who have shared
in the public councils since the year 1800. . . . In favor
of a cordial accommodation with Great Britain there has
certainly never ceased to be a prevailing disposition in the
Executive councils since I became connected with them.
In the terms of accommodation with that as with other
Powers, differences of opinion must be looked for, even
among those most agreed on the same general views.
These differences, however, lie fairly within the compass
of free consultation and mutual concession as subordinate to the unity belonging to the Executive department.
I will add that I perceive not any commitments, even in
the case of the abortive adjustment with that Power,
that could necessarily embarrass deliberations on a renewal of negotiations."

From these letters, the attitude of Monroe in entering Madison's Cabinet may be understood.   Committed to the doctrine that Madison had leaned toward France, and that this bias should be corrected,
Monroe and his personal party looked on Madison's
offer of the State Department as the pledge of a
change in policy which should have a rupture with
France for its immediate object, and the Presidency
for its ultimate reward.   Madison, on his side, understanding this scheme saw no objection to it, and was

unconscious of having committed the government to any position that could necessarily embarrass Monroe. Monroe's acceptance of this situation was as natural as his refusal would have been surprising, for no man who wanted office, and who saw the Presidency in his grasp, could be required to show rigorous consistency. Madison's attitude was somewhat different; and his assurance, in March, 1811, that he saw no commitment which could necessarily embarrass Monroe in renewing negotiations with England, showed not only that Madison, notwithstanding Robert Smith's assertions to Turreau, still counted on no war with England, but felt no suspicion that his measures within little more than a twelvemonth would lead him to a recommendation of war. The policy of commercial restrictions still satisfied his mind.

Madison was not alone in this ignorance. Monroe himself, still less conscious than Madison of a war spirit, expected to reach the Presidency by conciliating England. Even Robert Smith, to the surprise of the world, posed as the victim of his hostility to France, and hoped to become the centre of a combination of Smiths, Clintons, Federalists, and Duane Pennsylvanians, who charged that Madison was less friendly to England than he might have been. The President suffered much annoyance from the Smiths because he could not disprove their assertions or demonstrate his good-will for Great Britain.

As soon as Madison learned through Senator Brent

that Monroe made no serious difficulty in accepting the State Department, he sent for Robert Smith. A faithful account of the conversations that followed would add vivacity to the story, for Madison seemed at times to enjoy commenting not only on the acts of his opponents, but also on their motives; while Robert Smith, being easily disconcerted and slow in defence or attack, offered a tempting mark for arrows of temper. The first interview took place March 23,[1] and Madison made a long memorandum of what passed.

"I proceeded to state to him," recorded Madison,[2] "that it had long been felt and had at length become notorious that the administration of the Executive department labored under a want of the harmony and unity which were equally necessary to its energy and its success; that I did not refer to the evil as infecting our Cabinet consultations, where there had always been an apparent cordiality and even a sufficient concurrence of opinion, but as showing itself in language and conduct out of doors, counteracting what had been understood within to be the course of the Administration and the interest of the public; that truth obliged me to add that this practice, as brought to my view, was exclusively chargeable on him; and that he had not only counteracted what had been the result of consultations apparently approved by himself, but had included myself in representations calculated to diminish confidence in the administration committed to me."

[1] Serurier to Champagny, March 26, 1811; Archives des Aff. Étr. MSS.

[2] Madison's Works, ii. 494.

Robert Smith protested, in his somewhat incoherent way, against the truth of this charge; and the President, roused by resistance, spoke with more preciseness, instancing Smith's conduct in regard to Macon's bills in 1810, as evidence of the secretary's bad faith.

" With respect to his motives for dissatisfaction, I acknowledged that I had been, for the reasons given by him, much puzzled to divine any natural ones, without looking deeper into human nature than I was willing to do ; . . . that whatever talents he might possess, he did not, as he must have found by experience, possess those adapted to his station ; . . . that the business of the Department had not been conducted in the systematic and punctual manner that was necessary, particularly in the foreign correspondence, and that I had become daily more dissatisfied with it."

The man must have been easy-tempered who could listen to these comments on conduct, motives, and abilities without sign of offence ; but Robert Smith showed no immediate resentment, for when the President closed by offering to send him to St. Petersburg to succeed J. Q. Adams, who was to take Justice Cushing's place on the Supreme Bench, Smith showed no unwillingness, although he avowed his preference for the other vacancy on the bench soon to be caused by Justice Chase's death, or for the English mission left vacant by Pinkney's return. Madison declined to encourage these ambitions, and Smith retired to consider the offer of St. Petersburg. For several

days the President supposed the arrangement to be
accepted; but meanwhile Robert Smith consulted his
friends, who held other views on the subject of his
dignity and deserts.   When he next saw the President he declined the mission, declaring that acceptance would be only indirect removal from office, the
result of " a most shameful intrigue."   After trying
in vain the characteristic task of convincing him that
he altogether exaggerated his own consequence,
Madison accepted his resignation and left him to
carry out his threat of appealing to the country.
" He took his leave with a cold formality," concluded Madison, " and I did not see him afterward."

For ten years Robert Smith had been one of the
most powerful influences in politics, trusted with the
highest responsibilities and duties, seeming more than
any other single Cabinet officer to affect the course
of public affairs; when at a breath from the President his official life was snuffed out, his reputation
for ability vanished, and the Republican party, which
had so long flattered him, suddenly learned to belittle
his name.   Under the shadow of monarchical or
absolute governments such tales of artificial greatness
were common, and their moral was worn thin by ages
of repetition; but in the democratic United States,
and from the bosom of Jefferson's political family,
this experience of Robert Smith was a singular
symptom.

Never again did this genial gentleman sun himself in the rays of Executive power, or recover the smallest share of influence. He returned to Baltimore, where he lived thirty years longer without distinguishing himself ; but about three months after his retirement from office, in the month of June, 1811, he published an Address to the People, charging President Madison with offences more or less grave, and surprising every one by representing himself as having persistently but vainly opposed Madison's fixed purpose of making a virtual alliance with France. The evidence of the late Secretary of State, who might reasonably be thought the best informed and most competent judge, confirmed the Federalist and British theory that Madison was under secret pledges to Napoleon. So gravely did it compromise Madison that he caused Joel Barlow to write a semi-official reply in the " National Intelligencer ; " and although Barlow wrote in a bad temper, Madison himself wrote privately in a worse.

" You will have noticed in the ' National Intelligencer,' " he told Jefferson July 8,[1] " that the wicked publication of Mr. Smith is not to escape with impunity. It is impossible, however, that the whole turpitude of his conduct can be understood without disclosures to be made by myself alone, and of course, as he knows, not to be made at all. Without these his infamy is daily fastening upon him, leaving no other consolation than the malignant hope of revenging his own ingratitude and guilt on others."

[1] Madison's Works, ii. 513.

Robert Smith hardly deserved such invective. If the taunts of Madison, Barlow, and the Republican press and party at his incompetence were well-founded, the party had only itself to blame for putting such a man in so high a position. If triumphant in nothing else, Smith overthrew both Madison and Barlow by the retort with which he met their sneers, and retaliated the charge of incompetence.

" This advocate," replied Smith (in the " Baltimore American ") to Barlow (in the Washington " Intelligencer "), " would have us believe that many persons both in and out of Congress thought that Mr. Smith from want of talents and integrity was quite unfit for the Department of State, and that his appointment was the effect of an intrigue. Were there any truth in this remark, it could not fail to convince every person of the utter unfitness of Mr. Madison himself for *his* office. It in plain English says that from the officious persuasion of a few intriguers he had appointed to the most important and the highest station in the government a person without talents and without integrity ; and this person not a stranger, respecting whom he might have been misled, but one who had been his colleague in office during the long term of eight years, and of whose fitness he of course had better means of judging than any other person or persons whatever ; nay, more, — to this same person, without talents or integrity, was offered by Mr. Madison not only the mission to Russia, but the important office of the Treasury Department."

CHAPTER XVIII.

APRIL 1, 1811, Monroe took charge of the State Department. The first person to claim his attention was the French Emperor, and Monroe had reasons for knowing that diplomatists of reputed sagacity found use for uninterrupted attention when they undertook to deal with Napoleon.

Monroe stood in a situation of extreme difficulty, hampered not only by the pledges of his own government, but still more by the difficulty of dealing at all with the government of France. When Armstrong quitted Paris in September, 1810, being obliged to fix upon some American competent to take charge of the legation at Paris, he chose Jonathan Russell. The selection was the best he could make. Jonathan Russell possessed advantages over ordinary ministers coming directly from America. A native of Rhode Island, educated at Brown University, after leaving college he followed the business of a merchant, and in November, 1809, sailed from Boston in a ship of his own, which arrived at Tönning in Denmark only to be at once sequestered under Napoleon's Decrees. He passed several months in efforts to recover the property, and acquired experience in the process.

About forty years old, and more or less acquainted with the people, politics, and languages of Europe, he was better fitted than any secretary of legation then abroad for the burden that Armstrong had found intolerable ; yet the oldest and ablest diplomatist America ever sent to Europe might have despaired of effecting any good result with such means as were at the disposal of this temporary agent, who had not even the support of a direct commission from the President.

Russell felt the embarrassment of the position he was called to fill. Armstrong departed September 12, bearing Cadore's promise that the decrees should cease to operate November 1, and saying as little as possible of a condition precedent. The 1st of November came, and Russell asked the Duc de Cadore whether the revocation had taken place ; but a month passed without his receiving an answer. December 4, 1810, Russell wrote to the Secretary of State,[1] —

" No one here except the Emperor knows if the Berlin and Milan Decrees be absolutely revoked or not ; and no one dares inquire of him concerning them. The general opinion of those with whom I have conversed on the subject is that they are revoked. There are indeed among those who entertain this opinion several counsellors of State ; but this is of little importance, as the construction which the Emperor may choose to adopt will alone prevail."

[1] Russell to Robert Smith, Dec. 4, 1810; MSS. State Department Archives.

At about the same time Russell wrote to Pinkney at London a letter[1] expressing the opinion that, as the decrees had not been executed for one entire month against any vessel arriving in France, this fact created a presumption that the decrees were repealed. He could not be blamed for an opinion so cautious, yet he was mistaken in committing himself even to that extent, for he learned a few days afterward that two American vessels had been seized at Bordeaux, and he found himself obliged to write the Duc de Cadore a strong remonstrance on the ground that as this was the first case that had occurred since November 1 to which the decrees could have applied, the seizures created a presumption that the decrees were not repealed.[2] Russell's instructions from America, including the President's proclamation of November 2, arrived three days later, December 13, requiring him to assume the revocation of the decrees ; but only two days after receiving them, he read in the " Moniteur " of December 15 Cadore's official report to the Emperor declaring that the decrees would never be revoked as long as England maintained her blockades ; and again, December 17, he found in the same newspaper the Count de Semonville's official address before the Senate, declaring that the Decrees of Berlin and Milan should be the " palladium of the seas."

Yet Russell's position was not quite so desperate as it seemed. Certainly the decrees were not revoked ;

[1] Russell to Pinkney, Dec. 1, 1810; State Papers, iii. 390.
[2] Russell to Cadore, Dec. 10, 1810; State Papers, iii. 391.

but he had a fair hope of obtaining some formal
act warranting him in claiming their revocation.
Although Napoleon's motives often seemed mysterious except to men familiar with his mind, yet one
may venture to guess, since guess one must, that he
had looked for little success from the manœuvre of
announcing the revocation of his decrees as concerned
the United States.   Perhaps he dictated Cadore's letter of August 5 rather in order to prevent America
from declaring war against himself than in the faith
that a trick, that to his eye would have been trans-
parent, could effect what all his efforts for ten years
past had failed to bring about, — a war between the
United States and Great Britain.   The Emperor
showed certainly almost as lively surprise as pleasure,
when December 12 he received the President's proclamation of November 2, reviving the non-intercourse
against England.   His pleasure was the greater when
he learned that President Madison had adopted his
suggestion not only in this instance, but also in requiring of England the withdrawal of Fox's blockade of 1806 as a *sine qua non* of any future renewal
of commerce.   Delighted with his success, not only
did the Emperor take no offence at the President's
almost simultaneous proclamation for the seizure of
West Florida, but rather his first impulse was to lose
not a moment in fixing Madison in his new attitude.
He wrote a hurried letter [1] on the instant to Cadore,

[1] Napoleon to Champagny, Dec. 13, 1810; Correspondance
xxi. 316.

ordering him if possible to send fresh instructions
to Serurier, who was already on his way to succeed
Turreau as French minister at Washington : —

"Send me the draft of a despatch for M. Serurier, if
he is still at Bayonne. . . . You will show in this letter
the satisfaction I have felt in reading the last letters
from America. You will give the assurance that if the
American government is decided to maintain the independence of its flag, it will find every kind of aid and
privileges in this country. Your letter will of course be
in cipher. In it you will make known that I am in no
way opposed to the Floridas becoming an American possession ; that I desire, in general, whatever can favor the
independence of Spanish America. You will make the
same communication to the American *chargé d'affaires*,
who will write in cipher to his Government that I am
favorable to the cause of American independence ; and
that as we do not found our commerce on exclusive pretensions, I shall see with pleasure the independence of a
great nation, provided it be not under the influence of
England."

This hasty note still throws out flashes of the fire
that consumed the world. Silent as to the single
question that America wanted him to answer, the
Emperor not only resumed his old habit of dang-
ling the Floridas before the President's eyes, but as
though he were glad to escape from every Spanish tie,
he pressed on Madison the whole of Spanish America.
Once more one is reduced to guess at the motive of
this astonishing change. No one knew better than
Napoleon that the independence of Spanish America

could benefit England alone; that England had
fought, intrigued, and traded for centuries to bring
this result about, and that the United States were
altogether unable to contest English influence at any
point in Central and South America. He knew, too,
that the permanent interests of France could only be
injured by betraying again the Spanish empire, and
that nothing could exceed the extravagance of intriguing for the revolt of Mexico and Peru while his
armies were exhausting themselves in the effort to
make his own brother King of Spain. Such sudden
inconsistencies were no new thing in Napoleon's career. The story of the Floridas repeated the story of
Louisiana. As in 1803 Napoleon, disgusted with his
failure at St. Domingo, threw Louisiana to Jefferson,
so in 1810, disgusted with his failure at Madrid, he
threw Spanish America in a mass to Madison. What
was more serious still, as in 1803 Germany could
foresee that she must pay on the Rhine for the losses
of France at St. Domingo and New Orleans, so in
1810 the Czar Alexander already could divine that
the compensation which Napoleon would require for
Mexico and Peru would lie somewhere in the neighborhood of Poland. Thus much at least had been
gained for the United States and England. Napoleon
took no more interest in the roads to Lisbon and
Cadiz, and studied only those that led to Wilna,
Moscow, and St. Petersburg.

Read in this sense, Napoleon's instructions to
Cadore and Serurier told most interesting news; but

on the point likely to prove a matter of life and
death to Madison, the Emperor spoke so evasively as
to show that he meant to yield nothing he could
retain.   He ordered Cadore to talk with Jonathan
Russell about commercial matters : —

" Have a conference with this *chargé d'affaires* in order
to understand thoroughly what the American government
wants.   You will tell him that I have subjected ships
coming from America to certain formalities ; tnat these
formalities consist of a letter in cipher, joined with licenses, which prove that the ship comes from America
and has been loaded there, but that I cannot admit
American ships coming from London, since this would
upset my system ; that there is no way of knowing the
fact [of their American character], and that there are
shipowners who for mercantile objects foil the measures
of the American government ; in short, that I have made
a step ; that I will wait till February 2 to see what
America will do, and that in the mean time I will conduct
myself according to circumstances, but so as to do no harm
to ships really coming from America ; that the question
is difficult, but that he should give the positive assurance
to his Government of my wish to favor it in everything ;
that he knows, moreover, that several ships coming from
America since the last measures were known have obtained permission to discharge their cargoes in France ;
finally, that we cannot consider as American the ships
convoyed to the Baltic, which have double papers, etc.
It would be well if you could engage this *chargé* to
answer you by a note, and to agree that he disowns the
American ships which navigate the Baltic.   This would
be sent to Russia, and would be useful.   In general,

employ all possible means of convincing this *chargé d'affaires*, who I suppose speaks French, of the particularly favorable disposition I feel toward the Americans; that the real embarrassment is to recognize true Americans from those who serve the English; and that I consider the step taken by the American government as a first step taken toward a good result."

When Napoleon used many words and became apologetic, he was least interesting, because his motives became most evident. In regard to America, he wished to elude an inconvenient inquiry whether the Berlin and Milan Decrees were or were not revoked. Consequently he did not mention those decrees, although credulity itself could not have reconciled his pledge to wait until February 2, with his official assertion of August 5 that the decrees would be withdrawn on November 1. Such a course was fatal to Madison, for it forced him to appear as accepting the Berlin and Milan Decrees after so long protesting against them. So justly anxious was the President to protect himself from this risk, that in sending to Russell the Non-intercourse Proclamation of November 2 he warned the *chargé* against the doctrine of a condition precedent involved in Cadore's "bien entendu." The Emperor was to understand that the United States acted on the ground that "bien entendu" did not mean "condition precedent."[1] "It is to be remarked, moreover, that in issuing the Proclamation, it has been presumed that the requisi-

[1] Smith to Armstrong, Nov. 2, 1810; State Papers, iii. 389.

tion . . . on the subject of the sequestered property
will have been satisfied."

December 13, at the moment when Napoleon was
writing his instructions to Cadore, Jonathan Russell
was reading the instructions of President Madison.
No diplomatist could have found common ground on
which to reconcile the two documents. Madison's
knowledge of the Napoleonic idiom was certainly
incomplete. Whatever " bien entendu " meant in
the dictionaries, it meant in Napoleon's mouth the
words " on condition," — and something more. In
further assuming that the sequestered property had
been restored, President Madison might with equal
propriety have assumed that it had never been
seized. Russell did what he could to satisfy Madison's wishes, but he could not hope to succeed.

Bound by these instructions to communicate the
President's proclamation in language far from according with Napoleon's ideas, Russell wrote to Cadore,
December 17, a note,[1] in which he not only repeated
the President's assumptions in regard to the revocation of the decrees, but also ventured beyond the
scope of his instructions : he demanded an explanation of the language used by Cadore himself in his report to the Emperor, and by Semonville in the Senate.
As though such a demand under such circumstances
were not indiscreet enough, Russell strengthened the
formal and perfunctory protests of the President by

[1] Russell to Cadore, Dec. 17, 1810; MSS. State Department
Archives.

adding an assurance of his own that the United States, after cutting off their own intercourse with England, would not consent to " any commercial intercourse whatever, under licenses or otherwise, between France and her enemy."

Russell's note of December 17 was never answered by the French government, and, as was equally natural, it was never published by the President or made known to Congress. Fortunately for Russell, the Emperor was in good humor, and Cadore was in haste to convey his master's wishes to the American *chargé d'affaires*. December 22 Russell was summoned to the minister, and a very interesting interview took place. Cadore gently complained of the tone in which Russell's note had been written, but put into his hands, as its result and answer, the two letters written by the ministers of Justice and Finance, — which allowed American vessels to enter French ports, subject only to provisional sequestration, until February 2, at which time all vessels sequestered since November 1 would be restored. " When I had read these letters," reported Russell,[1] " I returned them to the Duke of Cadore, and expressed to him my regret that the general release of American vessels detained under the Berlin and Milan Decrees should be deferred until the 2d of February, as this delay might throw some doubt on the revocation of those decrees." Cadore replied that the time thus

[1] Russell to Robert Smith, Dec. 29, 1810; MSS. State Department Archives.

taken was intended to afford an opportunity for forming some general rule by which the character of the
property could be decided. Russell then complained
that by assigning the second day of February, — the
very day on which the non-intercourse with England
would be revived, — this event was made to appear
as a condition precedent to the abrogation of the
French edicts ; and thereby the order in which the
measures of the two governments ought to stand was
reversed. In reply Cadore repeated the general assurances of the friendly disposition of the Emperor,
and that he was determined to favor the trade of the
United States so far as it did not cover or promote
the commerce of England. He said the Berlin and
Milan Decrees, " inasmuch as they related to the
United States," were at an end ; that the Emperor
was pleased with what the United States had already done, but that he could not " throw himself
into their arms " until they had accomplished their
undertaking.

Nothing could be more gentle than this manner of
saying that the revocation of November 1 was and
was not founded on a condition precedent ; that the
decrees themselves were and were not revoked ; but
when Russell still pressed for a categorical answer,
Cadore declared at last, " with some vivacity, that the
Emperor was determined to persevere in his system
against England ; that he had overturned the world
in adopting this system, and that he would overturn
it again to give it effect." On the third point Cadore

was equally unyielding. Not a word could Russell
wring from him in regard to the confiscated property
of American merchants. "His omission to notice the
last is more to be lamented, as I have reason to believe that this conversation was meant to form the
only answer I am to receive to the communications
which I have addressed to him."

The conduct of Cadore warranted Russell's conclusion that "upon the whole this interview was not
calculated to increase my confidence in the revocation of the decrees." Although President Madison
reached a different conclusion, and on the strength
of this conference caused Congress to adopt the Non-
Intercourse Act of March 2, Russell's opinion could
not be disputed. At the end of another week Cadore
sent word that one of the American vessels, the
" Grace Ann Greene," arrived at Marseilles since
November 1, had been released ; and Russell wrote to
Pinkney that this release might be considered conclusive evidence of the revocation.[1] A month afterward he wrote to the Secretary of State on the same
subject in a different tone,[2] saying that the United
States had not yet much cause to be satisfied ; that
no vessel arrived since November 1 had been permitted to discharge her cargo, and that tedious delays
were constantly interposed. As for the property confiscated before November 1, Russell avowed himself

[1] Russell to Pinkney, Dec. 30, 1810; State Papers, iii. 417.

[2] Russell to Robert Smith, Jan. 28, 1811; MSS. State Department Archives.

afraid to make the reclamation ordered by the President: " I ascertained indirectly that a convention to this effect would not be entered into at this moment; and I thought it indiscreet to expose the United States, with all the right on their side, to a refusal." No action of the United States, he feared, could redeem the unfortunate property.[1]

Failure on these points was accompanied by a promise of success on others. The President had remonstrated against the Emperor's scheme of issuing licenses through the French consuls to vessels in ports of the United States; and Russell wrote to Cadore, Jan. 12, 1811, that such consular superintendence was inadmissible, and would not be permitted.[2] January 18 Cadore returned an answer, evidently taken from the Emperor's lips : [3] —

" I have read with much attention your note of January 12, relative to the licenses intended to favor the commerce of the Americans in France. This system had been conceived before the revocation of the Decrees of Berlin and Milan had been resolved on. Now circumstances are changed by the resolution taken by the United States to cause their flag and their independence to be respected. That which has been done before this last epoch can no longer serve as a rule under actual circumstances."

Although this letter said that the Berlin and Milan Decrees were repealed, — not on Nov. 1, 1810, but at

[1] Russell to Robert Smith, Feb. 13, 1811; MSS. State Department Archives.

[2] State Papers, iii. 501.   [3] Ibid.

some indeterminate time afterward, in consequence of the President's proclamation of November 2, — yet it officially declared that whatever the date might be, on January 18, when Cadore wrote, the revocation was complete. Russell sent the letter to the President, and the President sent it nearly ten months afterward to Congress as proof that the decrees were revoked. He could not send, for he could not know, another letter written by Cadore to Serurier three weeks later, which instructed him to the contrary : [1] —

" I send you the copy of a letter addressed by me to Mr. Russell, January 18, on the permits that had been at first delivered to American ships. I cannot assure you that the permits are no longer to be issued, although this letter gives it to be understood in an explicit manner. Continue to conduct yourself with the reserve heretofore recommended to you, and compromise yourself by no step and by no official promise. Circumstances are such that no engagement can be taken in advance. It is at the date of February 2 that the United States were to execute their act of non-intercourse against England ; but before being officially informed in France of what they have done at that time, we cannot take here measures so decisive in favor of the Americans as after news to February 2 shall have arrived from America. This motive will serve to explain to you whatever uncertainty may appear in the conduct of France toward the United States."

[1] Champagny to Serurier, Feb. 9, 1811 ; Archives des Aff. Étr. MSS.

From these official instructions the facts were easy
to understand. The decrees had not been revoked
on Aug. 5 or Nov. 1, 1810 ; they were not revoked
Jan. 18, 1811 ; they were not to be revoked on February 2 ; but the Emperor would decide in the spring,
when news should arrive from America, whether he
would make permanent exceptions in favor of American commerce. In principle, the decrees were not to
be revoked at all.

For four years President Madison had strenuously
protested that France and England must withdraw
their decrees as a condition precedent to friendly
relations with America. For four years Napoleon
had insisted that America should submit to his decrees as a condition precedent to friendly relations
with France. February 2, 1811, he carried his point.
The decisive day passed without action on his part.
Six weeks followed, but March 15 Russell still wrote
to the Secretary of State as doubtfully as he wrote in
the previous December : [1] "The temper here varies
in relation to us with every rumor of the proceedings
of our government. One day we are told that the
Emperor has learned that the Non-intercourse Law
will be severely executed, — that he is in good humor,
and that everything will go well; the next day it is
stated that he has heard something which has dis-
pleased him, and that the American property lately
arrived in this country is in the utmost jeopardy.

[1] Russell to Robert Smith, March 15, 1811 ; MSS. State
Department Archives.

Every general plan here is evidently suspended until the course we may elect to pursue be definite and certain."

Russell made no further attempt to maintain the fact of revocation. Indeed, if the decrees were revoked, American rights were more lawlessly violated than before. As ship after ship arrived from the United States, he saw each taken, under one pretext or another, into the Emperor's keeping : —

" To countenance delay, no doubt, a new order was issued to the custom-houses on the 18th ult., that no vessels not having licenses, coming from foreign countries, be admitted without the special authority of the Emperor. This indeed makes the detention indefinite, as when once a case is before the Emperor it can no longer be inquired after, much less pressed, and it is impossible to say when it may attract the Imperial attention. It is my belief that our property will be kept within the control of this government until it be officially known here that the Non-intercourse Act against England went into operation with undiminished rigor on the 2d of February."

Under such circumstances, the idea that the United States were bound by a contract with France — the principle on which Congress legislated in the month of February — had no meaning to Jonathan Russell at Paris, where as late as April 1 not a step had yet been taken toward making the contract complete. " I trust," wrote Russell, March 15, " that I shall not be understood in anything which I have written in this letter to urge any obligation on the United States to execute *at all* the Non-intercourse Law; this obligation is certainly weakened, if not destroyed, by the conduct of the Government here."

Russell never misunderstood the situation or misled his Government. Although Napoleon's habit of deception was the theme of every historian and moralist, the more remarkable trait was his frequent effort to avoid or postpone an evidently necessary falsehood, and, above all, his incapacity to adhere to any consistent untruth. Napoleon was easily understood by men of his own stamp; but he was not wholly misunderstood by men like Armstrong and Russell. He did not choose to revoke the decrees, and he made no secret of his reasons even to the American government.

In the spring of 1811 the Emperor was surrounded by difficulties caused by his interference with trade. The financial storm which overspread England in 1810 extended to France in the following winter, and not only swept away credit and capital throughout the empire, but also embarrassed Napoleon's finances and roused fresh resistance to his experiments on commerce. The resistance irritated him, and he showed his anger repeatedly in public. At the Tuileries, March 17, he addressed some deputies of the Hanseatic League in a tone which still betrayed an effort at self-control : [1] —

[1] Correspondance, xxi. 284.

" The Decrees of Berlin and Milan are the fundamental laws of my empire. They cease to have effect only for nations that defend their sovereignty and maintain the religion of their flag. England is in a state of blockade for nations that submit to the decrees of 1806, because the flags so subjected to English laws are denationalized; they are English. Nations on the contrary that are sensible of their dignity, and that find resources enough in their courage and strength for disregarding the blockades by notice, commonly called paper blockades, and enter the ports of my empire, other than those really blockaded, — following the recognized usage and the stipulations of the Treaty of Utrecht, — may communicate with England; for them England is not blockaded. The Decrees of Berlin and Milan, founded on the nature of things, will form the constant public law of my empire during the whole time that England shall maintain her Orders in Council of 1806 and 1807, and shall violate the stipulations of the Treaty of Utrecht in that matter."

The sudden appearance of the Treaty of Utrecht had an effect of comedy; but the speech itself merely reasserted the rules of 1806 and 1807, which time had not made more acceptable to neutrals. Again and again, by every means in his power and with every accent of truth, Napoleon asserted that his decrees were not and never should be revoked, nor should they be even suspended except for the nations that conformed to them. Though America had rejected this law in 1807, she might still if she chose accept it in 1811; but certainly she could not charge Napoleon with deception or concealment of his meaning.

A week after the address to the Hanseatic deputies, on Sunday, March 24, he made another and a more emphatic speech. The principal bankers and merchants of Paris came to the Tuileries to offer their congratulations on the birth of a son. Napoleon harangued them for more than half an hour in the tone he sometimes affected, of a subaltern of dragoons, — rude, broken, and almost incoherent, but nervous and terrifying : —

" When I issued my Decrees of Berlin and Milan, England laughed ; you made fun of me ; yet I know my business. I had maturely weighed my situation with England ; but people pretended that I did not know what I was about, — that I was ill-advised. Yet see where England stands to-day ! . . . Within ten years I shall subject England. I want only a maritime force. Is not the French empire brilliant enough for me ? I have taken Holland, Hamburg, etc., only to make my flag respected. I consider the flag of a nation as a part of herself ; she must be able to carry it everywhere, or she is not free. That nation which does not make her flag respected is not a nation in my eyes. The Americans — we are going to see what they will do. No Power in Europe shall trade with England. Six months sooner or later I shall catch up with it (*je l'attendrai*), — my sword is long enough for that. I made peace at Tilsit only because Russia undertook to make war on England. I was then victorious. I might have gone to Wilna ; nothing could stop me but this engagement of Russia. . . . At present I am only moderately desirous of peace with England. I have the means of making a navy ; I have all the products of the Rhine ; I have

timber, dock-yards, etc.; I have already said that I
have sailors. The English stop everything on the ocean;
I will stop everything I find of theirs on the Continent. Their Miladies, their Milords, — we shall be quit!
(*Leurs Miladies, leurs Milords — nous serons à deux de
jeu!*) "

This hurried talk, which was rather a conversation
than a speech, lasted until the Emperor's voice began
to fail him. He flung defiance in the face of every
nation in the Christian world, and announced in no
veiled terms the coming fate of Russia. His loquacity
astounded his hearers, and within a few days several
reports of what he said, differing in details, but
agreeing in the main, were handed privately about
Paris, and were on their way to St. Petersburg,
London, and New York.[1] One account varied in
regard to the words used about America : —

" The Decrees of Berlin and Milan are the fundamental
laws of my empire," began the second report. " As for
neutral navigation, I regard the flag as an extension of
territory; the Power which lets it be violated cannot be
considered neutral. The lot of American commerce will
be soon decided. I will favor it if the United States con-
form to those decrees; in the contrary case, their ships
will be excluded from the ports of my empire."

Russell sent to Monroe these private accounts,
adding a few details to show more exactly the Emperor's meaning. Writing April 4, he said that no

[1] Russell to Robert Smith, April 4, 1811; MSS. State Department Archives. Cf. Thiers's Empire, xiii. 27–33.

American vessel had been allowed an entry since February 4 unless carrying a license; that a secret order had then been given to the custom-house to make no reports on American cases; that the Council of Prizes had suspended its decisions; and that, notwithstanding Cadore's promise, licenses were still issued. "If the license system," concluded Russell, "were concerned, as the Duke of Cadore suggests, to favor American commerce during the existence only of the Berlin and Milan Decrees, it is probably necessary to infer from the excuse of that system the continuance of those decrees."

Left without powers or instructions, Russell could thenceforward do nothing. Remonstrance was worse than useless. "A representation of this kind," he wrote, "however mildly it might portray the unfriendly and faithless conduct of this Government, might have hastened a crisis which it does not become me to urge."

At length, April 25, despatches arrived from America enclosing the Non-intercourse Act of March 2 and the secret Act for taking possession of Florida. The President's accompanying instructions [1] ordered Russell to explain that the different dates fixed by the Proclamation and by the Act for enforcing the non-intercourse against England were owing to the different senses in which Cadore's letter had been construed in France and America, — the President

[1] Robert Smith to Russell, March 5, 1811; MSS. State Department Archives.

having assumed that the decrees would have been extinct Nov. 1, 1810, while the French government, "as appears from its official acts, admits only a suspension with a view to a subsequent cessation." These instructions, as well as Russell's despatches for the most part, were never communicated to Congress.

April 17, a week before these documents arrived, Napoleon made a sudden change in his Cabinet, by dismissing Cadore and appointing Hugues Maret, Duc de Bassano, as his Minister of Foreign Affairs. No one knew the cause of Cadore's fall. He was mild, modest, and not given to display. He "lacked conversation," Napoleon complained. Probably his true offence consisted in leaning toward Russia and in dislike for the commercial system, while Maret owed promotion to opposite tendencies. Maret's abilities were undoubted ; his political morality was no worse than that of his master, and perhaps no better than that of Cadore or of Talleyrand whom he hated.[1] He could hardly be more obedient than Cadore ; and as far as America was concerned, he could do no more mischief.

When Russell repaired to the Foreign Office, April 28, he was received by the new minister, who availed himself of his inexperience to ask many questions and to answer none. Russell had a long interview with no results ; but this delay mattered little, for the Emperor needed no information. No sooner had he

[1] Maret, Duc de Bassano; Par Ernouf., 285–299.

received the Non-intercourse Act of March 2 than he
ordered his ministers to make a report on the situation of American commerce.[1] The order was due
not so much to a wish of hearing what his ministers
had to say as of telling them what they were to
report : —

"The United States have not declared war on England, but they have recognized the Decrees of Berlin and
Milan, since they have authorized their citizens to trade
with France, and have forbidden them every relation
with England. In strict public right, the Emperor ought
to exact that the United States should declare war against
England ; but after all it is in some sort to make war
when they consent that the Decree of Berlin should be
applied to ships which shall have communicated with
England. On this hypothesis, one would say: 'The
Decrees of Berlin and Milan are withdrawn as regards
the United States ; but as every ship which has touched
in England, or is bound thither, is a vagrant that the
laws punish and confiscate, it may be confiscated in
France.' If this reasoning could be established, nothing
would remain but to take precautions for admitting none
but American products on American ships."

This view of the contract to which American faith
was bound, though quite the opposite of Madison's,
was liberal compared with its alternative : —

"Finally, if it should be impossible to trace out a good
theory in this system, the best would be to gain time,
leaving the principles of the matter a little obscure until

[1] Note dictée en Conseil, 29 avril, 1811 ; Correspondance
xxii. 122.

we see the United States take sides ; for it appears that that Government cannot remain long in its actual situation toward England, with whom it has also political discussions concerning the affairs of Spanish America."

The Emperor's will was law. The Council set itself accordingly to the task of " leaving the principles of the matter a little obscure " until the United States should declare war against England ; while the Emperor, not without reason, assumed that America had recognized the legality of his decrees.

CHAPTER XIX.

THE Emperor's decision was made known to the American government by a letter [1] from Bassano to Russell, dated May 4, 1811, almost as curt as a declaration of war : —

" I hasten to announce to you that his Majesty the Emperor has ordered his Minister of Finance to authorize the admission of the American cargoes which had been provisionally placed in deposit on their arrival in France. I have the honor to send you a list of the vessels to which these cargoes belong; they will have to export their value in national merchandise, of which two thirds will be in silks. I have not lost a moment in communicating to you a measure perfectly in accord with the sentiments of union and of friendship which exist between the two Powers."

This was all. No imperial decree of repeal was issued or suggested. President Madison cared little for the released ships ; he cared only for the principle involved in the continued existence of the decrees, and Bassano's letter announced by silence, as distinctly as it could have said in words, that the prin-

[1] Duke of Bassano to Mr. Russell, May 4, 1811; State Papers, iii. 505.

ciple of the decrees was not abandoned. Such were
Napoleon's orders; and in executing them Bassano
did not, like Cadore or Talleyrand, allow himself the
license of softening their bluntness. Russell knew
the letter to be fatal to any claim that the French
decrees were withdrawn, but he could do nothing
else than send it to London as offering, perhaps, evidence of the " actual relations growing out of the
revocation of the Berlin and Milan Decrees." [1]   He
wrote to Bassano a letter asking the release of the
American vessels captured and brought into French
ports as prizes since November 1, but he obtained
no answer.[2]   A month afterward he wrote again, re-
monstrating against the excessive tariff duties and
the requirement that American vessels should take
two thirds of their return cargoes in French silks;
but this letter received as little notice as the other.
Russell had the mortification of knowing, almost as
well as Bassano himself, the motives that guided
the Emperor; and July 13 he recited them to
the President in language as strong as propriety
allowed : [3] —

" The temper here toward us is professedly friendly,
but unfortunately it is not well proved to be so in practice. It is my conviction, as I before wrote you, that
the great object of the actual policy is to entangle us in

[1] Russell to J. S. Smith, May 10, 1811; State Papers, iii. 502.

[2] Russell to Bassano, May 11, 1811; State Papers, iii. 506.

[3] Russell to Monroe, July 13, 1811; MSS. State Department
Archives.

a war with England. They abstain therefore from doing anything which would furnish clear and unequivocal testimony of the revocation of their decrees, lest it should induce the extinction of the British orders and thereby appease our irritation against their enemy. Hence, of all the captured vessels since November 1, the three which were liberated are precisely those which had not violated the decrees. On the other hand, they take care, by not executing these decrees against us, to divert our resentment from themselves. I have very frankly told the Duke of Bassano that we are not sufficiently dull to be deceived by this kind of management. He indeed pretends that they are influenced by no such motive ; and whenever I speak to him on the subject, he reiterates the professions of friendship, and promises to endeavor to obtain the release of the remainder of our vessels captured since November 1. I fear, however, that he will not succeed."

Even in case of war with England, Russell warned the President to look for no better treatment from Napoleon, who might then consider America as " chained to the imperial car, and obliged to follow whithersoever it leads." He pointed out that concessions had never produced any return from the Emperor except new exactions and new pretensions. If war with England became inevitable, care must be taken to guard against the danger that France should profit by it. French trade was not worth pursuing. The tariff on imports, reinforced by the restrictions on exports, created a practical non-intercourse.

Napoleon's writings furnish evidence that the Em-

peror's chief object was not so much to entangle
America in war with England as to maintain the
decrees which he literally overturned the world to enforce. When he suspended their enforcement against
American ships in his own ports, he did so only because his new customs' regulations had been invented
to attain by other means the object of the decrees.
When he affirmed and reaffirmed that these decrees
were the fundamental law of his empire, he told a
truth which neither England nor America believed,
but to which he clung with energy that cost him his
empire.

Russell made no more efforts, but waited impatiently for the arrival of Joel Barlow, while Napoleon
bethought himself only of his favorite means for
quieting Madison's anger. August 23 the Emperor
ordered [1] Bassano to give his minister at Washington
instructions calculated to sharpen the cupidity of the
United States. Serurier was to be active in effecting
the independence of Spanish America, was to concert
measures for that purpose with the President, promise
arms and supplies, employ the American government
and American agents for his objects, and in all respects give careful attention to what passed in the
colonies ; yet in regard to Florida, the only Spanish
colony in which Madison took personal interest, Napoleon hinted other views to Bassano in a message [2] too
curious for omission.

[1] Napoleon to Maret, Aug. 23, 1811; Correspondance, **xxii. 432.**
[2] Napoleon to Maret, Aug. 28, 1811; Correspondance, xxii. 448.

" You spoke to me this morning," he wrote August 28,
" of instructions received by the American *chargé* on the
affair of Florida. You might insinuate the following
idea, — that in consideration of some millions of piastres,
Spain in her present condition of penury would cede the
Floridas. Insinuate this, while adding that though I do
not take it ill that America should seize the Floridas, I
can in no way interfere, since these countries do not
belong to me."

With this touch of character, the great Emperor
turned from American affairs to devote all his energies to matters about the Baltic. Yet so deeply
were American interests founded in the affairs of
Europe that even in the Baltic they were the rock
on which Napoleon's destiny split; for the quarrels
which in the summer of 1811 became violent between
France and the two independent Baltic Powers —
Russia and Sweden — were chiefly due to those om-
nipresent American ships, which throve under pillage and challenged confiscation. Madison's wisdom
in sending a minister to St. Petersburg was proved
more quickly than he could have expected. Between
March 1 and Nov. 1, 1811, at one of the most critical
moments in the world's history, President Madison
had no other full minister accredited in Europe than
his envoy to Russia; but whatever mortifications he
suffered from Napoleon, were more than repaid by
means of this Russian mission.

The new minister to Russia, J. Q. Adams, sailed
from Boston August 5, 1809, and on arriving at

Christiansand in Norway, September 20, he found up-
ward of thirty masters of American vessels whose
ships had been seized by Danish privateers between
April and August, and were suffering trial and condemnation in Danish prize courts. He reported that
the entire number of American ships detained in
Norway and Denmark was more than fifty, and their
value little less than five million dollars.[1] The Danes,
ground in the dust by England and France, had
taken to piracy as their support : and the Danish
prize-courts, under the pressure of Davout, the French
general commanding at Hamburg, condemned their
captures without law or reason. Adams made what
remonstrance he could to the Danish government,
and passed on to Cronstadt, where he arrived Oct. 21,
1809. He found a condition of affairs in Russia that
seemed hopeless for the success of his mission. The
alliance between Russia and France had reached its
closest point. Russia had aided Napoleon to subdue
Austria ; Napoleon had aided Russia to secure Fin-
land. At his first interview with the Russian Foreign
Minister, Adams received official information of these
events ; and when he called attention to the conduct
of the Danish privateers, Count Roumanzoff, while
expressing strong disapprobation of their proceedings,
added that a more liberal system was a dream.[2]

[1] J. Q. Adams to R. Smith, Oct. 4, 1809; MSS. State Department Archives.

[2] J. Q. Adams to R. Smith, Oct. 26, 1809; MSS. State Department Archives.

The Foreign Minister of Russia, Count Roumanzoff, officially known as Chancellor of the Empire, and its most powerful subject, favored the French alliance. From him Adams could expect little assistance in any case, and nothing but opposition wherever French interests were involved.   Friendly and even affectionate to America as far as America was a rival of England, Roumanzoff could do nothing for American interests where they clashed with those of France ; and Adams soon found that at St. Petersburg he was regarded by France as an agent of England.   He became conscious that French influence was unceasingly at work to counteract his efforts in behalf of American interests.

Adams's surprise was the greater when, with the discovery of this immense obstacle, he discovered also an equally covert influence at work in his favor, and felt that the protection was stronger than the enmity. By a good fortune almost equal to that which brought Monroe to Paris on April 12, 1803, Adams was officially received at St. Petersburg on October 25, 1809, only two days before the Czar first revolted against Napoleon's authority.[1]   Of this revolt, in the mysterious atmosphere of the Russian court, Adams could know nothing.   At the outset, obliged to ask the Czar's interference on behalf of the plundered American merchants in Denmark, he could regard himself only as performing an official duty without hope of more than a civil answer.   This was in fact the first result

[1] Tatistcheff, Alexandre 1er et Napoléon, p. 512.   Vandal, Napoléon et Alexandre 1er, II., 167 ff.

of the request; for when, Dec. 26, 1809, he opened the subject to Roumanzoff, the chancellor gave him no encouragement. The Danes, he said, had been forced by France to do what they were doing. France viewed all these American ships as British; and "as this was a measure emanating from the personal disposition of the Emperor of France, he was apprehensive there existed no influence in the world of sufficient efficacy to shake his determination." [1] Adams resigned himself to this friendly refusal of a request made without instructions, and implying the personal interference of the Czar with the most sensitive part of Napoleon's system.

Three days afterward, December 29, Adams saw Roumanzoff again, who told him, with undisguised astonishment, that he had reported to the Czar the American minister's request for interference in Denmark and his own refusal; and that the Czar had thought differently, and had "ordered him immediately to represent to the Danish government his wish that the examination might be expedited, and the American property restored as soon as possible; which order he had already executed." [2]

If Adams had consciously intrigued for a rupture between France and Russia, he could have invented no means so effective as to cause the Czar's interference with Napoleon's control of Denmark; but

[1] Diary of J. Q. Adams, Dec. 26, 1809, ii. 83, 87. Adams to R. Smith, Jan. 7, 1810; MSS. State Department Archives.

[2] Diary, ii. 88.

Adams's favor was far from ending there. The winter of 1809–1810 passed without serious incident, but when spring came and the Baltic opened, the struggle between France and the United States at St. Petersburg began in earnest. Adams found himself a person of much consequence. The French ambassador, Caulaincourt, possessed every advantage that Napoleon and Nature could give him. Handsome, winning, and in all ways personally agreeable to the Czar, master of an establishment more splendid in its display than had been before known even at the splendid court of St. Petersburg, he enjoyed the privilege, always attached to ambassadors, of transacting business directly with the Czar ; while the American minister, of a lower diplomatic grade, far too poor to enter upon the most modest social rivalry, labored under the diplomatic inferiority of having to transact business only through the worse than neutral medium of Roumanzoff. Caulaincourt made his demands and urged his arguments in the secrecy that surrounded the personal relation of the two Emperors, while Adams could not even learn, except indirectly after much time, what Caulaincourt was doing or what arguments he used.

Already in April, 1810, Adams reported[1] to his Government that the commercial dispute threatened a rupture between France and Russia. On one hand, Napoleon's measures would prove ineffectual if Russia

[1] Adams to R. Smith, April 19, 1810; MSS. State Department Archives.

admitted neutral vessels, carrying as they would cargoes more or less to the advantage of England ; on
the other, Russia must become avowedly bankrupt if
denied exports and restricted to imports of French
luxuries, such as silks and champagnes, to be paid
in specie. Russia, at war with Turkey and compelled
to maintain an immense army with a depreciated
currency, must have foreign trade or perish.

Napoleon wanted nothing better than to cripple
Russia as well as England, and was not disposed to
relax his system for the benefit of Russian military
strength. During the summer of 1810 he redoubled
his vigilance on the Baltic. Large numbers of vessels, either neutral or pretending to be neutral, entered the Baltic under the protection of the British
fleet. Napoleon sent orders that no such vessels
should be admitted. June 15 Denmark issued an
ordinance prohibiting its ports to all American vessels of every description, and August 3 another to
the same effect for the Duchy of Holstein. July 19
a similar ordinance was published by Prussia, and
July 29 Mecklenburg followed the example. The
same demand came from Caulaincourt to the Czar,
and the French ambassador pressed it without intermission and without disguising the dangers which it
involved to the peace of Europe. Alexander's reply
never varied.

" I want to run no more risks," he told Caulaincourt.[1]
" To draw nearer England I must separate from France

[1] Thiers's Empire, xiii. 56.

and risk a new war with her, which I regard as the most dangerous of all wars. And for what object? To serve England; to support her maritime theories which are not mine? It would be madness on my part! . . . I will remain faithful to this policy. I will remain at war with England. I will keep my ports closed to her, — to the extent, however, which I have made known, and from which I cannot depart. In fact I cannot, as I have already told you, prohibit all commerce to my subjects, or forbid them to deal with the Americans. . . . We must keep to these terms, for I declare to you, were war at our doors, in regard to commercial matters I cannot go further."

Thus the American trade became the apparent point of irritation between Alexander and Napoleon. The Russians were amused by Cadore's letter to Armstrong of August 5, saying that the decrees were revoked, and that Napoleon loved the Americans; for they knew what Napoleon had done and was trying to do on the Baltic. The Czar was embarrassed and harassed by the struggle; for the American ships, finding themselves safe in Russian ports, flocked to Archangel and Riga, clamoring for special permission to dispose of their cargoes and to depart before navigation closed, while Napoleon insisted on their seizure, and left no means untried of effecting it. He took even the extravagant step of publicly repudiating the very licenses he was then engaged in forcing American ships to carry. July 10, 1810, the "Moniteur" published an official notice that the certificates of French consuls in the United States carried by American vessels in the Baltic were false,

" and that the possessors of them must be considered as forgers," inasmuch as the French consuls in America had some time before ceased to deliver any such certificates ; and not satisfied with this ministerial act, Napoleon wrote with his own hand to the Czar that no true American trade existed, and that not a single American ship, even though guaranteed by his own licenses, could be received as neutral.

In the heat of this controversy Adams was obliged to ask, as a favor to the United States, that special orders might be given on behalf of the American vessels at Archangel. As before, Roumanzoff refused ; and once more the Czar directed that the special orders should be given.[1] This repeated success of the American minister in overriding the established rules of the government, backed by the whole personal influence of Napoleon, made Roumanzoff uneasy. Friendly and even confidential with Adams, he did not disguise his anxiety ; and while he warned the American minister that Cadore's letter of August 5 had made no real change in Napoleon's methods or objects, he added that the Americans had only one support, and this was the Czar himself, but that as yet the Czar's friendship was unshaken. " Our attachment to the United States is obstinate, — more obstinate than you are aware of." [2]

[1] Diary, ii. 143–160. Adams to R. Smith, Sept. 5, 1810; MSS. State Department Archives.

[2] Diary, Oct. 9, 1810, ii. 180–181. Adams to R. Smith, Oct. 12, 1810; MSS. State Department Archives.

Adams then saw the full bearing of the struggle in which he was engaged; his sources of information were extended, his social relations were more intimate, and he watched with keen interest the effect of his remonstrances and efforts. He had every reason to be anxious, for Napoleon used diplomatic weapons as energetically as he used his army corps. Only ten days after Roumanzoff made his significant remark about the Czar's obstinacy, Napoleon sent orders to Prussia, under threat of military occupation, to stop all British and colonial merchandise; and the following week, October 23, he wrote with his own hand to the Czar a letter of the gravest import: [1] —

" Six hundred English merchant-vessels which were wandering in the Baltic have been refused admission into Mecklenburg and Prussia, and have turned toward your Majesty's States. . . . All this merchandise is on English account. It depends on your Majesty to obtain peace [with England] or to continue the war. Peace is and must be your desire. Your Majesty is certain to obtain it by confiscating these six hundred ships or their cargoes. Whatever papers they may have, under whatever names they may be masked, — French, German, Spanish, Danish, Russian, Swedish, — your Majesty may be sure that they are English."

If Napoleon aimed at crippling Russia by forcing her into the alternative of bankruptcy for want of commerce or invasion as the penalty of trade, he followed a clear and skilful plan. Alexander an-

[1] Correspondance, xxi. 233, 234.

swered his appeal by pleading that Russia could not seize neutral property, and would not harm England even by doing so.[1] November 4, two days after President Madison proclaimed the revocation of the French Decrees, Napoleon rejoined:[2] —

" As for the principle advanced, — that though wishing war on England we do not wish to wage it on neutrals, — this principle arises from an error. The English want no neutrals and suffer none ; they allow the Americans to navigate, so far as they carry English merchandise and sail on English account; all the certificates of French consuls and all other papers with which they are furnished are false papers. In short, there is to-day no neutral, because the English want none, and stop every vessel not freighted on their account. Not a single vessel has entered the ports of Russia with so-called American papers which has not come really from England." [3]

Armstrong, quitting Paris Sept. 10, 1810, wrote to Madison in his last despatch a few significant words on the subject, [4] suggesting that Napoleon's true motive in reviving the energy of his restrictions on commerce was, among others, the assistance it lent to his views and influence on the Baltic. No other explanation was reasonable. Napoleon intended to force Russia into a dilemma, and he succeeded. The

[1] Alexander to Napoleon.   Tatistcheff, pp. 542, 548, 549. Vandal, 509.

[2] Napoleon to Champagny, Nov. 4, 1810; Correspondance, xxi. 252.

[3] Cadore to Kourakine, 2 Dec., 1810; Correspondance, xxi. 297.

[4] Armstrong to Smith, Sept. 10, 1810; MSS. State Department Archives.

Czar, pressed beyond endurance, at last turned upon Napoleon with an act of defiance that startled and delighted Russia. December 1 Roumanzoff communicated to Caulaincourt the Czar's refusal to seize, confiscate, or shut his ports against colonial produce.[1] At about the same time the merchants of St. Petersburg framed a memorial to the Imperial council, asking for a general prohibition of French luxuries as the only means of preventing the drain of specie and the further depreciation of the paper currency. On this memorial a hot debate occurred in the Imperial council. Roumanzoff opposed the measure as tending to a quarrel with France; and when overruled, he insisted on entering his formal protest on the journal.[2] The Czar acquiesced in the majority's decision, and December 19 the Imperial ukase appeared, admitting American produce on terms remarkably liberal, but striking a violent blow at the industries of France.

Napoleon replied by recalling Caulaincourt and by sending a new ambassador, Count Lauriston, to St. Petersburg, carrying with his credentials an autograph letter to the Czar.[3]

" Your Majesty's last ukase," said this letter, " in substance, but particularly in form, is directed specially

[1] Adams to Robert Smith, Dec. 17, 1810; MSS. State Department Archives.

[2] Adams to Robert Smith, Jan. 27, 1811; MSS. State Department Archives.

[3] Napoleon to Alexander, Feb. 28, 1811 ; Correspondance, xxi. 424.

against France. In other times, before taking such a measure against my commerce, your Majesty would have let me know it, and perhaps I might have suggested means which, while accomplishing your chief object, might still have prevented it from appearing a change of system in the eyes of France. All Europe has so regarded it; and already, in the opinion of England and of Europe, our alliance exists no longer. If it were as entire in your Majesty's heart as in mine, this general impression would be none the less a great evil. . . . For myself, I am always the same; but I am struck by the evidence of these facts, and by the thought that your Majesty is wholly disposed, as soon as circumstances permit it, to make an arrangement with England, which is the same thing as to kindle a war between the two empires."

Adams's diplomatic victory was Napoleonic in its magnitude and completeness. Even Caulaincourt, whom he overthrew, good-naturedly congratulated him after he had succeeded, against Caulaincourt's utmost efforts, in saving all the American ships. " It seems you are great favorites here; you have found powerful protection," said the defeated ambassador.[1] The American minister felt but one drawback, — he could not wholly believe that his victory was sure. Anxious by temperament, with little confidence in his own good fortune, — fighting his battles with energy, but rather with that of despair than of hope, — the younger Adams never allowed himself to enjoy the full relish of a triumph before it staled, while he

[1] Diary, Feb. 15, 1811, ii. 226.

never failed to taste with its fullest flavor, as though
it were a precious wine, every drop in the bitter cup
of his defeats. In this, the most brilliant success
of his diplomatic career, he could not be blamed for
doubting whether such fortune could last. That the
Czar of Russia should persist in braving almost sure
destruction in order to defend American rights which
America herself proclaimed to be unassailed, passed
the bounds of fiction.

Yet of all the facts with which Monroe, April 1,
1811, had to deal, this was the most important, —
that Russia expected to fight France in order to
protect neutral commerce. Already, Dec. 27, 1810,
Adams notified his Government that Russia had determined to resist to the last, and that France had
shown a spirit of hostility that proved an intention to
make war. A few weeks later he wrote that military
movements on both sides had begun on such a scale
that the rumor of war was universal.[1] Napoleon's
harangue of March 24, 1811, to the Paris Chamber of
Commerce was accepted in Russia as the announcement of a coming declaration, and the Russians
waited uneasily for the blow to be struck which the
Czar would not himself strike.

They waited, but Napoleon did not move. Hampered by the Spanish war and by the immense scale
on which a campaign in Russia must be organized,
he consumed time in diplomatic remonstrances which

[1] Adams to Robert Smith, Feb. 12, 1811; MSS. State Department Archives.

he knew to be useless. April 1, 1811, a week after his tirade to the Paris merchants, he dictated another lecture to the Czar, through Count Lauriston: [1] " Doubtless the smugglers will try every means of forming connections with the Continent; but that connection I will cut, if necessary, with the sword. Until now I have been indulgent; but this year I am determined to use rigor toward those who are concerned in contraband." A great convoy, he said, was at that moment collecting in English ports for the Baltic ; but the goods thus introduced would be everywhere seized, " even in Russia, whatever might be said to the contrary, because the Emperor Alexander has declared his wish to remain at war with the English as the only means of maintaining the peace of the Continent." A few days afterward, April 5, Cadore was ordered to write again: [2] " It is probable that the least appearance of a peace with England will be the signal of war unless unforeseen circumstances lead the Emperor to prefer to gain time." Alexander wished the moral advantage of appearing to be attacked, and he allowed Napoleon to gain time in these pretended remonstrances. Roumanzoff replied to them as seriously as though they were seriously meant. Once he quoted the American minister as authority for the genuine char-

[1] Napoleon to Champagny, April 1, 1811 ; Correspondance, xxii. 3.

[2] Napoleon to Champagny, April 5, 1811 ; Correspondance, xxii. 28.

acter of the admitted vessels. Napoleon treated the
appeal with contempt:[1] " Let him know that there
are no American ships; that all pretended American
ships are English, or freighted on English account;
that the English stop American vessels and do not
let them navigate; that if the American minister
sustains the contrary, he does not know what he is
talking about."

The American minister no longer needed to sustain
the contrary; he had passed that stage, and had to
struggle only with the completeness of his success.
Although a large British squadron kept the Baltic
open to commerce, few British merchantmen visited
those waters in 1811. Their timidity was due to
the violence with which Napoleon had seized and destroyed British property in 1810 wherever he found it,
without respecting his own licenses. In consequence
of British abstention, American vessels swarmed in
Russian ports. In July, 1811, Adams wrote that two
hundred American ships had already arrived,[2] and
that Russia was glutted with colonial goods until
the cargoes were unsalable at any price, while the
great demand for return cargoes of Russian produce
had raised the cost of such articles to extravagance.
America enjoyed a monopoly of the Baltic trade;
and Adams's chief difficulty, like that of Napoleon,
was only to resist the universal venality which made

[1] Napoleon to Maret, July 15, 1811; Correspondance, xxii. 327.
[2] Adams to Monroe, July 22, 1811; MSS. State Department
Archives.

of the American flag a cover for British smuggling. Adams seemed unable to ask a favor which the Czar did not seem eager to grant; for in truth the result of admitting American ships pleased the friendly Czar and his people, who obtained their sugar and coffee at half cost, and sold their hemp and naval stores at double prices.

The Russians knew well the price they were to pay in the end, but in the mean time Napoleon became more and more pacific. If war was to come in 1811, every one supposed it would be announced in the French Emperor's usual address to his legislative body, which opened its session June 16. The Address was brought in hot haste by special courier to St. Petersburg; but to the surprise of every one it contained no allusion to Russia. As usual, Napoleon pointed in the direction he meant not to take, and instead of denouncing Russia, he prophesied disaster to the victorious English in Spain : —

" When England shall be exhausted; when she shall have felt at last the evils that she has for twenty years poured with so much cruelty over the Continent; when half of her families shall be covered by the funeral veil, — then a thunder-stroke will end the peninsula troubles and the destinies of her armies, and will avenge Europe and Asia by closing this second Punic war."

This Olympian prophecy meant only that Napoleon, for military reasons, preferred not to invade Russia until 1812. As the question of neutral trade was but one of the pretexts on which he forced Russia into war, and as it had served its purpose, he laid it aside. He closed the chapter August 25 by directing his ambassador, Lauriston, to cease further remonstrance.[1] One hundred and fifty ships, he said, under false American colors had arrived in Russia; the projects of Russia were unmasked; she wanted to renew her commerce with England; she no longer preserved appearances, but favored in every way the English trade; further remonstrance would be ridiculous and diplomatic notes useless.

War for the spring of 1812 was certain. So much harm, at least, the Americans helped to inflict on Napoleon in return for the millions he cost them; but even this was not their whole revenge.

The example of Russia found imitation in Sweden, where Napoleon was most vulnerable. Owing to a series of chances, Bernadotte, who had happened to attract the attention of the Swedes, was made Prince of Sweden in October, 1810, and immediately assumed the government of the kingdom. Bernadotte as an old republican, like Lucien Bonaparte, never forgave Napoleon for betraying his party, and would long since have been exiled like Moreau had he not been the brother-in-law of Joseph and a reasonably submissive member of the Imperial family. Napoleon treated him as he treated Louis, Lucien, Joseph, Jerome, Eugene, and Joachim Murat, — loading them with dignities, but exacting blind obedience;

[1] Napoleon to Maret, Aug. 25, 1811; Correspondance, xxii. 441.

and instantly on the new king's accession, the French
minister informed him that he must within five days
declare war on England. Bernadotte obeyed. Napoleon next required the confiscation of English merchandise and the total stoppage of relations between
Sweden and England.[1] As in the case of Holland
and the Baltic Powers, this demand included all
American ships and cargoes, which amounted to one
half of the property to be seized. Bernadotte either
could not or would not drag his new subjects into
such misery as Denmark and Holland were suffering;
and within five months after his accession, he already
found himself threatened with war. " Tell the Swedish minister," said Napoleon to Cadore,[2] " that if any
ship loaded with colonial produce — be it American
or Danish or Swedish or Spanish or Russian — is
admitted into the ports of Swedish Pomerania, my
troops and my customs officers shall immediately enter the province." Swedish Pomerania was the old
province still held by Sweden on the south shore
of the Baltic, next to Mecklenburg; and Stralsund,
its capital, was a nest of smugglers who defied the
Emperor's decrees.

In March, 1811, Davout, who commanded at Hamburg, received orders[3] to prepare for seizing Stral-

---

[1] Napoleon to Alquier, Dec. 22, 1810; Correspondance, xxi.
328.

[2] Napoleon to Champagny, March 25, 1811; Correspondance,
xxi. 510.

[3] Correspondance, xxi. 506.

sund at the least contravention of the commercial
laws.   Bernadotte's steps were evidently taken to
accord with those of the Czar Alexander; and at last
Napoleon found himself in face of a Swedish as well
as a Russian, Spanish, and English war.   In the case
of Russia, American commerce was but one though a
chief cause of rupture;[1] but in the case of Sweden it
seemed to be the only cause.   In August, Napoleon
notified the Czar of his intentions against Stralsund;
in November, he gave the last warning to Sweden, —
and in both cases he founded his complaints on the
toleration shown to American commerce.   Nov. 3,
1811, he wrote to Bassano: " If the Swedish Government does not renounce the system of escorting by
its armed ships the vessels which English commerce
covers with the American flag, you will order the
chargé d'affaires to quit Stockholm with all the legation."   He returned again and again to the grievance:
" If Sweden does not desist from this right of escorting
American ships which are violating the Decrees of
Berlin and Milan, and maintains the pretension to attack my privateers with her ships-of-war, the *chargé
d'affaires* will quit Stockholm.   I want to preserve
peace with Sweden, — this wish is palpable, — but I
prefer war to such a state of peace."[2]

Once more the accent of truth sounded in these
words of Napoleon.   He could not want war with

[1] Tatistcheff, Alexandre 1er et Napoléon, p. 578.

[2] Napoleon to Maret, Nov. 3, 1811; Correspondance, xxii.
552.

Sweden, but he made it because he could not otherwise enforce his Berlin and Milan Decrees against
American commerce. Although a part of that commerce was fraudulent, Napoleon, in charging fraud,
wished to condemn not so much the fraudulent as
the genuine. In order to enforce his Berlin and
Milan Decrees against American commerce, he was,
as Cadore had threatened, about to overturn the
world.

This was the situation when Joel Barlow, the new
American minister to France, arrived at Paris Sept.
19, 1811, bringing instructions dated July 26, the
essence of which was contained in a few lines.[1] .

" It is understood," said the President, " that the
blockade of the British Isles is revoked. The revocation having been officially declared, and no vessel trading
to them having been condemned or taken on the high
seas that we know of, it is fair to conclude that the
measure is relinquished. It appears, too, that no American vessel has been condemned in France for having
been visited at sea by an English ship, or for having
been searched or carried into England, or subjected to
impositions there. On the sea, therefore, France is
understood to have changed her system."

Of all the caprices of politics, this was the most
improbable, — that at the moment when the Czar of
Russia and the King of Sweden were about to risk
their thrones and to face the certain death and ruin
of vast numbers of their people in order to protect

[1] Monroe to Barlow, July 26, 1811; State Papers, iii. 510.

American ships from the Berlin and Milan Decrees,
the new minister of the United States appeared in
Paris authorized to declare that the President considered those decrees to be revoked and their system
no longer in force !

END OF VOL. V.